CW00486211

"*Building a Portfolio Career* is a common sense approach to the enric without the pomposity and ponderot tired bromides, they illuminate a conv ..., ..., attainable enrichment of life."

Bill Sur, *retired Headhunter from Maryland*

"This is THE book for anybody who has ever wanted to take control of their work and their life. It covers every possible aspect from how and when to set up your business to stress management and healthy eating. As well as challenging you to think about where you are in your life and where you want to be it also encourages you to think of how any changes you make may impact on others around you."

Carole Comfort, *formerly Head of Welfare, British Aerospace*

"I couldn't put the book down and constantly used it as a reference guide. Reading the book released some new thinking and imagination, which changed my mind set and approach to my future. What I enjoy that ultimately suits me is the ability to mix and match work around my life. I enjoy the range of different work streams I have. I do what I want to do because I enjoy it."

Steve Grainger, *former Chief Superintendent, Metropolitan Police*

"Great work! I very much enjoyed reading it. It gives me new strength to pursue this career path, either as a real portfolio or as an addition to a standard paid employment (it reminds me that even if I enter into a standard employment with a company I have to make room for other types of work)."

Gerhard Barcus, *International Marketing Director*

"*Building a Portfolio Career* shows that with planning and determination, the portfolio life, with its potential for independence and fulfilment, can be an antidote to redundancy."

Mark Tran, *The Guardian*

For a complete list of Management Books 2000 titles
visit our web-site on http://www.mb2000.com

BUILDING A PORTFOLIO CAREER

Adrian Bourne
Christopher Lyons
Colin McCrudden

Management Books 2000

Copyright © Adrian Bourne, Christopher Lyons and Colin McCrudden 2005, 2009, 2016

All rights reserved. No part of this publication may be reproduced, stored in a retrieval system, or transmitted in any form or by any means, electronic, mechanical, photocopying, recording, or otherwise without the prior permission of the publishers.

First edition published in 2005 by Management Books 2000 Ltd
Second edition published in 2009 by Management Books 2000 Ltd
This new edition published in 2016 by Management Books 2000 Ltd
36 Westerm Road
Oxford OX1 4LG, UK
Tel: 0044 (0) 1865 600738
Email: info@mb2000.com
Web: www.mb2000.com

This book is sold subject to the condition that it shall not, by way of trade or otherwise, be lent, resold, hired out, or otherwise circulated without the publisher's prior consent in any form of binding or cover other than that in which it is published and without a similar condition including this condition being imposed upon the subsequent purchaser.

British Library Cataloguing in Publication Data is available

ISBN 9781852527594

NOTE TO READERS

The opinions, advice and guidance expressed in this book are intended as a guide only. Every effort has been made to ensure the accuracy of the contents and associated material. The publishers, authors and contributors accept no liability for any injury or loss sustained as a result of using the information in this book. The website addresses and contact links are correct at date of publication.

CONTENTS

INTRODUCTION

The continuous fluctuations in the global economy and the ever-changing nature of work conspire to make the world a different place from when this book was first published in 2005 and then revised and reprinted in 2009. Taking stock and planning your life and career has never been more important and the opportunity to explore the portfolio route is more timely than ever.

The positive manner in which previous editions of our book were received, together with the wider spread of Portfolio Working as a credible career choice, confirm this authoritative 'How To' book as an asset for the growing numbers of those becoming 'Portfolio Professionals'.

We hope that this updated edition, which includes a new section on 'The Power of Social Media and How to Harness It', will be well received, thereby further cementing the book's acknowledged reputation as an easy to read practical guide.

The world was introduced to the concept of work as a portfolio in Charles Handy's farsighted book *The Age of Unreason* in 1989. The changes in work patterns he predicted have led many thousands to adopt the lifestyle he envisioned and his definition of a "work portfolio" as *"a way of describing how different bits of work in our life fit together to form a balanced whole"* is now a reality to many. We are proud that our book has swelled the ranks since it was first published and helped to elevate the concept to a credible professional status.

Our co-author, Colin McCrudden, played a great part in this journey up to his untimely death in April 2010. His contribution of talent, knowledge, humour and friendship was immense. The legacy of his thoughts and experience of portfolio life is thankfully captured in the book. We have left his Portfolio Journey on page 208 just as he wrote it. It shows how his portfolio life opened up time for the most important things in his life, his family.

Building a Portfolio Career incorporates much recent learning and reflects the new world order.

It shares with new readers the experiences of the authors and contributors together with the wide-ranging feedback we have received.

As authors we have ourselves made the transition from senior full-time roles to living the Portfolio Life, and have experienced the benefits of this approach to balancing work and personal lifestyle. So it has been especially pleasing to meet and discuss our experiences with many individuals embarking on this journey and we have included new material by contributors who have been inspired to make the change.

Who will this guide help most?

Building a Portfolio Career is a practical guide for anyone open to exploring and planning a change in the balance of work and home lifestyle, now or in the future.

You may be employed, full or part-time, unemployed, retired, worried about your next twenty years or just in need of a change. You may have been in one role, profession or company for many years and believe that change may be around the corner, but have no clear idea of what comes next. This book is essential reading for those considering their next steps. As Handy observed, *"Retirement, unemployment and redundancy only make sense in job-work terms. The optimist's scenario sees work and leisure and adequate money for all, with lots of room for individual variation ..."*

In preparing the editions of this book we drew on meetings with Charles Handy and his wife Elizabeth, and the lively, stimulating exchange on how predictions come true, on where the trends point next and the flexibility of portfolio living. As we explained the purpose of the book, Charles observed *"I get a lot of people who've read my books asking 'How do I fill my portfolio?' It sounds as if you're writing a 'how to' book for the portfolio life."*

This is, indeed, a 'How To' book, a practical guide for the journey of becoming a Portfolio Professional.

In Part 1, we introduce you to the Portfolio Life, invite you to look at a broader view of your future, and advise how to use the book to maximum benefit. Part 2 offers a range of models to help you understand how the Portfolio Life can meet your goals and aspirations. In Part 3 we share personal experiences, which help your transition to becoming a Portfolio Professional. Part 4 has specialist contributors advising on living the Portfolio Life and running your own business.

Throughout the book you will find contributions from a range of different people chronicling their personal experiences and stories of their personal Portfolio Journeys. The contributors offer the benefit of their wide experience in their own individual styles. They have given freely of their time and talents to provide a unique insight into this alternative approach, with wisdom and practical insight. We are truly grateful for their guidance.

We hope that you will enjoy the book and your own personal journey.

Adrian Bourne
Christopher Lyons

PART 1

INTRODUCING THE PORTFOLIO LIFE

1

BUILDING AN UNLIMITED LIFE

A man is a success if he gets up in the morning
and goes to bed at night,
and in between does what he wants to do.
Bob Dylan

The whole you ...

This book is unashamedly and selfishly about YOU. It's not a life coach book; it's both broader and more practical than that. It encompasses your professional life and your personal life. It's about the 'You' which draws together not just your business life, not just your career, but the wider compass of what makes you YOU – your family, friends, environment, contacts, and the broader world to which you relate.

Through its pages you can change your career, your future, your life – by putting your career into a new perspective, by finding a new way of arranging your work around your life, rather than the other way round.

The first edition of this book reflected a world where changes in life priorities, in demographics, but above all in the culture of employment, pointed the way to a new format of career which offered increased control and greater freedom.

Now, as we prepare another new edition, what was at that time a change of direction, made at leisure as a matter of a choice, has become for many a pressing need, a reaction to forced changes in personal circumstances.

The new age of uncertainty concentrates the mind

The economic and workplace changes of recent years have changed our fundamental view of the background to our lives. The box has been opened and cannot be closed again. Gone for ever are guarantees of job, assumptions of employee-employer loyalty, career progression and training as part of the role, final salary pension schemes and many more. The old contracts and presumptions are in the past.

Young people about to start their working lives have a new and worrying view of a world where jobs disappear overnight, irrespective of employee loyalty, talent or experience. Graduates who have spent time and money building a skill find it out of demand and apparently worthless.

Those at the other end of their working lives – 50 and above – are of course the most vulnerable. They are at the top of the list for redundancy and the bottom of the pile for alternative employment.

As a result millions of people are redefining their priorities and rethinking their jobs and lives. People at all stages of their lives are taking control of their own careers.

Greater focus

This world of uncertainty, and the greater sense of personal career planning, makes us do something which we usually avoid or put off. It focuses minds and causes us to review our lives and work – to decide and concentrate on our priorities.

For those with large mortgages and small children this may bring a greater concentration on steady earnings and continuity of employment. Less ambition perhaps. A greater willingness to please the boss and bring success to the employer. Or a tactical move to a safer, more grounded situation in a teaching, social or community role.

In contrast to this, those who lose their jobs are exposed to a new and unwelcome world where their talents are no longer as highly regarded and where their future opportunities have shrunk alarmingly.

There are of course grey areas between these two extremes, but, within them, common factors for all in this new environment.

Above all there is a renewed realisation that we are all in charge of our own career. The marketing and self-branding that we may have put off in the past is now obligatory. If we are to survive in this harsher world of work, presentation of ourselves can no longer be limited to a paper CV. Networking, the use of social media, and creative presentation of our talents and experience are now a must.

But if we are to survive and prosper in this new world more is needed than a simple career review. We owe it to ourselves, and to those around us, to carry out a more basic career reassessment. In fact, to go further even than that – a reassessment of just what we want from our working lives.

Seeking the positives

Good things come out of bad and if harder times cause reassessment of priorities this can bring positive outcomes.

Above all, reassessment means taking more control over our working lives and this, in turn, should cause us to choose to take more control of our futures. Taking responsibility for our future out of the hands of employers and into our own hands can now be a far more attractive prospect.

So it should not be a surprise to see a generation of rapidly increasing numbers of entrepreneurs and portfolio workers finding that the portfolio life offers the freedom, control and choice they are seeking.

For those who lose their prized jobs through no fault of their own, this need to take more control can be even more crucial. Even if a new job can be found, the odds are that it will require still more compromise and a worse fit between job specification and talents. Income for now, but less satisfaction in the future.

This 'How to' book helps you to plan how income and satisfaction can both grow in the future.

A greater in-depth reassessment of priorities is required. After all, this is the rest of your life that is in play and you should at least ensure that every option is considered.

Straitjackets

Careers, as they used to be understood, are becoming more and more rare. The best current definition of a career is 'the general progression of one's working life.' As you look back at your own career, you'll see a series of jobs, situations, positions, functions, or roles.

We spend our lives performing roles, but others determine the nature and scope of those roles. We can still be highly successful because we humans are good at adapting to circumstances. However, few of us end up in the career we always wanted. It's rare to find a degree subject being practically applied in a role five years later. How many of us at some time accepted the less preferred position because the money was better?

However much you've enjoyed it, whatever your successes, if you stand back and examine your life, and specifically your working life, objectively and dispassionately, it's unlikely that it has given scope for all your talents. You've worn the straitjacket. You've put to one side some of your dreams and abilities in order to fit the roles assigned to you.

A Gallup survey presented the following statement to employees of large organisations:

'At work I have the opportunity to do what I do best every day.'

Only 20% of respondents replied that they 'strongly agree' with the statement. What they do best is too often left at home or used outside the work environment.

You may have experienced *Bring YourSELF to Work Day*. Its purpose?

'By taking part, you will have permission to be more fully your authentic self by showing others more of who you are outside your work life and by sharing more of your dreams and aspirations with others at work.'

For many of us, our under-utilised talents, dreams and aspirations won't go away, won't let themselves be sidelined. We look for ways to use them in other parts of our lives. We run events, start societies, have hobbies, join committees, take evening classes, do charity work, some even write books. Our lives are a hybrid of paid work, unpaid work, planned leisure activities, and what we often term 'spare time'.

So whilst our lives may feel in balance, in reality they rarely are. We don't have our talents matched by what we do for work, and we don't have the correct balance between income and time – the balance which enables us to meet our priorities and our goals. That's why it's time to get the balance back.

Shortening and shrinking

However tight the straitjacket, however strong the imbalance, we adapt, commit, enjoy and succeed. The roller-coaster carries us through the ups and downs, tight corners and narrow squeaks. They're all part of life's rich pageant.

It's only when we take the helicopter view of ourselves and our lives that we see the imbalance and consider that there may be an alternative. That 'Helicopter Moment' comes at different times for each of us. It's usually triggered by family events, by job circumstances, by personal crises or spiritual shifts. Whatever the trigger, one of the underlying catalysts is Time. Research reveals that we start to have a greater awareness of our own mortality between the ages of thirty and forty. Our perception is that time is shortening. Similar to that of a holiday drawing to an end, we feel the need to make the most of it.

The other significant catalyst is what we term 'shrinking'. A feeling of stricture, limitation, narrowing, an awareness of doors closing. There comes a time when it's far more difficult to move into a new industry; when the top job becomes out of reach; when a desk job or sideways move comes on to our horizon.

If you haven't had your Helicopter Moment yet, don't put the book down. You're in the best position – you can be prepared and ready to address the shortening and shrinking before it hits you.

Your Portfolio Career

A portfolio career provides the antidote to shortening and shrinking. Opportunities re-appear, doors open, life balance is re-born, straitjackets removed.

There's a double opportunity contained in these pages – to put your working life in balance within your broader life – finding the whole you rather than the role, and within that to use the whole pool of your talents, many previously unused or under-used.

An attractive goal, perhaps. But how will you achieve it? How will you find that balance? How will you unlock those hidden talents?

Unleash your full potential

Your talents are enduring and unique to you and your greatest potential for growth is through identifying and utilising your greatest strengths.

We'll help you to identify those strengths, building on the talents you've been using in your current employed roles, and unearthing the hidden gems, which have been waiting for a chance to shine. Once you have these clearly in front of you, then you have the raw material to become 'Unlimited' – a word you'll find we use again and again in the course of this book.

Look at all your talents, not just those you've been using. Get to the core of your talents. Stop thinking of yourself as an Astrological Survey Supervisor (an ASS?), a PEM, JAE, FDD, or whatever other title your current business card expounds. To get the most from the many talents you have gained over your employed years, we have to look deeper, go back to basics, find the hidden treasure, the attributes that form the nucleus of your talents, experience and wisdom.

Unlock the wealth in your head

Wealth n. a great amount, a profusion

Too often, all the word 'wealth' means to us is money, assets, material goods. But few of us regard ourselves as wealthy; it becomes a mirage, moving away as we get tantalisingly closer.

It's also a fact that wealth only becomes truly productive when we realise it. We can be wealthy beyond measure, sufficient to give us a feeling of security and well-being, but until we get the cash from the bank and put it to work, our wealth has been of little purpose.

※ *Yet we are all immensely wealthy. We are all fortunate to have deep in our heads a host of pulsing brain-cells which contain our true wealth, a wealth safe from bank collapses, inflation, or theft.*

We each have a wealth of talents, a wealth of knowledge, a wealth of expertise, a wealth of experience, of contacts, of worldly wisdom. In fact, wealths beyond measure. You can't see them on an MRI scan. You can't get them out and count them to check they're still there. The great plus about them is that they are always growing, even though some are hidden, forgotten, even suppressed.

Releasing all your talents

Everything you have done, seen, experienced, since your earliest days has added to your stock of talents, knowledge and skills. Some have been gained through training, but the real core strengths come from your personality. We've already seen that they are not necessarily put to good use during our employed lives. But they're still there.

In later chapters you'll identify the full range of your talents, and be asked to really open your mind and to envisage how they can be put to work. You'll build a unique blueprint for your future. Being Unlimited is about having a role that suits your talents rather than somebody else's job spec.

Pause for a moment and think of the people you know who demonstrate quite different roles outside their employed role. Neil (name changed) is a not-too-brilliant salesman who just about holds on to his everyday role. In complete contrast his life outside work consists of running a large national youth organisation demanding a range of skills not required or demonstrated in his sales role.

Or Steve, a head-down IT boffin (you know the type) who in his leisure time burst into life as a stand-up comedian. Once this was discovered, he launched a new career as a brilliant after-dinner entertainer and now, portfolio-ing, teaches public speaking to executives.

> ✱ *Then there's the P-word: Passion. How many of us really bring passion into our employed lives? Have we got anything to be passionate about? Some may have, but the majority not.*

Enjoyment, interest, perhaps; but not Passion. After all, passion comes from inside us. Whatever the management may hope, it can't be artificially created by motivational speeches at a company conference. Most of us tend to be passionate about a different range of activities from those of our employed lives.

Write your own Job Specification

Job descriptions – written or unwritten – are devised by employers. That may well be yourself in your current management function, so you will understand what follows. A job description is written and the employer seeks to find the employee who best fits the description. If the recruitment is well designed and the recruiter sticks to the brief, the employer will hope for an 80% to 90% fit.

However, research shows that the typical employee fit, on the other hand, is less than 50%. The employee celebrates the gain of a job, promotion, extra income, and ignores the mismatch. After all, the employer is not interested in whether the employee enjoys doing all the 20 items on the job description; just that they have the majority of the talents described.

The interview for a portfolio role is quite different. It's one where you sit in both seats – employer and prospective employee. (Perhaps a mirror is needed.) As employer, you can make a statement to yourself which no employer would normally make:

✱ ***'Describe your talents and what you enjoy doing. Then I'll invent a role to fit them all.'***

A role that only fits YOU

If you're going to become Unlimited, if you're going to unleash your full potential, then you need a job that is so bespoke, so individual, so unique, that only you can fill it.

We call it **'Your Portfolio Life'** because it contains a fusion of what you want to do, what you have the talents to do and, most importantly, how you can reach your whole-life goals.

Thousands of people are already portfolio-ing. We'll learn more about portfolios in Chapter 2, and throughout the book we'll be meeting some of the people who have left their limited life behind, become Unlimited, and made the Portfolio Life work for them.

But this is individual to you, and the book will guide you through the process of drawing up your own unique job description for your portfolio future.

Wealth of opportunity

One wealth you possess which hasn't been mentioned yet is the wealth of opportunity. We don't always take our opportunities in life. We're held back by inertia, fear of failure, fear of the unknown, family pressures – all sorts of reasons for not taking the positive step.

Our deepest fear is not that we are inadequate. Our deepest fear is that we are powerful beyond measure. It is our light, not our darkness, that most frightens us. We ask ourselves, who am I to be brilliant, gorgeous, talented, and fabulous? Actually, who are you not to be?

Marianne Williamson
quoted by Nelson Mandela in his inaugural address

This book is about preparing for an opportunity – an opportunity you personally create, boldly making the move to seize the moment. Or it can be one imposed from the outside through redundancy or retirement. Many good opportunities are 'grasped' when the alternatives look less attractive.

As you work your way through the book, you will appreciate that the opportunity of becoming Unlimited, of identifying the real you, is one that offers considerable rewards.

Enjoy the rewards

One of our Portfolio Professional friends had been portfolio-ing for a year or so when he came out with the classic statement which sums up the Portfolio Life so well.

> ✱ *I never imagined that I could do what I enjoy, what I'm good at, and people would value me for it ... and pay me.*

Behind this statement lies the flexibility which only having a portfolio of different roles can bring. How much do you want to earn? Identify your talents well, market them, and your only limit is the amount of time you want to devote. Yes, portfolio-ing can be about earning well; if income is your prime goal.

Most portfolio people aim to earn as much as they earned in their employed life. But their other goal is to make the most of that diminishing resource, **Time**. Working until you drop is an unattractive prospect. Without getting too New Age about it, don't you want to see the sunrise and watch the flowers grow? Don't you want to see more of this world before you depart from it?

It is the achievement of equilibrium between income and time which lies at the heart of a life in balance. You can only achieve the balance which suits your life, if you have control of these two key factors.

The Portfolio Lifestyle offers you *control over your income and your time*, by building a working life that fits what you want out of your life rather than a role fulfilling the needs of others.

How to use this book

So far, a brief introduction, and the identifying of an opportunity. In the next chapters we will help, assist and guide you towards this opportunity.

The next two chapters of Part 1 introduce you to the concept of the Portfolio Life, encourage you to look more closely at some of the issues that you may be facing, and answer essential questions for your decision.

In Part 2 we use a series of models to help you focus on where you are now and where you want to be, assisting you in your decision on whether and when Portfolio Life could be the right course for you. There's guidance on planning your portfolio and choosing suitable roles.

Part 3 is about implementing your decision, the questions faced at the transition stage, and the Portfolio Bridge that allows you to plan your journey at your own pace.

Part 4 is full of specialist guidance to assist you in running, and succeeding in, your new Portfolio Life.

To summarise ...

- By now you know the subject of this book – it's YOU.

- We've seen how traditional jobs in organisations are like straitjackets, limiting the full use of our talents and potential, and leaving us seeking wider fulfilment and better balance.

- You've been introduced to the concept of the Wealth in your Head – the myriad talents, knowledge, skills and wisdom you have available to put to work for you.

- The challenge is to channel that wealth to become Unlimited; to fashion a role unique to you, and to reap the considerable rewards.

- That role is your Portfolio Life.

But just what is this 'Portfolio Life'? Where did it come from, and why? Who does it? Who is suited to it? The next two chapters provide the answers.

Brian Palmer's
Portfolio Journey

Charles Handy has much to answer for.

For a start, he wrote a book called 'On being 50 in the 80s'. Which I was, at the time. His book was inspirational. To me, at any rate. Fresh from a gruelling three-year tussle with corporate America, I was ripe for change. The idea that one could set one's own agenda, mix the cocktail of one's life oneself, was heady stuff. Then there was the quotation from Goethe on the wall of one of my favourite clients:

> **'...when one definitely commits oneself then providence moves too. All sorts of things occur to help one that would never have otherwise occurred ... all manner of unforeseen incidents and meetings and material assistance which no man could have dreamt would have come his way. Whatever you can do or dream you can, begin it. Boldness has genius, power, and magic in it. Begin it now.'**

So, okay – what next?

Time to take stock, time to decide what to commit to.

Time to ask the basic question: "How would you like it to be?"

In my own case, it was a mixture of things. Earning a living would be nice, at least for a few years until my pensions became due. BUT ... I wanted never to work full-time for a corporation again. I wanted to work towards becoming a serious artist rather than a leisure painter.

I had an idea for a new kind of business, but it would take time to put together. Could these all be reconciled? No way to find out but to do it ...

I made up a very fancy CV and wrote to everyone I knew. Plus a few head-hunters specialising in non-executive directors. Both in a very positive way, and with a tone of confidence I was far from feeling.

Then I started serious work on my Big Idea, signed up at Art College one day a week and continued to go to industry functions looking as prosperous as possible. Best of all, I went on holiday with my wife to France. For the first time in thirty years we told nobody where we were going (because we didn't know) or when we were coming back (ditto).

What happened? As to the motoring trip to France, serendipity kicked in, and we had the most marvellous time and the opportunity to think things through and really discuss our plans.

Publicising my availability had several consequences. An offer to be considered to head up a company very similar to the one I'd just left. (Politely declined.)

A slow-motion wrestle towards being a non-exec director of a company that was 'going public'. Two ongoing consultancies and a couple of smallish assignments. Not a bonanza, but the start of a portfolio.

And it left time to go to Art Classes, be involved in local issues, and work on my Big Idea. In the course of which, I discovered that it was by no means only middle-aged male professionals who liked the idea of portfolio living. The most wonderful PA/Administrator joined me from a much better job because I was able to promise her Wednesdays free to learn Bereavement Counselling. Radical, at the time.

After nine months gestation, we got the Big Idea together and launched it, supposedly on civilised, fairly relaxed, Charles Handy portfolio living principles. Unsurprisingly, it didn't turn out quite like that.

New Solutions, as the company was called, dominated my life for the next seven years. It was enormous fun, but it made for a very full existence. The portfolio contracted, Art School became night school, travel plans went 'on hold', local involvements fell by the wayside.

Seven exciting years on, New Solutions was sufficiently successful that I was able to pass it on to our management over time, on condition that they should let me gradually phase out, go to Art School properly on Mondays and Tuesdays, and work towards a Degree.

It took another seven years. I graduated in June '98, and have a new main career as an artist, with a couple of business and local interests for variety. (I'm glad I don't have to live on my art earnings though.)

When I started on this personal odyssey, now labelled Portfolio

Living, I wrote myself a memo in the form of some verses, one of which read:

If you really want to travel – Do it now.
Or life's mysteries to unravel – Do it now.
Cut the knots and start creating.
You can't keep procrastinating.
FOR THE MEN IN BLACK ARE WAITING – DO IT NOW.

And incidentally, Goethe was right.
Try it and see.

Brian Palmer is a working artist and printmaker (he has exhibited at the RA Summer Exhibition), a recently-retired (after 42 years!) Non-Executive Director of Young's Brewery, and a writer and lecturer on the local history of Highgate.

2

THE PORTFOLIO LIFE

When making your choice in life, do not neglect to live.
Samuel Johnson

A definition

We've talked about unleashing your full potential, unlocking the wealth in your head and enjoying the rewards of your unique talents. We've seen that there is a way of getting greater control of your life and achieving a better balance.

So what is the dream job that makes all this possible?

It's one that gives people a freedom and flexibility not present in the employed life. It's a role that offers a panorama of the whole of life, its demands and its goals – rather than just concentrating on the working part. It's one which starts with its adherents reassessing the satisfaction and reward they want from their remaining years and what they want to contribute to family, friends, and the society around them. In short, the opportunity to have a truly life-enhancing and life-deepening future role.

Charles Handy coined the term 'Portfolio Life' in his book *The Age of Unreason* in 1989. He explained his concept in this way:

> *'... a portfolio of activities – some we do for money, some for interest, some for pleasure, some for a cause... the different bits fit together to form a balanced whole ... greater than the parts.'*

Handy realised that for many people the changes taking place in employment patterns, in society, in Western culture, demanded a new type of role, one which could provide them with a much more holistic, more fulfilling lifestyle.

Portfolio workers are individuals who undertake a range of different projects for different organisations or clients. Essentially self-employed, they can undertake one project at a time or be working on several projects for various employers simultaneously.

Handy used the terms 'Portfolio Work', 'Portfolio Career', and 'Portfolio Life'. But what of the people who adopt this new role? Since Handy, its early adopters have described themselves, in somewhat reserved terms, as 'having a portfolio lifestyle'.

✱ *Now, with more and more joining the portfolio ranks each year, we award them the professional title their role merits, recognising them as 'Portfolio Professionals'.*

The rise of the Portfolio Professional

Portfolio Professionals don't wear a uniform. We can't recognise them by their eggheads or loud voices or demonstrative gestures. But PP-hunters know where to look. They know that PPs are rarely seen on rush-hour trains; that they're more likely to be on the golf course when it's quiet. Don't look for them at airports on busy bank holiday weekends. Although PPs probably fly more (for leisure pleasure) than their peers do, they can, as we have already learned, choose their time.

But when you do spot them, you should register the fact that PPs are the fastest-growing group in the UK economy. Not bad for an army of people who still have no official title.

Look in government statistics and you will find part-time, full-time, temporary; you'll find plumbers, consultants, designers and gardeners. But no Portfolio Workers. What you will find is a rapidly growing number of people classed as 'self-employed'. Numbers in self-employment have risen by over 25% since 2000. In addition, there has been a major rise in new business registrations, now running at a rate of 400,000 per year, with statistics showing that 63% of all new businesses have no employees, just an owner. Hidden Portfolio Professionals?

In Part 4, we'll see that one of the early decisions for a PP is whether, for tax purposes, to be classed as self-employed or whether to buy a £100 off-the-shelf company and become a director. For our purposes now, we can simply recognise that both statistical groupings contain many tens of thousands of Portfolio Professionals. The growth of their numbers has been a consequence of a plethora of changes taking place over the last twenty years in society, culture, economics, demographics and employment. Let's examine some of them.

Changing work priorities

The children of post-war Britain quickly learned that their goal should be a steady job, providing a regular income for life.

In return for a projected lifetime's loyalty from the employee, the more enlightened employers began to offer more than just an income during employment; completing the full stint of service resulted in an income through retirement as well. Supporting the working practices was the work ethic, and its associated lures of money, status and recognition. With shorter life expectancy, work filled most of the anticipated human span, and was both the income-generator and the major channel of social interaction and self-fulfilment.

The new social forces unleashed in the 1960s and 1970s challenged the old establishment and the accepted order. They also brought into question many of the previously accepted tenets, including the work ethic. Values were changing.

During the 1970s and 1980s, average disposable income increased by two-thirds. It brought holidays in Spain, consumer durables to make lives easier, and a car outside most front doors. With income came choice. But for many the attraction of higher disposable income began to wane. The treadmill of the constant demand for disposable income and the need to be 'better than the Jones' left many feeling trapped in mindless jobs, jobs demanding a level of energy and focus that leaves little time for anything else.

We began to see time as the alternative to income, with an

increasing realisation that the two must be kept in balance if we are to have fulfilled experiential lives.

✱ *Work is one path to self-fulfilment, but often involves sacrificing other parts of life which can be equally or more fulfilling.*

Above all, with the new freedoms came a requirement to set our own definitions of success. Success was no longer to be measured only in consumables. On the new checklist of life there were items which were only a dream for preceding generations: enjoyment, excitement, experience.

Overlaid on this came the recessions of the last three decades and the realisation that even those most highly prized of employees, the city traders, could face redundancy. We knew now that the old covenant was no longer. We had to look after ourselves. All jobs are temporary whatever the contract of employment may say. The employer's commitment to us lasts as long as we are economically productive, and our commitment to the employer is equally short-term.

So the established order is changing to a world where to change jobs, companies and even industries during a working lifetime becomes the norm. At the same time, the definition of work is altering as the distinction between full-time work and part-time work narrows. Job sharing, flexible working and home-working have increased the range of choice between income and time.

In the private sector the age of final-salary pensions has passed and with it comes a new era when later ageing and improved health leads to an expectation that we will retire later and have to wait longer for our state pensions. However, from research findings, we see that even the lucky generation do not choose to sit back in full retirement. Given the choice, most would opt to go on working; demanding flexibility and choice.

Little wonder that a big question is now being asked more frequently:

Should we live to work, or work to live?

I haven't done half the things I want to do with my life.
Is it just work, retire, die?

Anon

A job title should not be a justification for being alive. The hours, the stress, are all part of a treadmill that draws us away from real life, and the things we want to do. Life is short, and we should not waste it.

Surveys consistently reveal that people's primary objective is to spend more time with their family and friends. Unfortunately, wearing 'job blinkers' narrows their minds to see only incremental change – a few less hours work, another day's annual leave – as a credible option. With family and mortgage, the idea of swapping income for time seems remote. But this doesn't mean that the desire isn't there. It's only when you pause the treadmill to consider your life in more depth that the real focus and true priorities come through. Many of us have sat on the beach on holiday and questioned what our life is about. Or were you too busy keeping in touch with the office?

In recent research, over 50% of respondents said that they intended to take a gap year. Gaps are now being taken through all the stages of life. Life as a continuous working career is no longer. Breaks from it are positives, not negatives. Gap years are just one response to a self-examination revealing that there is something missing. The prospect is a more exciting life path which simply involves doing what's enjoyable and achieving that dream.

But how does one achieve the kind of flexibility, which gives more time with family and friends, or become a 'serial gapper'? It's the kind of flexibility that doesn't come easily from the limited life of working for an employer. But it can come from designing an *Unlimited life* as a Portfolio Professional.

Chris Ashcroft's
Portfolio Journey

I joined the Royal Navy in 1980, promising myself that I would only stay as long as I was still still enjoying it. So every few years, I took a hard look at life, work and the balance between the two before embarking on the next challenge. By 2011, I found myself at the Ministry of Defence in London, with the Thames river taxis the only ships in view.

Although I enjoyed Service life, the opportunities to balance work and fun diminished as the Armed Forces downsized. I had a choice; carry on, enjoying my work less each day, or make some serious changes and fulfil my promise. That promise, made 24 years earlier, drove me to re-examine what I wanted from life. I realised that the most important thing was to take back control.

I had made lots of contacts in the defence industry and consultancy companies whilst at the MoD; there was always someone offering to take my CV. This was my introduction to professional networking and it was about this time that I met my first Portfolio Professional; indeed, it was the first time I had even heard the term.

Mind made up, in 2003 I requested early voluntary retirement. The Armed Forces give excellent support to those who decide to leave voluntarily or otherwise. They provide an array of courses from the basics of writing CVs through brick-laying and plumbing to short professional courses. However while the package serves well those wanting salaried employment or those starting their own businesses, it offers little guidance or information on portfolio working. I enrolled on a Career Transition Workshop. The course helped me recognise my worth and translate my Service skills into civilian market language – a Serviceman's understanding of 'good leadership' and 'excellent communications skills', for example, are considerably different to how civilian companies consider the same skills.

That done, I went back to see my new-found friend, the Portfolio Professional, who gave me invaluable help and guidance. I had received lucrative job offers within the defence industry, but they offered the same control (or lack of control) over my day-to-day life. I opted to pursue portfolio working, and set about analysing my military work skills.

I soon realised that, in addition to my training for war-fighting, I had also developed skills in:

- *basic accounting*
- *HR*
- *maritime security*
- *personnel development and training*
- *project management and consultancy*
- *interim management (life in the Forces is a series of interim management posts!)*

They are all transferable to the civilian market. This analysis helped me realise that I had been portfolio working for years. The only real problem was that I had not been in control of the portfolio or my spare time.

I analysed just what I wanted from life and what I needed financially. It was not just salary that I had to consider. The Force also provides free medical and dental care, some free travel, reasonable leave allowance and a whole range of other packages all of which have a financial value and have to be taken into account when deciding to leave. Only you will know what life/work balance is right for you, but you have to assess it and plan ahead.

During the final weeks with the Navy, I formally rejected two excellent job offers. Even now, I admit to near panic. I was vindicated when both companies responded by offering consultancy assignments. I decided to set up my own limited company as a vehicle to manage my professional services. By the time I came to 'sign off' from the Navy, I was already working on my first contract. It spanned some 8 months abroad with lots of opportunities to develop my portfolio during UK breaks. Since leaving the Navy in 2004 I have completed a variety of consultancy jobs, some as short as half a day, as well as pursuing my next great adventure. I have also completed periods of full -time employment as a director, usually in small companies undergoing rapid change. I always look for a key project to provide the basic needs, both financially and in work interest, then I seek smaller projects/jobs that also provide a reasonable income. Add to that the constant networking for business development, which enables me to catch up with old friends, and it makes for an enjoyable and challenging lifestyle and gives me plenty of time for my real passion – off-piste skiing. Together my work and leisure represent a portfolio of interests and most importantly for me, I have regained control.

> **Chris Ashcroft retired from the Royal Navy in 2004 with the rank of Commander. He has been director at 3 'micro' companies and both Operations & Technical Director at a maritime security company. He continues to work as a business consultant in the maritime security and underwater defence industries. His current activities comprise Chairmanship (& Director) for a Freehold Company which owns one of the largest mansion blocks in Kensington, active membership of various committees spanning housing through to the Society for Underwater Technology, and day-to-day work as COO/Director for the Security Association for the Maritime Industry.**

Charles Handy

In *The Age of Unreason*, Charles Handy set out his vision of how the economic and social changes he had experienced during his own working lifetime, would extrapolate into the future.

Although frequently described as a 'management guru', Handy is much more a social philosopher, taking a broad view of society and the position within that of business, the corporate world and the individual. He foresaw how the advent of the Knowledge Society would change the whole basis of employment and, together with changing demographics, would substantially alter the pattern of our working lives.

> *'We'll all leave organisations earlier and we're all likely to have 30 years on our own now. So I believe that from the age of 50 onward every man and woman will have to learn to manage their own life.'*

He suggested that 'portfolio' may be an appropriate word to re-describe work in a fuller sense. Treating his various occupations as you might shares in a portfolio, Handy seeks to optimise the return, not only in financial rewards but also in personal satisfaction and contribution to society.

> *'A work portfolio is a way of describing how the different bits of work in our life fit together to form a balanced whole.'*

Portfolio concept

Charles Handy was not the first Portfolio Person; he was simply the first to use the term. Charles worked for Shell, reached the age of 50 and, like many others, wondered whether what he was doing was really useful, and whether it was what he wanted to do for the rest of his life.

Despite his high-level role, Charles still recognised himself as a cog in the wheel, part of a process. He quotes a time when his wife Elizabeth asked him three key questions:

- Are you proud of your work?
- Are the people you work with special?
- Is the organisation doing really good things?

His answer to each of these was 'all right'. To which Elizabeth Handy pointedly asked whether he was prepared to settle for the rest of his life being just 'all right'.

But there was the green grass on the other side. He was in mid-life, a stage at which we start to think more about the remaining years. By 50, even though career and health are still going for us, there's something at the back of our minds that triggers each time there are decisions to be made. It reminds us that there are 'end-points' for life, for work, for relationships.

In later chapters, you will be identifying your own personal goals for the rest of your life. If there's one word that summarises Charles Handy's goals, it is *'independence'*. Frightening, perhaps ... but wonderfully liberating. Unlike many gurus, he practised what he preached and adopted the independent life, the life that he characterised with the word 'portfolio'.

Work ... in Handy chunks

'What matters now is how we use our time,
not how much of that time we use.'
Charles Handy

Handy's first issue was with the word 'work'. Work was important, a fundamental part of life. But 'work' is commonly identified with the single job which we go out to do – too limiting a definition. Yes, the job is one form of work, but there are others. What we usually term 'work' is more accurately described as 'paid work', and while working for pay is essential, it should certainly not be the whole point of life.

So an important part of Handy's thinking was not opting to become self-employed or taking a form of early retirement. It was in using that independence to 'chunk' his life into the important elements, which would meet his goals for himself and for those around him.

His new definition identified **four types of work**:

- **Paid work**
- **Study work**
- **Gift work**
- **Home work**

A further step saw him dividing his time between these four elements and imposing strict limits on each. If all four were important to the balance of his life, then each had to have its allotted space and time. The Portfolio Life brought choice and a major element in that choice was how to spend time.

> *'Some people will spend money to save their time, others will spend their time to save money.'*

Paid work

Having a sufficient income is an important element in all our lives. But we find ourselves sacrificing other areas of our lives in order to stay on the consumption treadmill. Handy, on the other hand, asked himself the simple question: 'How much income is necessary to meet my needs?' Having done so, he was able to define the proportion of his time that would be spent on paid work. This had to leave him at a comfortable level for himself and his family, but the more time he spent making money, the less time was available for doing the things he really wanted to do.

Study work

The move to a knowledge-based society has made knowledge workers prime candidates for the Portfolio Life. Employers look to buy in broader skills from out-sourced knowledge workers. Some knowledge will naturally erode in life outside the corporate nest, but experience and worldly wisdom are enhanced within a broader Portfolio Life.

Workers selling knowledge must constantly renew that knowledge. Portfolio Professionals need to be not just up with the pace, but ahead of it. Their wide variety of activities, tasks and projects necessitates continuous learning and self-development. Occasional spare time is not sufficient; study work needs its due allocation of their life.

Of course study work should include study for the unpaid parts of the portfolio. The Portfolio Life offers the opportunity to realise dreams – studying to turn leisure photography or an interest in cooking into a serious, and even a paying, proposition. So many of us want to learn more, whether through evening classes or a degree course. The great thing is that these can be chunked into a portfolio.

Gift work

A key element of Handy's design for his own portfolio was to formalise the need to 'put something back'. Many feel that it's an important part of our role in society, and that an occasional financial contribution to good causes is not enough; but we rarely allocate sufficient time for it.

Gift work comes in many different guises. For many it is donating, on a pro bono basis, the skills which form the core of their paid work. For others it can be totally unrelated to their paid work, offering variety as well as that feel-good factor. But it only happens if time is made for it.

Home work

Handy's fourth type of work is best defined as 'family and home maintenance'. Each of us has a responsibility for managing our home and contributing to the life of our family and those around us. Portfolio Workers have the choice of using their unique talents to bring in sufficient income to pay others for home maintenance, or using some of their time to contribute to it. In the case of family life, a well-balanced portfolio can only be achieved by chunking real time to spend with family, which won't be eaten into by other apparently more pressing elements.

Time for yourself

🟔 *There's a fifth chunk in most portfolios: chunking time for yourself as well as for work.*

'Time for yourself' includes not only family time but also personal time; time for holidays and non-work pastimes. The whole principle of chunking life is to allocate and ring-fence time for each important element.

Portfolio Life in reality

Charles Handy chunked his life, varying the chunks from year to year dependent on his own goals and priorities and, increasingly, on those of his wife, Elizabeth. She has built her own portfolio, developing her passion for photography into a professional business, and they have co-authored a number of books. They still adhere firmly to their agreed chunking. The proportions of work may have changed over time but the time principles on which their Portfolio Life is based still hold firm.

Portfolio Professionals: the facts

* **Portfolio Professionals are not retired.** There are PPs who, moving through the stages of their PP years, may choose to reduce paid work and concentrate their talents in unpaid and gift work. But they are definitely not retired.

* **Being a Portfolio Professional is not about opting out and setting up a smallholding on a remote island.** Of course, PPs who combine the smallholding with part-time lecturing on organic foods at the local college and sit on an advisory panel for a major supermarket, clearly have a meaningful portfolio.

* **Portfolio Professionals design a portfolio which suits their purposes and not those of an employer.** PPs have more freedom

and more flexibility than an employee. That's a key part of being Unlimited. It is also different from single-business self-employment, full-time contract working or interim management, although elements such as these can be useful temporary additions within a portfolio.

- **Portfolio Professionals work smarter.** Life-work balance comes from planning what is wanted out of life and having control over how it is achieved. Doing what you enjoy doing is working smarter; and the chunking helps to keep the balance right.

- **Portfolio Professionals have different success criteria.** Salary, position and title are no longer important. PPs define their own criteria for success and measure progress against these. Income might be an important criterion to recognise at their annual review of themselves, but so could ticking off another few countries visited or time spent with friends.

- **Portfolio Professionals can have as much job security as employees.** With a well-designed portfolio, risks are spread, putting precious eggs in more than one basket. At the bottom line, PPs are selling their talents. Nurtured and updated, they put together a far more marketable proposition than the last job title.

- **Portfolio Professionals don't have to start with a step into the unknown.** There's an easy route to becoming a PP, by taking advantage of existing employment. This can be the seed-bed for any portfolio. PPs use their spare time to build new parts of their prospective portfolio, and change the priorities of their working day to ensure more networking, wider industry involvement, formal training etc. If they can arrange for their past job to become a part-time element of their new Portfolio Life, the step into the unknown can be a gentle and well-prepared one.

- **Portfolio Professionals need not lack community.** Many employees see their working environment as providing a social interaction which they would find hard to replace. They view working at home, the end of a telephone, and the tapping of emails as an isolating prospect. But the Portfolio Life provides the PP with the choice of how much contact they require. It's up to them. PPs choose which part of their life – paid, gift, or home – will provide the contact and community they seek, and they build this into their portfolio. Above all, the prospect of choosing the people you work with, and escaping office politics, can be wonderfully liberating.

Portfolio-ing – the great and good

You have already read a number of the Portfolio Journeys. They're from contributors who made the move and are sharing their experiences with us. A cross-section of the portfolio-ing community, getting on with their lives, enjoying their chosen roles, contributing to the community around them, and benefiting from the rewards of the lifestyle.

Our contributors are not names you will necessarily know, but that doesn't mean that the lifestyle is not one for the better known. Here are some examples.

- **Sir Trevor Brooking** certainly had a successful career but early retirement, inevitable for footballers, brought him to portfolio-ing. Director of West Ham, BBC pundit and anchorman, chairman of sports bodies including Sport England, Director of Football at the FA. He even fitted in a temporary assignment as caretaker manager of West Ham. Trevor's portfolio also includes extensive Gift Work, particularly related to charities supporting disabled people and youngsters. A well-balanced portfolio based around sport.

- **Germaine Greer** has been portfolio-ing for most of her adult life. University connections, for example as a Professor at Warwick University, have maintained the Study Work chunk, while writing books and presenting on television have formed much of her Paid Work. Germaine is a great example of using the Portfolio Life to do things outside the norm, whether her gardening column for Private

Eye many years ago or her surprise appearance on Celebrity Big Brother. You can't get a more varied portfolio than that.

- **Michael Portillo** is a good example of a Portfolio Professional who lost his job – as an MP. He fought back to win another seat, but gradually developed his portfolio while still carrying out his job as an MP. He finally 'retired' from the House in 2005. Michael's portfolio has included non-executive directorships, judging book awards, writing newspaper columns, and doing Gift Work for a number of organisations. As a television presenter, he is well known for his Railway Journeys, This Week (the political discussion programme), Dinner with Portillo and many more. But what stands out is the way he has incorporated his enthusiasms into his portfolio: as a theatre critic, on the board of an orchestra, and developing his love of opera into introducing Wagner for the BBC.

- **Sir Gerry Robinson** is now one of the UK's best-known business personalities through his BBC series, *I'll Show Them Who's Boss*. His high-flying business career saw him leading large corporate organisations, coming to public prominence with his move to Granada and the take-over of Forte. As he withdrew from full-time executive positions, his portfolio broadened to include the Chair of the Arts Council, his TV presenting, and a number of non-executive roles including Chairman of Allied Domecq. Although seen by many as a hard-nosed businessman, Gerry's priorities reflect those of many other Portfolio Professionals: 'In my view, the only time really worth spending is time with your family.'

- **Sir Tony Robinson** (no relation) has his place in TV history as Baldrick in Blackadder. His acting career has been long and successful, starting as one of Fagin's gang in Oliver!, followed by a long list of film, stage and TV credits. But Tony's portfolio of roles is much wider. He's written and narrated children's stories, been active in the actors' union, Equity, and on the national executive of the Labour Party. His passion for popularising knowledge saw him developing his enthusiasm for archaeology into the successful series, *Time Team*. His Gift Work includes Oxfam, Comic Relief, and many more. This broad portfolio may have been based on his acting fame, but has now taken Tony into many other areas where he's been able to pursue his passions, enthusiasms, and beliefs.

These, with many thousands of others, get a kick from the variety and flexibility, which the Portfolio Life offers. Their portfolios have clear connections with their earlier careers, their networks are important, but they have then branched out into wider roles and other areas.

This is about YOU

This book isn't about a concept, about Charles Handy or Michael Portillo. It's about YOU.

This is your life. This is your future. This is your opportunity.

There's a wonderful book by Allen Carr that has helped many people give up smoking. They come to it after years of attempts with tablets, patches, or hypnotism. As you make your way through the 459 pages, there's a growing awareness that the time for decision is getting closer with the turn of each page. Then, there in the penultimate chapter, it arrives. You can go no further. The remaining cigarettes must be destroyed, or you'll never give up.

Your portfolio decision is not so time-critical. Portfolio-ing can come at any stage of life. All we ask is that by the end of this book you have made a decision on whether or not this would be a good option for you. As you will see, that decision can mean starting immediately, or deferring it to give time for planning and preparation. In fact, the magic element in the portfolio decision is that the longer you take to make it the more compelling it becomes.

So the pressure's off. Sit back and enjoy the ride.

To summarise...

- In this chapter we took a step back to take a broad view of what the Portfolio Life is all about.

- Viewing its historical context and its relevance in today's world gives perspective and confidence.

- It's your life but, with the guiding principles firmly in your mind, you'll make a better job of designing your own portfolio later in the book.

- Concepts such as chunking are valuable learning points. They're not about time management, but life management.

In Chapter 1 we introduced the benefits of you becoming Unlimited.

In Chapter 2 we've explained the concept of the Portfolio Life and the reasons for its success.

In the next chapter we put these together and show you how the Portfolio Life can work for you.

Stephen Grainger's
Portfolio Journey

I joined the Metropolitan Police Service (MPS) in 1977 at the age of 18 having had a brief career in banking in the City after leaving school. I found myself at a very young age patrolling the streets of South and West London, quickly being promoted to Sergeant at the age of 23. I climbed up the ladder of promotion through varying areas of policing such as training and development, corporate change programmes, community policing, staff officer to senior officers, Heathrow Airport and traffic management.

My last 5 years were particularly significant given that at 30 years service one could effectively retire, aged 48, and seek new career opportunities. In the last four years of my career I reached the rank of Chief Superintendent in the Capital of London. I had operational command roles as head of police training and Royalty Protection – the last position being in charge of policing for all London Palaces, Windsor Castle, Scotland and personal protection duties in the UK and abroad.

When I realised the '30 year barrier' was approaching rapidly and with 18 months to go I started to focus on retiring. I sought the help of a friend, Heather White, who has contributed to the editions of this book. As a result of her assistance, and my own reading of the book, I quickly realised the portfolio life style was a very attractive way ahead after a career in policing. I couldn't put the book down and constantly used it as a reference guide. Given the institutionalised career life style I had enjoyed in the Police, reading the book released some new thinking, innovation and imagination, which changed my mindset and approach to my future life. I felt relieved in a way because the 'norm' in the Police is to think of getting another 'job' at retirement and I didn't want to do that!

With advice from Heather and this book, I planned my retirement for January 2007. During the previous year I was exposed to a number of networks and key individuals, through which I developed my confidence and new skills in preparation for leaving the MPS and stepping out into the new world of self-employment. Firstly, I looked at my contact list and who I knew. I literally sat down and did some serious networking with them. This led to my first potential piece of work with an iconic Sporting Club in the UK, which gave me the confidence to develop further consulting work as I then knew I had a sound income and working foundation to move forward. I eventually left the MPS in April 2007 with four significant contracts/associations in place ranging from security consultancy to FSA compliance/ alternative investments consultancy.

I distinctly remember my first day after leaving the MPS. Stepping out of the house and down to the local railway station for a meeting up in the City felt really odd, exciting and exhilarating. These are the only words I can use to say how I remember feeling. Changing my lifetime behaviour to this portfolio way of life that I had signed myself up to filled me with a huge amount of energy and determination to develop as much work as possible.

As time went on I developed the passion of the portfolio lifestyle. I shared my experiences with many of my colleagues who were still serving senior officers in the MPS and ended up having several 1-1 with these ex colleagues (who were considering retirement). This has led to a point where I feel now I am a 'champion' for the portfolio lifestyle and have advocated it as a significant life changing process to many serving officers as well as friends and business colleagues from similar institutions.

What I have found is that the portfolio lifestyle allowed me to have a diverse and flexible way of life. I went on holiday virtually where and when I wanted to. I don't have to answer to anyone every day other than myself. You have to be self-disciplined about what you do and the management of your time. For me, I have a life that I am in charge of, which fits in with our lifestyle. I meet a vast range of people in many occupations and enjoy making connections. Heather White often describes me as a 'good connector'! I never did this before because in the Police Service one never really stepped outside into the commercial sector.

What I really enjoyed was the ability to mix and match work around my stage of life. I enjoyed the range of different work streams

I have. I did what I wanted to do because I enjoyed it and never took on work I wouldn't enjoy.

The success of this portfolio working secured a new permanent career, which was too good to miss. To move from a large organization to suddenly a less than 'risk averse' style of career, allowed me to find out more about myself. It broadened my professional competencies to enable me to tackle most things. A superb experience and once again I thank all those who helped me with the initial decision to jump into the world of self – employment in 2007.

Finally, I hope readers realise they can do it and actually enjoy their semi-retirement as I am doing!

Thank you Building a Portfolio Career.

Stephen Grainger is a retired Chief Superintendent of the Metropolitan Police Service. His first step in portfolio was working as Managing Director of a small company of associates involved in security, risk-threat management and event management consultancy services. He had a diverse portfolio including leadership training and FS consultancy. He is now Head of Security at the All England Lawn Tennis Club in South West London.

3

YOU AND THE PORTFOLIO LIFE

Travel, change, interest, excitement!
The whole world before you,
and a horizon that's always changing!
Mr Toad, *The Wind in the Willows*

In Chapter 2, we gave you an insight into the concept of the Portfolio Life and you met some people who have adopted it successfully. However, it's you who has the opportunity to become Unlimited.

This chapter focuses on **you**, encourages you to look more closely at where **your** life is now and where it's taking you, and it seeks to answer some of the questions, which will be most pressing for **your** decision.

Crossroads and controls

You are at a crossroads. You may not have known you were, but by reading *Building A Portfolio Career* you now have a decision to make. Your road through life has seen many crossroads already, in your personal and work life.

You've been faced with choices; some straightforward, some more difficult. At each crossroad, decisions were necessary – income, location, prospects. After each crossroad, regrets and second thoughts soon dull as we make the most of the road we have chosen.

At some time, many of us have faced a crossroads where one of the signposts said, *'Do your own thing'*. We looked up the road; pot holes stood out, and dim street lighting meant that we couldn't see our destination clearly. We chose the apparently straighter road of continued employment.

Crossroads are increasingly common in today's world of work. Stop signs and T-junctions are increasingly in evidence. Change of direction is forced on us, and sideways is often the only choice. We look for the best alternative route on which to set out again.

More frequent crossroads are not the only difficulty facing us. The controls are often no longer in our hands, and the older you are, the more those decisions affect you, and those who depend on you.

The right road?

In retrospect, your decisions turned out to be the appropriate ones and you're on the right road now. You enjoy your current role, work with people you enjoy working with, handle the stress, the long hours.

But is that how it is? Will there be another promotion? Will you be with your current employer until retirement? Is your job truly fulfilling? Is your industry exciting, innovative, ethical? When they write your obituary, will you be proud to have spent your life doing what you're doing now?

The freedom of the open road

This book presents you with another crossroads. It presents you not with a career choice but with a **life choice**. It demands honesty, unbiased analysis, and an assessment of what you really want from your broader life and from your remaining working life.

Can you be a Portfolio Professional? The next few chapters will assist you in making that decision.

Freedom is something that few experience in their working lives. That's why so many who choose self-employment describe it as a liberating experience. Yes, you have the freedom to make your own mistakes. You're in charge. You determine the tasks, control the projects. You have the freedom to make the choices.

Your current job

Let's take a brief look at your current job. What do you get out of it?
Do you love it dearly? Or do you spend a good part of your working day passing the time and planning for the weekend?
Ask yourself the three 'Elizabeth Handy questions'.

- *Are you proud of your work?*
- *Are the people you work with special?*
- *Is the organisation doing really good things?*

Add another two questions:

- **Do you really enjoy what you're doing?**
- **Are you doing what you really enjoy?**

If your answers are positive and you see continuing in your employed role as being your preferred choice, that's good. Just bear in mind that others may not because, as an employee, the choice of whether you continue in your job does not solely rest with you. And the older you get, the less it's in your hands.

Jobs get outgrown, people are promoted beyond their competence level, see the sideways move coming, suffer from office politics or begin to question their organisation's ethics.

Have you ever found yourself thinking: *'There must be more to work than this.'* Or even: *'There must be more to life than this.'*

Cushion and handcuffs ...

But how soft is your cushion? The organisation is taking good care of you. There's a salary and all the trimmings. Enough to provide a level of inertia and make any move to portfolio-ing a real leap of faith.

And then there are the handcuffs. A very few are held by golden handcuffs with financial inducements. Most other handcuffs are slowly rusting. As the cushion becomes less soft, the handcuffs – pension, private health scheme etc – start to bite. Negative reasons for staying where you are come to the fore. It's difficult stopping being a wage-slave.

Of course, you can always wait to be pushed, for somebody else to make the decision for you.

... or trampoline?

But what if, when you bale out, the Portfolio trampoline awaits you? The opportunity not only to bounce back in financial terms but also in life. The opportunity to get the balance right.

Prospective PPs envision trampolines not cushions, and see handcuffs for what they are: restraints to creativity, innovation and a holistic life.

Is it for you?

Let's look at bit closer at how you might go about making your portfolio decision. For most people hearing about the Portfolio Life for the first time there's an immediate attraction. We all value independence. We all value flexibility. We all want to spend more time doing what we enjoy and less time doing what we don't enjoy. Most of us want something more out of life than a 9 to 5 job. So although there are lots of buts and lots of questions, by this stage the Portfolio Life is looking worthy of further investigation.

That's the Portfolio Life as a practical working concept. But what about you? What about you as a Portfolio Professional? Is it a good fit for you? Have you got what it takes to succeed?

You're unique, and the life-stage you're at makes your goals even more individual. Those individual goals will be revealed by the models in Part 2. Here we look at some of the issues behind them.

The Careers Game

You've probably bought property in Mayfair when playing *Monopoly*, and solved the knifing in the conservatory in *Cluedo*. But did you ever play *Careers*? Not as high-profile, but a best-seller in its day and still around. Success comes from setting goals for your career at the start of the game, and being the first to achieve them all. The choice is relatively simple: a balance between Fame, Fortune or Happiness. You decide your own success formula and race to be the first to achieve it. It's your choice, and you win or lose based on that choice.

It's rather similar to what we seek to achieve in this book. Using the **Top 10 Hits Model** in Part 2, you will be assisted to set your goals for the rest of your life. For the first time you have an opportunity to set balanced goals and be a winner by meeting them. Fame is probably not a goal for the average Portfolio Professional. Fortune and Happiness certainly are.

Waning weekends

There are two problems with weekends: they're only two days long... and they're running out. How many have you got left?

Assuming life expectancy of 75 years, you have the following weekends to look forward to:

- If you're 40 ... 1800 weekends
- If you're 50 ... 1300 weekends
- If you're 60 ... 780 weekends

Suddenly weekends take on greater importance. But they're still only two days long – and, annoyingly, everybody has them at the same time.

The standard response is that you should make the most of them, watch less television, lie in bed less, be more constructive and proactive. But there's an even better way: put more weekends in your life, or at the very least move your weekends into more useful parts of your diary. Why are weekends always between weeks? Combine them and chunk them and they become real time again.

The **Lifetime Circles Model** in Part 2 lets you review the use of your time.

Things to do before you die

It is no coincidence that books with the phrase 'before you die' in their title are appearing everywhere. They are driven from one side by the knowledge that life is running out and from the other by a growing realisation that we can do something about it. Imagine a book entitled *1000 Places to See Before You Die* being published in the 1970s before the advent of cheaper air travel and before a more relaxed attitude to careers.

Do you plan to wield your driver on the *1001 Golf Holes You Must Play Before You Die*? Or visit the *Fifty Places to Fly-Fish Before You Die*? Or are you one of the many people who have worked out their own list and published it on the web? If you haven't got a web presence to publish it, have you at least got a list? It's a big world out there and if you wait too long, it may be too late to do some of the more active things on your list. Will you fit them all into your five weeks of annual leave?

You can look at what you really want to do with the rest of your life using the **Last Big Birthday Party Model** in Part 2.

Your current life

Take a critical look at your current life. Put compromise and second best to one side for a moment. As you review it, don't accept that 'that's just the way it is'. You can go through a whole lifetime using excuses like that.

- Does your life consist of doing what you want to do?
- If you think it does, do those around you agree?
- Do you give yourself brownie points for making it to the open evenings at school?
- But what about the children's soccer or hockey games?
- Are your weekends interrupted by desk work or calls from the office?
- Overall, are the things you're doing with your life a good match for your (unwritten) priorities?

The **Wheel of Life Model** in the next chapter is designed to guide you on your life roles and priorities.

Your questions answered

So it still looks attractive. Yes, you want some of those things this promises. Yes, you'd like to give it a go or at least consider it further. But you've still got lots of questions.

? Can anybody start the Portfolio Life?

Successful Portfolio workers are all ages and come from all walks of life.

The Wealth in Your Head can be built on long experience, or newly acquired through formal or informal training. As we'll see when we look at what motivates PPs, most will use their existing industry or role as a base but seek additional avenues to meet their broader aspirations.

Most moves into Portfolio Work take place over the age of forty, when skills have been learned, experience gained, and the wealth in the head established. This is the time when many begin to pose themselves the bigger questions as age and its consequences come into sight for the first time: *'This isn't a rehearsal. What do I really want to do with my life? How can I see more of my children before they leave home? Shouldn't I be giving something back?'*

? How different is it?

Having reached the other side and become a Portfolio Professional, there's no doubt that it's a different style of life. That's its attraction and reward, but it may take you some time to adapt.

Much of the practical side you've been handling already. If you're active outside work – in hobbies, pastimes, societies, spiritual life – and have an active family life and a phalanx of close friends, then you've already built a portfolio of activities. Women, in particular, are experts in multi-tasking, and with so many now engaged in part-time jobs, they are truly portfolio-ing, possibly never having heard the description.

? Is the timing right for you?

The stage of life you reach before making your move into portfolio-ing significantly affects your decisions regarding the type of portfolio you plan and the chunking of your time. A key freedom that comes with the Portfolio Life is the freedom to set your own life stages.

There is a new breed of young Portfolio Professionals, many taking up the independent lifestyle after graduating, failing to be attracted to a single mainstream occupation. University career advisors now have the Portfolio Life on their schedule and can give limited advice. Starting at this stage has the upside of great enthusiasm and a completely clear playing field. The obvious downside is a smaller range of marketable talents to sell.

By now, you will have appreciated that the Portfolio Life is extremely individual. Your specific circumstances, talents and goals determine at which stage a move to portfolio-ing is on for you. However, as a general rule, the 30s are the most difficult time for people to make that move. Mortgages are large, children are small. These also tend to be the years of quick advancement, before any career ceiling begins to show. Unless your particular circumstances make the time right for you, just lap up all that experience and knowledge, maximise your networking contacts and build your industry reputation. But never forget the major option you have.

Between 40 and 50 is the best time to start considering the Portfolio Life seriously. Whether you are still on the up-path of your career, or feeling it slowing down, this is a time when it's important for you to understand your future options. In the next ten years the odds are that you will come to a major career crossroads, possibly not of your making. Then you need the options in front of you. So this is the time to be preparing the ground, following the advice later in this book, and ensuring that you have your Portfolio Bridge ready when needed.

Even if you appear to be surviving the fragile fifties with your job intact, somebody from HR will call you in sooner or later to discuss that word 'retirement'. If you're not careful, that will be your working life over. The late 50s or early 60s are not times to try to get a new job, and they are more difficult times to set yourself up in a new style of life. Unless, that is, you've been making portfolio plans and preparations and are ready to launch your Portfolio Life when push comes to shove.

? What skills will you sell?

Everything you need to be a Portfolio Person is in your head. The skills, the experience, are already there and these are what people will pay you money for.

Yes, they will pay for you.

You will swap salary for fees and, in doing so, gain a new sense of identity. They won't be paying for some brand or job title, however grand. They'll pay for you, because you have skills and experience, which they need to apply to their organisation.

> ✳ *The big plus of the Portfolio Life is that the Wealth in Your Head can be put to work in a variety of ways – and all of them to suit you, your ambitions, your needs.*

In what is still called 'full-time employment', the wealth in your head is increasingly under-valued the older you get – in the Portfolio Life its realisable value increases.

It's all a question of turning your skills and experience into a service or product which people will pay good money for.

? How marketable will you be?

If you're concerned about the security of your Portfolio Life, then 'employability' is a watchword to follow. Whether you're in the employed life or planning a Portfolio Life, your value is in your employability. What you need is marketable skills, ideally in areas in which you can develop specific and unique expertise. If they are in fast-developing, fast-changing market areas then you can get ahead of the game and exhibit expertise. Organisations are unbundling anything they can, cutting back to their core activities and contracting-in services and expertise. The Portfolio Professional has never had a better window of opportunity.

Your value in the marketplace will be driven by the relevance of your skills. From an income-generating viewpoint, you need to identify markets where your skills will be most valued. This may mean that you look to areas outside your existing industry or sector. Many PPs have a core of projects within their networked, existing industry, but then extend their skills into other higher-paying areas.

In Chapter 6 we guide you through building your own portfolio of roles.

? What about income?

That balance between income and time is at the heart of optimising the rewards from your Portfolio Life. Looking across the gulf as you prepare to leap, time doesn't look to be a problem, apart from having more on your hands than you want. It's income that looms large in your thoughts, and no doubt in the thoughts of those dependent on you.

You design your own Portfolio Life and set your own income expectations. They may be to earn as much in gross earnings as you do from your current employed role, provided, of course, that this leaves time for your unpaid work and your other goals. So this is the core of your choices. Be realistic about your potential earnings, but also about your expenditure and priorities.

In the employed life, your choice is often restricted. Portfolio Life gives you the choice. Work longer, earn more, fly business class, two weeks holiday. Or work for less time, earn less, fly economy, five weeks holiday.

While many PPs look to earn what they were earning in employment, there are many who take the decision to sacrifice some of that income. They may need less to maintain their standard of living, are willing to downsize their housing with family gone, or simply have lower costs when not employed. Longer life expectancy has its part to play also. The logic of leaving an inheritance is less pressing when it becomes a case of your fifty-year old children using it to buy a bigger car. So SKI-ing (spending the kids' inheritance) has got more common in recent years.

✱ *If SKI-ing's too much for you, you might consider that at least it's time to put a stop to further EKI-ing (earning the kids inheritance).*

Clearly careful thought and planning are necessary and there's advice on this in Chapter 7.

? What's driving you?

You're well into Chapter 3. Hopefully you're already thinking differently about your work and your life. Think back for a moment to why you picked up this book and why you have continued to read it.

What's driving you to consider the Portfolio Life?

It could be negative reasons, feeling limited, in the proverbial rut, or because you feel time breathing on your back. Your plug may have been pulled, in which case there's a positive because your leap hasn't the same risk. You have, of course, the option of looking for another position in the employed world. But what a wonderful time to give full consideration to becoming a PP.

Perhaps you are driven by a submerged dream, by something you've wanted to do all your life, which could now come to reality.

✱ *The dream that is your driver doesn't have to be the main element of your portfolio; tail can wag dog in the Portfolio Life.*

There are PPs out there whose reply to 'What do you do in your Portfolio Life?' will be to put their non-earning life first. They're living their dream, and the earning bit is whatever they can do to let that dream live a little longer. There are lots of portfolio-ing actors.

Are you driven to realise your passion? Often it's there in your leisure life, and in many cases contains a large element of creativity. You have a passion for photography, for writing, for designing clothes. It's been a spare-time passion, but you'd get a thrill from it becoming a larger part of your life, and from the challenge of doing it professionally and being paid for it.

Is time pressing you to leave a legacy of yourself? Something that will allow you to look back and say 'I made a difference' or 'I was here'. It may be something creative or charitable or simply more time with family or in the community.

? Have you got it in you?

Many of the big steps we take in life appear beforehand to be leaps across dangerous rapids. When viewed from the other side, the waters look calmer and the gulf not so broad. Many of the Portfolio Journeys throughout the book are from people pleased to be on the other side. But for you, the gulf looks just as big as ever. As you read through the book, we'll be assisting you on your journey. But it will still be a leap. There are major financial implications; and if you can overcome those, there are major lifestyle implications.

So, courage and self-conviction come high up on the list of the qualities you need to make the move.

The size of your personal step depends on your own circumstances and on your goals for your new life. There are many ways to make it easier and less risky:

- preparing from inside your current role, particularly through networking, professional bodies and industry contacts
- taking early retirement and an early pension to give you a secure minimum income level on which to build
- contracting a part-time role with your current employer gives you income and helps you build your reputation as an independent.

In the end, how big you see the leap depends on how attractive life on the other side looks. Complete the models in the book and assess the practical advice on establishing your Portfolio Life. If you reach the stage where you can say *'Yes, this is for me; I can see so many good things coming from it'*, then the risk reduces and the leap doesn't demand the same degree of courage.

? What qualities are necessary?

Opportunity knocks. You have the talents to put to use. What other qualities will you require to be a success?

- **Risk-tolerance required.** That doesn't mean that the Portfolio Life is inherently risky; it just appears riskier. In the employed life, you're only one economic downturn, or personality conflict, or corporate restructuring away from unemployment. But you get on with the job and forget about the possibility, whereas in portfolio-ing there's always some uncertainty.

- **Willingness to accept new challenges.** Not only as part of the move to a PP life, but as a permanent part of your new life. There's less continuity of employment and income, and the constant challenge of the next hurdle, the next prospect, the next re-invention of your talents.

- **Networking is part and parcel of the Portfolio Life.** It's not just an element in running your business; it's one of the requisite skills to ensure success. If you don't enjoy – yes, enjoy – networking, then your portfolio will be thinner and less healthy than it should be. There's valuable advice on networking in Part 4.

- **Self-development has to become a constant element in your portfolio.** Your Study Work will determine your employability and how marketable your skills are. This is far easier if you get a kick out of your study time rather than tolerate it. Some great portfolios have been built on finding a niche area of knowledge and establishing yourself as the 'niche guru'.

- **You must not only have marketable skills; you must be able to sell them.** Marketing advice is available later in the book, and in many other tomes. If you have doubts about your selling abilities, you need to concentrate on selling yourself: people buy people first. You must also overcome selling's biggest obstacle, the fear of rejection. There are tips on how to sell yourself and your portfolio in Part 4.

- **You need lots of self. You must be self-starting, self-inspired, self-directed.** Many of you will be fortunate to have a supportive family team close by your office for when times are difficult and inspiration gets thin. The ability to bounce back and get out there again is vital. Without it, your portfolio will not meet the income levels you require and your other associated goals will be more difficult to achieve.

- **Multi-tasking is at the heart of the word 'portfolio'.** What is a portfolio without it? You have to enjoy working on several tasks/projects at once. Yes, you may be used to doing that within your current employed role – but all within a limited area. In a well-spread portfolio, however, the multi-tasking will be in diverse areas, presenting a quite different challenge.

? What are the pros and cons?

We are talking about portfolios, so we have to include the traditional warning:

> *'Past performance is no guarantee of future performance. The value of a portfolio can fall as well as rise.'*

Continuing the share portfolio analogy, preparation and planning are absolutely vital. You need to spend time deciding the overall portfolio strategy, not jump straight into the portfolio itself. You need to research the proposed parts of your portfolio to avoid making any wrong choices. You should spend time understanding the businesses involved and the market opportunities arising. You need to spread your risk; no good investor would buy shares in only one industry area. You need to be able to handle that risk, the falls as well as the rises, accepting that some parts will do better than others and that it is the total portfolio result which really matters.

Pros	Cons
• Variety & flexibility • Control & autonomy • Better life-work balance • Personal growth • Leisure time • Continued learning • No boss or corporate politics • Excitement • Achievement • Pleasure doing what one likes	• Risk • Change • Lack of stability • Variable income • Lack of company benefits • No regular routine • Feelings of isolation • Uncertainty • Constant need to network • Time pressures

The risk warning is one we must ensure you understand. Pushing your boat off from the security of the employed life is not always straightforward. There are those who can't handle the insecurity of it, and head back to shore before too long. Others just don't get on with paddling alone and need the apparent camaraderie of established organisations.

✱ *Some see it as a job change rather than a life change, and so never get the full rewards portfolio-ing can bring. You have been warned!*

On the other hand we know that job security in the employed world is not what it was, and gets less the older we get. We know that the rewards of doing your own thing...being recognised as you rather than your title... doing what you want rather than what others want you to do -- all these are worth the risks involved.

To summarise...

- There were lots of 'yous' in this chapter. It was time to make it personal, to bring you face-to-face with how the Portfolio Life might fit for you.

- There were lots of questions too. You have much to think about if you're tempted to consider the move.

- While the authors are enthusiastic advocates for the Unlimited life, it's your turn to make the step. We've tried to clarify some of the upsides and downsides of the decision that faces you later in the book.

Is the Portfolio Life for you? Will you explore so that you have a plan ready when you need it? Will you invest some time in your own long-term plan?

Working with the models in the next three chapters will get you much closer to an answer.

Nick Handel's
Portfolio Journey

A friend gave me a truly inspiring book for Christmas. 'The Alchemist' by Paolo Coelho is an allegory about an Andalusian shepherd boy on a quest for untold treasure. It is about listening to our hearts and being alive to the omens that appear along life's path. My friend inscribed the book: 'Today is the first day of the rest of your life. Go where you will, my friend!'

At the age of fifty-five, the wisdom contained in those 170 pages made me reflect that, when we are forging careers, we're too busy living for the present to appreciate the significance of experiences and events that shape our lives.

A lofty introduction, perhaps, to 35 years with the BBC which began in 1967. I was a wannabe film-maker who had passed up university to follow a dream in broadcasting. The first few years were uphill working by day, attending evening classes in cinematography and growing increasingly frustrated.

One day, a colleague showed me a job advertisement for a junior producer in Local Radio. Not exactly the target of my broadcasting ambition, but an omen it certainly was. I landed the job and made an important discovery: the principles of communication, whether with audiences, artists or colleagues, are essentially the same in radio as in television. I also learned an invaluable new skill: journalism.

Journalism is an extension of story-telling and I was no stranger to that. As a teenager, I had earned pin-money by working as a children's entertainer. My conjuring skills were fairly disastrous – but I could hold a young audience spellbound by enacting stories with string puppets...

Omen number two presented itself in a pub off Hanover Square in 1971. I was in my cups and regaling our News Editor with the story of a malevolent six-year-old who had stamped on my disappearing walking cane. News travelled fast. Next day, I was hauled before the Station Manager. 'I hear you spin a good yarn,' he said, 'I want you to take over the daily children's slot. You start on Monday.'

For the next two years, I wrote and presented countless stories for the under-tens and, now firmly committed to a life in Radio, soon found myself making Light Entertainment programmes for Radios 2 and 4. What, if anything, would become of those early years of film study at Regent Street Polytechnic...?

Cue omen number three! I had just ruined a perfectly good pullover by drenching it in water to regress Esther Rantzen to her early days as a Radio sound effects girl when she had once improvised the sound of lovers splashing across a marshy field by using a wet pillow (for wet pillow read my soggy jumper). I still don't know whether it was creativity or my eccentric programme-making style that made her invite me to join the That's Life! team, but invite me she did. Almost at once, I found myself directing films for BBC1's top-rating weekend consumer show. Among my triumphs were a Yorkshire Terrier that said 'Sausages' and an Old English Sheepdog that drove a car. Happy days!

The next thirty years were spent producing and directing documentary and entertainment series on a wide range of subjects. I worked with many of the biggest stars in drama, entertainment and sport and ran some of the BBC's most prestigious events including the annual Children In Need Appeal.

Why did I leave at 54? The BBC was a more freelance culture, the programme commissioning process was becoming more tortuous and budgets and deadlines were growing tighter and tighter. However, another omen was looming on the horizon. Many budding directors and producers were dropping by to seek opinion and advice. This was a great joy and opened my eyes to the value of all that experience locked away in my greying old head. Perhaps it was time to plough some of it back into the industry I love...

The day after my leaving party was disconcerting. Where had the last three decades gone? Had I made the right decision? Who was I? Why were there blank pages in that once-packed diary? What was I going to say to people who asked me, 'What programme are you working on at the moment...?'

I soon began to relish reconfiguring my professional DNA into a busy and fulfilling `semi-retirement` which has included running directors` *courses both for the BBC and for many independent companies - and a children`s novel (something I`d always meant to do but never found that time). The process of writing it opened my eyes to another skill I`d learned without realising it: all TV production techniques can be applied just as effectively to the written word. My portfolio journey has now taken a turn into education – where these concepts are helping primary school children gain confidence and ability in creative writing. They are available as a resource for teachers which I call 'Calling the Shots!' (www.pogolearning.com). Actually, I think it could also be a good motto for portfolio workers!*

Nick Handel was a senior producer/director in factual entertainment with the BBC. He now runs production courses within the television industry and education sector. He is the author of 'Newskids on the Net'.

PART 2

CHARTING YOUR PORTFOLIO

Welcome to the 'working' section!

Chapters 4 and 5 offer you the chance to work with some useful models. They will help you learn more about yourself and what you want for your future.

How many hours over recent years have you put into preparing long-term plans for your work, for your business, for other people?

Your own plan deserves even more.

Why not be as comprehensive and structured as you would be for others?

If you do all the exercises, we have a cunning way of bringing all your input together into a comprehensive summary of what is right for you. You'll find that in Chapter 6.

Or you can take the less comprehensive route and just pick out a few to do —whichever way, the investment in time to understand more about yourself and your goals will be time well spent.

A good plan has to look at where you are now, where you want to get to, and what you aim for when you get there.

The models and diagrams in the next three chapters can be the foundation of such a plan. Here's a map of how your exploration can take you there in Part 2:

Where you are now

You'll build greater understanding of:

- the value of your skills and experience
- how to make the most of your unique talents
- the balance of all the roles you play in your life (and what you might want to change)
- the values that are most important as drivers for your future

Where you want to be

You'll be clearer on:

- which skills to transfer into new areas
- how to spend more time in areas of special talent
- your new balance for life-work and time-money

The Plan for your Portfolio Life

You'll be able to realise:

- your top goals for the rest of your life
- a new life-work balance
- the portfolio that fits goals and balance best for you

Figure 1

Charting your way ahead

In the next three chapters, you'll be working with the models and some special charts. Love charts and forms? Don't we all?! But these are not to trap you in, but to open you out. They're important building blocks in making your decisions. You know that old adage that you'll get out what you put in: repeated irritatingly often and irritatingly proven to be true. So why not try the models, complete the charts, and see if they stretch your mind.

How you do them is up to you. We reckon you won't want to mark them in the book – and who knows who you might pass this book on to, or where it might end up! If you'd like a set of the models and charts to work with, download via our website – see the contacts page at the back of the book.

We suggest you start up a 'Portfolio Plan' file to record your journey and to keep all the steps together.

📁 *When we think it would be useful for you to add something to your file, we've flagged with this symbol.*

You will find it helpful to keep a pad of paper and a pen close by. Why not go really mad and buy some of that wonderful vellum paper, and one of those free flowing pens that seem to glide across the page and make you feel like Michelangelo or Leonardo sketching their dreams. All great decisions are worth the best of thinking, the best of materials and the best of time.

You can work with the book while cooking with the other hand, feeding the baby, filling the car with petrol, chatting to friends on your mobile... just as you can mix single malt whisky with Coke, top a fillet steak with a fried egg, wear open-toe sandals with a dinner jacket.

Or you can take a special hour just for your own planning, shut away the world for a while, put on your favourite music, stretch and relax, engage all parts of brain and enjoy the experience.

Your choice, but we do have a recommendation.

Get the result you deserve, because you owe it to yourself!

Note: The models used in Chapters 4 to 8 are proprietary to The Success Group, the UK arm of The Global Coaching Partnership.

4

WHERE YOU ARE NOW?

A journey of a thousand miles must begin with a single step.
Lao-tzu (604 BC – 531 BC)

The journey to your Portfolio Career sounds like an exciting path of exploration. You stand at the start with those contrasting feelings of excitement, expectation, and fear of the unknown

That's good, because you'll need all the energy and the curiosity they bring as you explore. You're taking a positive step to get the balance right for the rest of your life; how good will it feel when you can to answer that 'how are you?' question in a new way: not 'Stressed and overworked because of the Boss' but 'Challenged, liberated (and, yes, perhaps overworked!) because I am the Boss.'

It's your turn to think about your 'current reality'.

- What am I best at?
- What do I enjoy?
- What do I want to do more of?
- What do I want less of?

This chapter will help you know more about who you are now and what you have already to equip you for making the most of your portfolio life.

Past experience

First, let's bring together some pieces of data that you might have already – you'll need them later for the Planner:

- any 360° assessment where everyone you work with above, side and down says what they think of you
- psychometric test results such as Myers-Briggs, Firo B.

If you have them, dig them out of the loft, the file or the 'wherethehellarethey' and have a read. Do they sound like you, and is that you now or when you last did them? Don't be too modest to accept the strengths or too defensive to acknowledge the weaknesses.

🖙 *It's useful to jot down some quick conclusions and keep them in the file.*

Now find a copy of your latest CV; don't worry that it might need updating. We can use the CV of your past jobs to find out what skills lay behind the job titles.

Jobs tend to have descriptions that hide the tasks and skills within. For example, under the title 'sales manager' lurk many different skills, including researching and analysis, managing people, negotiating, interpersonal skills, networking, communication and running projects.

Let's look at your skills within three past jobs (Figure 2). From these jobs, explode out what you really did and which skills you used most in them.

Title of job	Tasks in job description	Skills used	Experience gained
Job 1			
Job 2			
Job 3			

Figure 2. Three past jobs

Open your mind to think behind the job descriptions and complete the three columns.

📂 *Add any other skills that come to mind and put all your conclusions on a separate chart. This will be your* **Skills and Experience Chart** *for the Portfolio Planner.*

Know your special talents

Isn't it funny that we often concentrate on what we can't do so well, rather than what we do best?

We're well conditioned throughout life to this emphasis on the negative. Remember the school report that praised your good subjects, but said you had to spend more time and energy on all your poor subjects, the ones you hated, the ones that didn't come naturally...

Or the appraisal at work that spent 10 minutes on your successes and 110 on your failures; then the 'future development' part said something like 'Your creative and innovative skills are excellent but we need you to be an all-rounder. You need to work on your numeracy, it's 'Accounting for non-Accountants' training for you.'

So it's no surprise that we spend more and more time on what we find difficult instead of what we're really good at. What a waste, for us and for anyone who's paying us.

If only you could unleash your full potential and enjoy the rewards of your unique talents; do the things you enjoy, the things you're best at and leave others to take on areas where you're just competent or worse.

You can, but first you have to identify what those talents are, unearth and celebrate them after those long years of people pushing them under bushes.

We'll do this with the **Special Talents Model**.

What do we mean by talents?

We mean your underlying talents that are transferable, to a number of different jobs and to different life roles. They are part of you whether you are at work, at home, at leisure, wherever, whenever.

Talents are not the same as skills. These are often linked to a job and based on knowledge. The car mechanic may have a skill in repairing engines, based upon his talent for understanding how things work; a teacher may have a skill in motivating her class to learn, because of her talent in relating to children.

An executive, skilled in negotiation, is using her talent for empathy and understanding motivations.

Your talents are there waiting already – the wealth you can discover. Remember the little boy who watched Michelangelo carefully carve away the rugged stone to create a sculpture of a beautiful horse.

'How did you know the horse was inside there?' he said.

We just need to take away some of our conditioning and prejudices to reveal what's inside us.

We can look at the definitions of talents and activities in four categories, as set out in figure 3 on page 86 and page 87.

Having looked at the definitions, get out a piece of paper for notes and take 30 minutes to think about yourself, honestly without being too modest or too hard on yourself. There are no right or wrong answers. Think what other people might say about you. Ask a 'sounding board' buddy what he or she thinks.

Look for the talents inside the activities. For example:

- skill with figures may reflect talents in numeracy and analysis
- people skills may come from talents in being approachable and open
- skills in ideas denote talents in creativity and inventiveness.

When you really helped that friend in need, was it because you had a skill in listening, or a talent for empathy, or perhaps a bit of both?

Think of what people mean when they say, *'That's you all over ... how do you do that ... that's the unique you.'*

Look for those hidden areas that you take for granted, because they're so natural, 'like falling off a log' to you, but distinctively talented to someone looking at you.

We're not talking job descriptions here. 'Project Manager' is not a talent, but understanding what makes a project team tick is. 'Sales Director' isn't, but knowing how to spot a buying signal is.

SPECIAL TALENTS	EXCELLENT
• Activities where your performance is excellent and you keep getting better • Energising and exciting for you – maximum fulfilment and a joy to do • People impressed and excited when around you • Others don't know how you do it you are so good at it • Never tire of doing it or get bored *Identify your special talents by associating them with the following emotions and observations that you experience when doing them:* **Love** It is something that you love doing, most of the time and under most circumstances. **Energy** The activity usually generates more energy than it uses. **Ease** This activity is easy. Comes naturally without conscious effort. **Results** It's rare that you don't produce the results that you are looking for, and often produce more. **Development** These skills are always growing. The more time you spend on it the better it seems to get. **Feedback** These areas are often commented upon by others. People tell you that you are good at doing this.	• Activities where your performance is way above normal standards • Others ask you to do it for them – recognise you are better than most • Not difficult for you t • o do, but you are not wholehearted – wouldn't enjoy doing it all the time *Identify your excellent activities by associating them with the following emotions that you experience when doing them:* **Excitement** Stimulating because you believe that you have superior skills **Team work** You discover other individuals with excellent abilities that you can work with **Reputation** These abilities bring you praise and acclaim **Opportunity** Others want you to work with them or want those skills for themselves

INCOMPETENT	COMPETENT
• An activity where no matter how long you work at it, you are not going to be successful • Can't do even if taught • Very high energy for poor results • Others would recognise as a weakness *Identify your incompetent activities by associating them with the following emotions that you experience when doing them:* **Frustration** It's difficult to make headway **Stress** You experience a high degree of tension, often fatigued easily **Conflict** Breakdowns in communication with others occur frequently **Confusion** Perspective is easily lost	• Activities where your performance only comes up to minimum standards • High energy for adequate results • Others would rate as satisfactory *Identify your competent activities by associating them with the following emotions that you experience when doing them:* **Competition** Many other individuals have an equal amount of ability: limited opportunities **Anxiety** Worried about making mistakes and falling behind **Repetition** It always seems the same **Boredom** It's difficult to be enthusiastic, you can't easily see opportunity for growth and development

Figure 3. Definitions for Special Talents Model

When you're happy with your rough notes, plot your talents and activities in the appropriate box on the **Special Talents Chart** (figure 4). (If you haven't done so already, download the template from www.PortfolioProfessionals.org.)

Special talents	Excellent
Incompetent	Competent

Figure 4. Special Talents Chart

How does that look? Are there any surprises?

- What is there in your Special Talents that you want to make more of in your future portfolio career?
- Where would you like to see talents move between the boxes?
- What is there in the bottom two boxes that you want to leave behind, leave to others who have those as their special talents?

Remember talents gained in one role can transfer into a new sphere – our Executive Negotiator can use her empathy talents in counselling married couples, as well broking deals with trade unions.

📁 *Let's put the **Special Talents Chart** in the file so we can use it for the Portfolio Planner later.*

Lucy Field's
Portfolio Journey

Living the portfolio life is an innate part of a career in contemporary dance. I have had the privilege of working across many different skill sets with a wide variety of companies.

In the contemporary dance world there are only a tiny percentage of long-term contract performance jobs. From the get-go I was made highly aware, during my vocational degree, that 'the more strings you have to your bow, the better.' In a dancer's professional career, freelance work is built from many different projects as a performer, choreographer, teacher and beyond. This is partly through economic demand with comparatively low salaries, but mainly driven by passion and interest. You are very much what holds the key to your success; capitalising on your talents and treating yourself as a business. .

In my journey the portfolio lifestyle has always been present. I have moved through freelance, self-employment, and full-time roles that have a portfolio approach. Using this book to transition from full-time to freelance, I have found the pie chart 'Wheel of Life' exercise (on page 93) very useful in analysing my Handy 'chunks' of time – capturing where I think I am and where I want to be. Dancers are often clear about their talents and interests early on and are open to morph and shift with changes to them as time goes on. As a nod to Simon Sinek ('Start with Why'), this 'why-pie' dictates the rest of 'how-pie' and 'what-pie'. In my essential pie are the following slices; dance (obviously), music, theatre, writing, leadership, curiosity about how things work and an unbridled desire to tell all and sundry about it.

I began my journey as 20-year old freelancer, where the main emphasis of my 'paid work chunk' was teaching for an educational workshop agency. I taught approximately 17,500 young people in over 250 schools across the UK in just under two years and had to be highly organised with my time, planning and travel. This was a hefty chunk, and I wanted to increase the more risky performing 'chunk', so I developed the choreography slice to give me more opportunities. Choreography is fantastic for developing problem-solving skills and resourcefulness. I made and fundraised my own work in my local neighbourhood and used creative workshops with young people to test out ideas.

Growing conscious of early burn-out, I wanted a geographical focus, and an opportunity came up for me at DanceXchange as Dance Artist in Residence. Although a full-time post, the portfolio philosophy was at its centre. Within this role I was able to develop my choreography, project management and teaching skills with relative freedom within the boundaries and objectives of the organisation.

I began to recognise that balance is hugely important, and through the support of an industry life coach, realised my move to Birmingham had created an imbalance in my work-home life as my boyfriend (now husband) remained in London. Through coaching I rebalanced the unhealthy side of the dance mind-set; a tendency towards perfectionism, putting in 200% effort at any cost and never saying 'no' (lessons I am still learning!). I was keen to get my teeth into developing talent, and I became Pre-vocational Training Coordinator at The Place, enabling me to move back to London.

In this full-time role, which lasted for 6 years, I was part of the beginning of a fantastic development in UK dance training managing one of the first Centres for Advanced Training. Once again, the portfolio philosophy was present, and I was able to develop my range of skills further including governance, curriculum design, financial management, talent identification, production, commissioning and marketing. Simultaneously, I was on a local authority arts grants panel, and taught at another dance school in the evening.

Towards the end of this period the balance had certainly tipped again, and my pie felt dominated by work. I decided to take the risk of going freelance again, using my knowledge and experience to support others in their portfolio journey. This was a difficult decision to make, and felt a little controversial. I had a fantastic job that had rendered plenty of success but I felt I wasn't in the driving seat. I took the leap and used this book to help me make the transition.

The first thing I did was re-visit my 'inner-pie' and get clear on what it was I wanted. I then looked at what my areas of business were going to be (which remain today); dance management, dance and young people, writing and presenting. I spent a good deal of time strategising; listing my values, writing my own business plan, coming up with my brand and marketing strategy and evaluating my progress. I re-launched my freelance self with an email, entitled ' A Valentine's Day card from Lucy,' and within 24 hours I was booked to interview Arlene Phillips for the Imagination festival. Since then I have worked on a range of projects for Rambert, English National Ballet and co-founded Inside Dance (an online magazine show). I felt such freedom in being able to design my time, I had no limit to my enthusiasm to work. I also discovered a women-focussed workspace, a great place to network with many other portfolio women out of my sector. Sometimes portfolio life can be isolating and being with other women gave me lots of ideas and perspective.

I became a Mum in 2012. This has pros and cons as a freelancer – you can design workload to suit your physical demands, but financially it can be very hard. During my pregnancy, English National Ballet and Rambert were hugely supportive. I returned to work gradually in 2013 and I found this transition the biggest challenge as I had a new 'Mum chunk' to get my head around. Now my pie includes balancing family with my roles at Rambert and Dance Woking. Being a Mum makes me more productive, as now, more than ever, my time has definite limits. It has also moved me to write about being a Dance Mama and collate the stories of others in my blog.

I am lucky in that I have always known what I wanted to spend my life doing.

Some lessons learned so far are:

- time is our greatest commodity,
- sometimes it is perfectly fine to say 'No,'
- seize and create opportunities,
- and clarity, clarity, clarity.

Lucy is Learning & Participation Manager at Rambert, Chair of Dance Woking, Founder of Dance Mama and lives with her family in Surrey. www.lucyfield.com @ihearttalent.

Learning from the whole of your life

An opportunity you've given yourself in your planning is to put your whole life in the plan.

We're adept at compartmentalising and segmenting our life into pieces.

We may say:

- *I leave half of me in the car park; won't need it at work.*
- *I'm a different person at work to the real me at home.*
- *I must reduce work time to find time for my real interests.*
- *I have to go to art classes to keep my creativity alive.*
- *I don't like leaving early to do my charity work.*
- *Oh to get out of this suit when I get to the weekend.*
- *TGIF and I can be myself again.*

One of our Portfolio Professional friends had built up a talent for helping couples in their relationships; he trained in dialogue techniques and communication between couples, active listening, questioning, conflict management – this, he felt, was his charity work, his spare time stuff, the outside teaching work he did with his wife. Meanwhile, he was battling with the usual menu at work: interpersonal wars, conflict, lack of communication, interface problems and looking for training in it – this was, he felt, the work he was paid for, his weekday stuff, the inside work of his career.

He didn't see the connection because he'd built a wall between his charity and his paid employment. The two worlds were separated in his mind until he planned his portfolio, and realised that all experiences were available for whatever the portfolio became.

We all under-exploit our abilities and knowledge by putting them in boxes of our own making.

As a Portfolio Person you can look holistically, you can use all of your assets in any venture you want to pursue.

✱ *Put all of you in the plan!*

Your roles in the Wheel of Life

The **Wheel of Life Model** looks at the roles you play in all parts of your life and helps you see where you might want to change the balance.

In any one week we have different roles in different parts of our life: lecturer, gardener, handyman, cook, father, mother, brother, sister, sportsperson, spouse, citizen, friend.

Some roles are paid, some are unpaid; some we may think of as 'work' some as 'leisure'.

Let's think about all parts of your life, work and spare time all together, and see how much of your 24 hours a day they are taking. You may want to change the balance in your portfolio day!

Take the drawing of two circles, as illustrated in figure 5.

Then think about the percentages of time you spend in a typical day now in your different roles: x% as manager, y% as parent, z% as sportsperson and so on.

Plot these percentage shares by segments in the NOW circle – just roughly, no marks for absolute numeric accuracy or geometry!

Then think about the future; the time when you want to change from your current life-work balance. What percentages have to change? Note down how the future 100% splits out. Then plot this on your FUTURE circle.

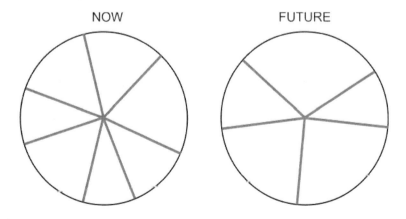

Figure 5. Wheel of Life Model

What conclusions are there in the changes?

- Note how the paid and unpaid areas change ... and perhaps overlap.
- Perhaps you need to invent new segments or drop some you have now.
- What might you want to build into your future life?

Capture these – use whatever colours turn you on.

🖙 *Put your conclusions on the* **Wheel of Life Chart** *in your 'Portfolio Plan' file so you can use the thoughts on the Portfolio Planner later.*

Learning from our successes and disappointments

Looking at our past Successes and Disappointments helps us learn about our needs and our interests, as well as reinforcing what we know about our talents and our strengths.

SUCCESSES		
Success	Why is it important to me?	How did I achieve it?
DISAPPOINTMENTS		
Disappointment or regret	Why was it important?	What could have worked better?

Figure 6. Successes and Disappointments Model

Use the Successes Grid first

Think back over your life to find 6-7 successes – times when you are proud of yourself. They can be achievements or difficulties overcome. Think across all parts of your life, professional and personal. Put these in the first column.

Complete the middle and right columns to show why each one was important to you and what was it in you that made it happen.

Are there any common themes about what equals success for you?

Consider whether these show a core need that you have; for example, it might be for power, for recognition, or to help others.

What strengths, talents or attributes have helped you be successful?

You might have identified them in your **Special Talents Chart**; if so this just reinforces how important they are to you. Or perhaps you've been reminded of some additional talents to add to your Special Talents.

Make a note of your conclusions.

Now let's move to the Disappointments Grid

Disappointments are useful for the positive self-knowledge they can bring.

Apart from Edith Piaf *('Non, Je ne regrette rien')*, we can all remember some things we did that were disappointing, and some that we're disappointed we never did.

Think back over your life for disappointments or regrets – times when you did not achieve all you wanted. Think across all parts of your life.

Put a number of them in the left hand column and then fill in the other two columns.

Do you know what didn't work? Think about how you could possibly have changed things. Anything you could still do/change and want to?

The right hand column can help show the knowledge, experiences, skills or insights you now have that can help in the future.

Is there anything you would like to go back and pick up again – hobbies, friendships, achievements?

Or are there regrets about things you've never done; dreams unfulfilled, 'never had time to start it', or 'never believed I could do it'.

Unblocking the past

The author Julia Cameron (*The Artist's Way*) doesn't believe in never believing!

She claims that we all carry blocks with us that tell us we can't be the writer, artist, athlete we'd love to be. That casual word from a parent at an impressionable age, the teacher who laughed at our efforts, the embarrassment of failure at a young age – all blocks that life inflicts on us, all blocks that we can remove.

Another of our Portfolio Explorers, looking for his future route, regretted the fact that his career had been a block to being a flute player in the orchestra, his boyhood dream. Ambition, drive and the need for money had taken him up the marketing career route in the food industry. His orchestral dream was a disappointment on his chart.

But in rethinking what could work better, he put together marketing talent and a love of music and thought how many concert halls, bands, music publications needed marketing?

Another Explorer is a Managing Director with a wine diploma, presentation skills and business experience. There's a potential client base waiting for him to bring his sparkling expertise together for informed entertainment at business conferences and trade dinners

So the **Successes and Disappointments Model** helps us identify needs and confirm our talents; we can pick up pieces of ourselves, interests, passions that we might think lost, and can bring them back into our future planning.

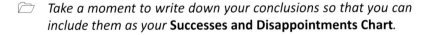 *Take a moment to write down your conclusions so that you can include them as your* **Successes and Disappointments Chart**.

Your Best Job Yet

This model concentrates on your Paid Work, to help discover what you're best at, and what you want to use more of in your future roles.

We're going to take you back to your 'best job yet' and look a bit deeper at identifying the experience and skills that you have … and those you want to make more of.

When you look back over every type of job you've done, paid or unpaid, which one fills you with that warm glow of memory and satisfaction? Which one fitted you so well at that time? Close your eyes and take yourself back over the job, try to recall the highs, and put out of mind for the moment the lows. Remember the plaudits, the applause, the fun, the laughter, when you were really on top of the job.

Take a few moments to recall it, and then look at the list in figure 7 below. Have a go at ticking the characteristics that capture why the experience was the best job you've had. Then go to the right column and tick those characteristics that gave you most satisfaction, enjoyment and/or pleasurable challenge.

	What made it the best job	What I enjoyed most
The goal was absolutely clear.		
Success or failure was obvious and measurable.		
I played a significant part in setting the goal.		
I provided a lead in what was required to make it happen.		
I was a constructive member of the team.		
I was a key influence on a group of people helping motivate them.		
I was forced to deal with new/many situations and people.		

It created increased personal pressure.		
I had to influence people without authority.		
The range of tasks was varied, diverse or ambiguous – no easy answers.		
I had a clear idea of what I had to do and why.		
I was in a highly visible role.		
It required breaking new ground.		
I had to use skills outside my normal 'expertise'.		
I had to learn significant new knowledge quickly.		
I had to make difficult decisions in the face of uncertainty.		
I had to work with a significant boss- good or bad.		
Something important was missing forcing me to be resourceful.		
I played a key role defining the strategy and planning tactics.		
I played a key role in keeping people focused on the goal.		

Figure 7. Your Best Job Yet

See if you can identify what skills or characteristics helped you succeed in that job. There may be some that were relevant for you then but not now. More important, there will many that you want to take forward into your future roles.

What do they tell you about who you are, what you're best at, and the needs you want to fulfil? These are core things that you need to be satisfied if your future roles (paid or unpaid) are to be the right ones for you.

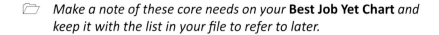   *Make a note of these core needs on your* **Best Job Yet Chart** *and keep it with the list in your file to refer to later.*

Valuing our values

The models so far have given us a sharper focus on our talents, strengths, needs and interests.

To complete the picture of 'Where I am now', we need to look at our core drivers, our values. We think about words such as security, recognition, freedom, status, power, creativity, fun.

Someone said that we want to be famous in our twenties, rich in our thirties, respected in our forties, wise in our fifties and have peace of mind thereafter.

Our drivers evolve at different stages of our lives.

The change you are considering is an opportunity to bring your future roles closer to your guiding values.

You'll find your values by thinking about those things that bring you greatest satisfaction (helping others, having integrity, being open, keeping your word and so on) and things that bring you most conflict (when you feel torn between who you are and what you're being asked to do).

Your view of which are most important to you may have altered over the last years ... but you may not have noticed.

How important are money, location, titles, working with people, your own fulfilment?

There is some important balancing to be considered:

- time versus income
- constraint versus choice
- control versus freedom
- taking versus giving something back.

Create your own list of your Guiding Values and see where the changes might be.

Put them in the left hand column of the grid shown in figure 8, and give them an importance out of 5 (5 is high); see how things change between 5 years ago and 5 years from now

You'll have your own key values but we've given you a few to start with.

Value	Score 5 years ago	Score 5 years from now
Secure income		
Status		
Responsibility at work		
Competitiveness		
Peace of mind		
Sense of community		
Giving something back		
Freedom from controls		
Spiritual fulfilment		
Fun		

Figure 8. Your Guiding Values

Look at your results and see if you can select ten Guiding Values that you think will be most important to you in the future.

If our future life and roles are in line with our values, we will feel integrated and whole. If the future conflicts with our values, we will feel unfulfilled and frustrated.

📁 *Put those ten core values on the* **Guiding Values Chart** *and – you've guessed it! ......*

Doing what we love ... and being paid for it

I'd rather be a failure at something I enjoy than be a success at something I hate.
George Burns

Isn't it a great thought that we can do more of what we love and be paid for it!

How does it feel in the job you're in now? How much time are you doing what you love, what you're best at? What might be getting in the way?

Do we have to wait for others to take away those blocks or can we do it ourselves?

✱ *Can we do what we enjoy, what we're best at, what others value us for ... and get paid enough for it? The answer is yes. The question is why doesn't everyone do it?*

Is it lack of opportunity, lack of confidence, a sense of masochism, a lack of faith or is it some strange work ethos that we're conditioned into?

Consider these contrasting sequences:

• I struggle with things I'm not good at.	• I enjoy doing things that come naturally.
• Things I don't enjoy are a lot of hard work.	• I tend to do well what I enjoy.
• People value effort and sweat.	• People value me when I do well.
• People will pay me for things I find hard.	• People will pay me for things I enjoy.

Which is the most believable? And which is the most positive? Too often we believe that if it's not hard work, it's not valuable; if it's not difficult, I don't deserve reward.

Can we be so lucky as to have the enjoyable result, or do we too easily accept the struggle?

Do we value effort and sweat because we're caught in that crazy 'collusion of busyness'?

Or can we escape our conditioning and believe in using our special talents?

Your new Unlimited life is the chance to believe and to act on it.

To summarise ...

- We've seen how to plan our future in a holistic way.

- We have a fuller, more positive view of who we are now.

- Our charts have gathered information on our talents, experience, interests, values and needs by exploring:
  - skills and experience
  - special talents
  - successes and disappointments
  - best job yet
  - wheel of life
  - guiding values.

After Chapter 4 you have some clear insights into where you are now.

In Chapter 5 you can start to look ahead to where you want to be.

5

WHERE YOU WANT TO BE

Only those who will risk going too far can possibly find out how far one can go.
TS Eliot

This chapter takes you forward to see just how far you want to go.

There are three models that complete the charts you'll need for the Portfolio Planner. They will help you project forward, dream of what you really want and start a forward plan of how you can get there.

In every decision, we need to play three roles: dreamer, realist and critic.

You'll need the latter two in later chapters when you're getting practical.

For now, you need to tap into the dreamer in you. The part that can project long-term, can see the big picture, and open the mind to new alternatives.

Walt Disney, who knew a thing or two about dreaming, said that the function of a dreamer is to, *'see clearly in his own mind how every piece of business in a story will be put.'*

The classic example of projecting to a seemingly unattainable goal is John F Kennedy on the moon-landing, when he predicted a man on the moon by the end of the 1960s: a vision that was long-term projected forward, a big 'what' rather than a big 'how'... and it seemed impossible to everyone who heard him say it!

Reaching for the stars

We're looking a long way ahead, not just at the next role or even the next 5 years.

This is your chance to look at the rest of your life as a whole and to really understand what you want to achieve in it: your personal, professional and lifetime goals.

That may sound challenging and a bit grandiose, but if you're not going to do it, who will, and if you never try to reach for the dream, who knows?

Leo Burnett, who founded the advertising agency of that name, had a logo that showed a hand reaching for some stars, and the words:

'If you reach for the stars you may not get one...but you won't come up with a handful of mud either.'

So we're going to reach out and forward, put some substance to our dreams and think how we might attain them.

✳ *The secret to planning the successful journey is to project forwards to your dream, and work backwards to your plan.*

Starting at the end and working backwards loosens us from the ties of today; we can soar above where we are now and look down at a bigger picture.

People who've successfully planned their lives (you've seen them and wondered how?) know it's about setting a destination and having a map of how to get there. The journey is not about following the map rigidly – that wouldn't be great fun.

The route on the map will change as you go and you'll discover ways you never imagined that lead you forward. You may choose to change your angle slightly as you reach a crossroad; you learn from experiences and synchronicities as you travel. But if you've set your destination with a plan you believe in, you'll know which overall direction is right. If your life direction is to go North, you'll know when you get to a crossroad to head North West or North East ... and definitely not South.

In his book *Good to Great*, Jim Collins describes the concepts that define successful companies. These can be represented as follows:

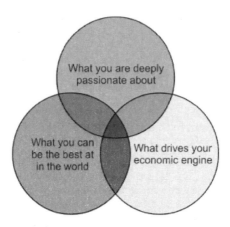

Figure 9. Defining concepts

The same factors can define your successful future life and your successful future business. Where the circles intersect is where your future success lies.

This chapter uses models that can help open new horizons ... and help draw the map of how to get there.

The first one is about your birthday party, your last big party!

Your last big birthday party

What do you want to achieve before you die?

A sobering thought or a great opportunity to make the most of life!?

Remember how Chapter 3 talked about those '1,000 places to visit before you die' lists and '1,001 golf holes you must play'?

Have you sat watching one of those '1001 things to do before you die' programmes and wondered ...?

How many have I done already, and how many are there still to do: when can I fit them in; how many weekends are there until I'm 75? How many holidays will I manage to squeeze in?

A coach in Toronto, Dan Sullivan, has a question that he says most people have an answer for, *'What age are you going to be when you die?'*

And the next question is, *'Does assuming that affect the way you are leading your life?'*

With life expectancy lengthening, someone 'retiring' in their mid 50s can have as many years' active life ahead as they've just spent at work.

Are we making the best use of our remaining time, or are we just spinning wheels thinking everything we want to do will occur naturally in its own good time, if we keep looking? And if we don't know what we're looking for, how will we recognise it?

The model in figure 10 can help us identify what we want from the future and start to plan the stepping stones.

It asks you to imagine your birthday party of the future, probably the last time you expect to get everyone together – you'll see there are a number of questions to stimulate your thinking.

MY LAST BIG BIRTHDAY PARTY

Imagine you are coming towards the end of your life. You decide to have a big party or equivalent celebration for a special birthday, e.g. 70th, 80th or 90th.

- How old are you at this landmark birthday? (Try to push it as late in your life as you are comfortable with)

- What is your status physically? Mentally? Financially?

- Who do you want at the party and why – what areas of your life do they come from?

- What are the reasons the guests have for coming to the party?

- What do you want them to be saying about you, what they have shared with you and what they will remember you for?

- What do you want to be able to say/remember about your life in your birthday speech?

Download a template from www.PortfolioProfessionals.org

Figure 10

Write out your answers to the questions; enjoy being able to project forward with all the benefits of being more healthy and alive than you will be then!

What do your answers tell you about your life and achievements?

- Are all the things you want to celebrate and be remembered for already well on the way?

- Or have you been diverted?
- Is that income-time balance the culprit? Time poor and money rich?
- Do your guests reflect the people you spend time with now?
- Or are you spending most of your time with people you may never see again when this part of work stops?
- Did the events you want to remember (or be remembered for) fit with where your time and energy is going now?
- Or are you going to get to those, when you're less exhausted by today?

What about those big things you want to do with your loved ones: the dreams, the ones you'll look back on in the photo album and smile contentedly.

If they haven't begun already, when might they start?

Consider how many years you have been thinking about them and how many years have you still got to go. Going to wait until you retire? When might that be?

Make sure you're not gambling with your time, your health, family's health, and all the other eventualities you can't predict.

We are very careful about making provision for our financial security. Our pension is an investment for the future. In the same way, our health and our relationships need investment for the future; deposits need to be put in at this point to realise the benefits later.

Take a moment to close your eyes and ask yourself:

> ✳ *If those are the people, events and achievements I'm going to celebrate at the end of my life, when and how am I going to make it happen?*

Will you be able to make the time you need working for an employer and leading the corporate life? Or do you need to make a change?

🗀 *Let's put the conclusions from the* **Last Big Birthday** **Party Chart** *in the 'Portfolio Plan' file*

There was a management seminar in Switzerland of high-potential General Managers in their late 40s.

They did some paper planning and looked at their future life goals and the way current life was getting in the way of them.

The facilitator fed back the results to them, relating the common experiences of sacrifices of time with the children, missed family events, marriage break-ups, the quest for earning money instead of enjoying time, the missed childhoods and the children who hardly knew their parents.

A hush fell on the room, a quiet sad stillness......broken by a voice:

'I see it now. I've missed life with my boy. As soon as I get home, I'm going out in the garden with the bat and ball and pads and we'll play cricket: used to turn my arm at a googly when I had time at the cricket club.'

'How old is your son?' asked the facilitator.

'Sixteen.'

'I think you may be too late.'

Your top 10 hits

Let's use the results from The Last Big Birthday Party to set some goals for the journey.

Many of us enjoy dreaming of the destination but never make the steps to get there. Perhaps it's because some of the questions the routemap requires seem big and daunting:

- where we want to live
- how much money do we really need (and how much do we want)
- how we want to spend our time
- who do we want to spend the time with
- what pattern of work : full-time, part-time, employee, self-employed
- what mix of paid work, home work, gift work, study work?

Thinking of all the steps you do want to start taking, write 20 things that you want to achieve in your lifetime: use the conclusions you had from Last Big Birthday Party, remember what you learnt from your Successes and Disappointments.

Now prioritise the twenty to the **Top 10 Wonderful Must-do Hits**, some of which you may have started, others are still waiting.

Write them large on a sheet of paper with a blue pen (for blue sky thinking!).

  📂   *This is your* **Top 10 Hits Chart** *you'll need to review when we get to the Planner*

Stepping stones

This chapter brings up some big issues, issues that affect others close to us, issues that make us fearful, excited and in need of confidence. We'll come to those later but they're a great positive sign of change and movement.

If we understand the direction and the feelings it evokes, we're on the way to planning actions.

And they do need planning!

Without a plan, we can go round in a maelstrom of doubts and fears, in circles of indecision and inertia.

With an aim for the future, decisions lead us to the right stepping stones. For example:

? If you want to be a recognised expert on the Great Wall of China at 80, it helps to know in which decade are you going to walk it, when are you first going to visit China, when are you going to contact the travel agent, and when to begin the research.

? If you want to be a published author, when are you going to draw together those jottings and ideas, publish articles, contact publishers, research the topics?

? If you're going to retire to that barn in France, when will it become a holiday home, is learning French a good idea, and planning holidays there to explore the area, and meeting some French estate agents? When will you start?

? If you're to be exhibited at the Royal Academy Summer exhibition before you're 60, going to art class one evening a week in your 40s would seem a good start.

? Having a star you've discovered named after you is not impossible in your 50s, but unlikely unless you've made the time to buy that telescope or join that Astronomical Club in your 30s.

What do I want more of … and less of?

We're going to look in more depth at the action plan through the Lifetime Circles.

The Top 10 Hits will have highlighted some of the conflicts in where we want to be long term, and where our short term is going. We're going to look at what you really want to change in the next three years.

Let's enjoy a fantasy journey.

What would be your perfect week in three years time? What would happen, would you be alone or with others, how would the hours be filled? What's the balance of work and leisure?

Imagine there are no constraints and think about the fantasy week you dream of.

You're going to look at some circles and picture the change you want to make in your time and energy for the future.

So let's adopt the dreamer position: head and eyes up, relaxed comfortable posture … and dream ahead.

Follow these steps to find where your life and energy might be out of balance now, and how you can make the change you want.

Step 1

Sit back, relax and picture that ideal life-work harmony and what it really means.

Take out a sheet of paper and write a summary of your ideal future week.

If you're feeling artistic, draw a picture (as abstract as you like) that captures the fantasy.

What are the feelings you want to have, where would you be, who with, what would you be doing, how would you spend your time?

List the significant activities in that future life.

For example, looking at those chunks of work, how much would be work time at work, work at home, study work, gift work, family life, socialising with friends, sport, leisure, culture, spiritual and religious time.

What percentages do you want for each – you might take that as percentages of time or of energy.

Write down your percentages. Then make a pie chart with your future ideal percentages in FUTURE. Put them into roughly equivalent segments.

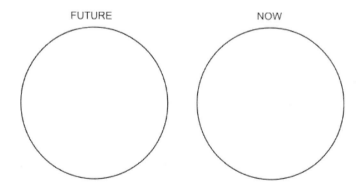

FUTURE   NOW

Figure 11. Lifetime Circles Model

Step 2

Now look at today, at last week: how did the percentages work there?

How did that week feel? What energised you, what exhausted you?

Put those percentages in their segments in NOW.

Step 3

Compare your circles. What conclusions can you draw about the current balance and the future dream?

These points may help your conclusions.

- Is work too dominant at present; is this what I want?
- Will it change, or do I have to?
- Is there enough energy for leisure and renewal?
- Where can I find that essential energy?
- Are there family and friends I'm losing touch with?
- How can I meet them more often?
- If I was to be living my ideal balanced life what has to change?
- How long can I live with being out of balance?
- When might the dream become a reality?
- What do I need to stop doing that takes energy away from planning my future?

So, what have you learnt:

- about time and energy and how you want to change the balance
- about your passions and needs
- about what you want more of in your life
- and what you want less of?

🗁 *Another big chart for our file. Record those conclusions on the* **Lifetime Circles Chart** *as:*

- what I want more of
- what I want less of

Your Portfolio Crossroads

This chapter started out by projecting forward a long way.

We've arrived back closer to today, armed with a clearer vision of where we want to be and the first steps we can take to begin on the path.

By now you may be thinking how Portfolio Life might give you the flexibility and freedom that your new priorities are crying out for.

It's an attractive thought ... but what about that realist and critic we mentioned before, and kept to one side. What are the questions that they keep asking us about making such a change – urgent and vital questions?

> **?** What will the family say?
> **?** How would I manage without a regular salary?
> **?** Identity and status: what do I say to 'what do you do now?'
> **?** What happens when the phone doesn't ring and I've no emails coming in?
> **?** How can I replace the chats with colleagues?
> **?** What's the secret of successful networking?
> **?** How do I sell and market myself?
> **?** What's it like running an independent business instead of being employed?

How do these questions make you feel?

- A realistic assessment of the hurdles to a new life?
- A leap too far at the moment?

If your investigation has shown that where you are now and where you want to be are quite similar, perhaps the Portfolio Life isn't right for you at this stage.

Fulfilment for some can come within the more predictable security of fully employed life. Your time and income balance may be firmly on the income side for the next few years.

If this is your immediate route, the models and analysis will have left you clearer about why it's right for you, clearer about how it fits your needs and aspirations.

Stay with the evolution from where you are now, but keep an eye out too for when your views or circumstances might prompt a rethink. Perhaps you'll look at the Portfolio Life as a long-term option to be revisited later.

If you feel that a future picture is emerging of exciting challenges of freedom and stretch and learning, you'll want to explore Portfolio Life more.

If you do, you are not alone. Others have trod this path, asked the questions, and found there is a way.

The following chapters will help you find it.

Your portfolio is the way you can release yourself from today's shackles and realise your dreams, achieve a better balance, develop new skills, and develop yourself.

Can you do that, fitting into the job spec someone else has designed?

Or do you want to forge your own blueprint and discover how the world helps you find the path to use it?

To summarise ...

- You've projected forward to your dream so you can work backwards to your plan.

- Your Last Big Birthday Party showed what you really want from the rest of your life.

- The Top 10 Hits highlighted the priorities.

- The Lifetime Circles identified the changes you want in your balance.

- Now it's your choice whether the Portfolio Life is the best way for you and whether this is the right time.

In Chapter 6 you'll look at the actual constituents of your Portfolio and the answers to the challenges it raises.

Julia Cleverdon's
Portfolio Journey

I remember so well the December afternoon when the coach, who had been commissioned by me as Chief Executive of Business in the Community, came to talk over the actions I needed to take in the organisation. I had known him as a Managing Director and through his work on a major community project. What I was not prepared for however, was a kind and apparently casual remark as we finished our conversation, "And what about your career, Julia, you've done this job for fifteen years – what are you thinking about in your plans forward?" I found myself in floods – unable to either answer the question or to find a handkerchief. Thinking about it now, I can see more clearly why the question caught me on the raw, and how lucky I was that he asked it.

It is very easy for those of us caught up in the excitement and challenges of leading an organisation that one loves to miss the passing of the years and the shifting of the tectonic plates. I had joined Business in the Community in 1988 when it employed thirty people and engaged 140 member companies. I was appointed Chief Executive in 1992, and worked very closely with our inspirational President, the Prince of Wales, and with five different Chairmen. We grew the business and the campaign to more than 850 companies, 400 employees and £25 million turnover. Each succeeding Chairman urged me to stay and I willingly agreed; the death of my husband, leaving me with two young daughters, ensured that my only overwhelming priorities were my girls and work.

It was into this situation that my coach asked the question. I knew that a new Chairman was due and that I must decide, at 56, what I wanted to do. Would I stay for another three years – and end my career at 60 in that role or be brave and see if I could do anything else with my talents? I can honestly say that without help from the book and the coaching I would never have managed to face up to the thought of a different future. We saw each other once a month, and I talked and he listened and then reflected back in helpful and insightful notes the implications of what I said and what I proposed to do! Marvellous exercises to make you think – like writing your birthday party speech at 70 – forced me to realise the significance of my oft quoted line 'Every work of art is a child of its time' and that I had done my time.

Then what could I do instead? Did I really want to try to be a non – exec Director or concentrate time on the campaigning passions which I cared about? Would I be capable of chairing another voluntary organisation or was I too much a very hands-on Chief Executive? If my happiest time was spent making speeches on causes I cared about would anybody pay me to continue to make speeches? How would I manage in my future life with a hailstorm of paper and too many appointments crammed into a day without my right hand executive assistant for the last seventeen years? All these thoughts and many more whirled through our conversations and were converted into a plan with timings and milestones.

Six months after starting the coaching programme, in summer 2007, I made the decision to stand down and I finally left BITC in March 2008. I had used the months in between to redefine my work with the Prince's Charities, begin working with top levels of Government to develop the strategy on mobilising business with education and develop my role as Chairman of Teach First. So my portfolio was underway and I enormously enjoyed the experience of doing something focused and new.

My Executive Assistant and I decided that we would stick together and see how to make it work. Speaking engagements began to come in and we got braver about asking for a fee. I established my portfolio and achieved a new lifestyle that balances my work, home and personal life closer to the way I want it.

From my experience on the journey, I would encourage potential portfolio people to have faith that :

- *your talents and experience can be transferred and amplified beyond your current role.*

- *when you know what you want to do, the world will bring*

opportunities to make it happen, including a new support team and paying clients!

- *you have just got to get going: the first step is the hardest and then the road rises up to meet you.*

- *a plan with timings and milestones will make a clear path through the myriad of questions and options...and give you a feeling of control.*

- *as your portfolio evolves, you benefit from reviewing its balance annually and keeping on track through regular updates with a Coach.*

Dame Julia Cleverdon's portfolio involves working across Business and Government. She brings together influential movers and shakers to inspire new thinking and galvanise action. She is a speaker, ambassador and campaigner on her areas of passionate interest. After her term as Chair of Teach First, she is now Vice Patron; she is Vice President of BITC, Special Adviser on responsible business to the Prince's Charities, and Chair of National Literacy Trust.

6

PLANNING YOUR FUTURE PORTFOLIO

Two roads diverged in a wood, and I –
I took the one less travelled by,
And that has made all the difference.
Robert Frost

In Chapters 4 and 5, you've learnt a lot about yourself:

- where you are now: *talents, experience, interests, values*
- where you want to be: *needs, what to have more of, what less of*

In this chapter, you're going to gather all that learning onto the Portfolio Planner and use it to plan the best portfolio for your current reality and your future dream.

You're going to bring together all your data from previous chapters, explore the options for your portfolio roles, and see how it all fits into a Portfolio Plan.

It's an important part of your journey whatever point you are at now.

You may have decided to pursue the Portfolio Life straight away.

You may be considering making the change in the next year, or sometime in the future.

Even if you've decided to stay in full-time employment for now, the Portfolio Planner can be a useful tool to evaluate what works for you.

The Portfolio Planner

If you've completed all the exercises, now you get your reward with our comprehensive planning tool.

If you took the Fast Track and just did a few exercises, read forward to see how our Planner can assist you, and you may decide to go back and do the ones you missed

Have a look at the Routemap on page 123 (figure 12), which shows how all your work on models and charts comes together.

The grid on the right-hand side, called The Portfolio Planner, has 'role options' across the top axis and eight headings from 'Experience' to 'Other Factors' in the left hand column.

The boxes to the left of the grid represent charts you'll have gathered as you worked through the models in Chapters 4 and 5. We'll start filling these in a bit later but before we do, let's spend some time on the choice of roles for the top axis.

Choosing roles for your portfolio

By this stage, you understand what the Portfolio Life is all about, you've looked at where you are in your life, and where you would like to be.

So, your biggest remaining question will be: 'What are the roles I want to pursue for this wonderful life I have in prospect?'

It's time for you to design your future roles.

As we've said earlier, the special thing about portfolio-ing is that the role you will design is unique to you. There won't be another one quite like it. So we won't be giving you an A-Z of every possible job, from actor to zookeeper. What the next few pages aim to achieve is to get you to think as broadly as possible about your portfolio, to really open your mind. After all, if you've gone out each morning of your life to a single job, however complex and demanding, then running a portfolio is quite different. It requires shifts in your thinking, covered here and in Chapter 7.

------------PORTFOLIO PLANNER------------

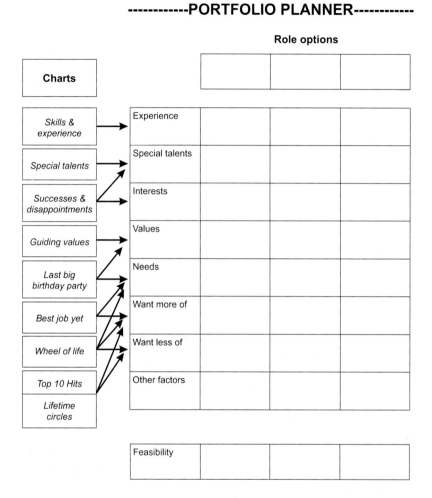

Figure 12. Portfolio Planner Routemap

If you're in employment and are looking tempted to become Unlimited, then you can use a more relaxed approach; you have time to develop some of the roles which tempt you. On the other hand, if you've already left employment and are actively pursuing the alternative of the Portfolio Life, then you need to put the job pressures out of your mind for the rest of this chapter. This is your portfolio future and you don't want to blow it by grabbing at the first thing going. Yes, there may be financial pressures, but this is still your chance to open a new door and get the balance right.

Some principles before we get under way. As far as possible, stick to the guiding principle from earlier chapters: 'do what you enjoy'.

That should be your aim. You may not achieve it straight off in your first portfolio days; compromises may be necessary. Perhaps you won't be able to do 100% of what you enjoy; but whatever you achieve, it's unlikely that you will have to compromise as much as you have done in your employed life. As you develop your portfolio and gain confidence, then you can look to achieve the second part of the phrase: 'with people you enjoy working with'.

Michael Korda said:

'Your chances of success are directly proportional to the degree of pleasure you derive from what you do.'

As a Portfolio Professional you're looking for both.

So this section is about making choices for, and designing, the roles for your portfolio. You've already made the decisions on what percentage of your life that should make up. You've identified your talents and skills, your successes and disappointments. Have all these at your side as you turn the next few pages. Make notes as you go on any roles which come to mind as you open your mind reading the next few pages.

Your portfolio for all of your life

Let's begin with a truism: you can only start from where you are now. So where is that?

In employment? Age? Family circumstances? Income – and savings?

Our stage of life makes a big difference to our portfolio planning. We've seen that in earlier chapters, with the whole message of life and opportunities running out. It's not just about age, it's about how we feel about life and what we seek to achieve in it.

Age is significant. There's no doubt that starting a portfolio at fifty is easier than at sixty. Ageism does exist and is faced by everybody seeking employment. However, the advantage of the Portfolio Life is that you're not seeking full-time employment, and you will find in so many portfolio roles that grey-haired experience can be a plus. There's a particular advantage if you're 45 or older because doing your own thing is about the only way you'll be certain of being able to keep doing what you want to do, for as long as you want to do it. However, if you're moving towards the 'senior' part of your life, then it's probably not the time to be choosing to be a tennis pro or male model.

You'll read in Chapter 7 of the importance of carrying your family with you in your portfolio decision, and some of the difficulties to be aware of. If you're approaching the Portfolio Life in its fullest sense, then you appreciate that it's more than just a job. So much of your portfolio future is going to be a life together that, when choosing your roles, you need to consider carefully the demands and expectations of your immediate family. If they want to share more of you, then an interim role which requires you to be living away from home all week may bring in the cash, but will not meet your family's requirements. If your partner works full-time, this could provide the regular income you will no longer have, but how will you achieve your goal of spending more quality time with him or her? Perhaps you could both make the move and become Portfolio Partners?

It's a portfolio, stupid

How many times has the word 'portfolio' appeared in this book? Like you, we've lost count. So it's even more surprising how often in discussing the move with potential Portfolio Professionals, their thinking revolves around a single role. A lifetime of employment has brainwashed them into thinking that way.

Charles Handy described his portfolio as 'different bits of work', and that's what you should be looking for as you consider potential roles. A mix, a blend, a collection – potentially with a theme, but we'll come to that shortly. For now, regarding the Paid Work part, let's just say: money comes in a variety of different bundles from a number of different sources.

It's no coincidence that most of the world's finest wines are blends. On the positive side, blending allows the winemaker to optimise complexity, ageing potential, concentration and length. It enables the whole to be greater than the sum of the parts. Significantly, for our purpose, one of the winemaker's main aims in blending is to create a wine with the ideal balance. On the negative side, blending minimises variations in vintages, the effect of weather, diseases and other problems.

Healthy portfolios are blends. Blends can give you the variety that may have been missing in your employed life; they contain a little of this and a little of that, allowing you to include passions, interests and hobbies. As with wine, they provide an insurance against temporary setbacks. Industries wax and industries wane, businesses grow and contract. This may have posed you a problem in your employed life, but having a suitable blend of role in a well-balanced portfolio should avoid that happening in your new life.

The great Château Pétrus is a 95%/5% blend, whereas many top champagnes have equal blends of three grape varieties. In the same way, your portfolio can have a mix of big and small in terms of time, and of high & low in terms of earnings. There isn't a single rate for the job, and you will probably be the first to concede that your twenty years experience as an actuary should earn you a better rate than your developing dream of being a street performer. But if you choose to sell only your actuarial services, then you will not gain the full benefits from the Portfolio Life. Moreover, you're possibly one step from the stage, the West End beckons, your dream could become a reality, could match your alternative earnings, and become the prime role in your portfolio.

Many portfolios combine the rough with the smooth. One friend works as a caretaker three days a week, in a bookseller's at weekends, and writes his novel in every other moment. There's no reason to think 'white collar' for 100% of your portfolio if that isn't the right fit for what you're wanting to achieve in life.

The Ideal Portfolio

It's your portfolio, chosen by you and built on your experience and your goals. So we simply offer a few thoughts on what, in the medium to long term, an ideal portfolio might consist of.

- **Have at least one no-brainer.** Perhaps it's not your favourite way of spending your working day, but you can pick up business fairly regularly and it pays.

- **Have a number of customers.** If you have just one, you're back to being employed. Single customers can be attractive, but they're risky. They can go out of business, your contact can fall under a bus, or one of your assignments may not go down well. Eggs & baskets territory!

- **Concentrate your working time on what you enjoy doing.** We keep saying it, but enjoying, in the broadest possible sense, is a big part of what the Portfolio Life is about. As soon as you can afford to financially, bias your portfolio towards the things you enjoy most. How you divide time between your different roles is up to you. Push the boundaries as much as possible towards enjoying.

- **Only pursue what's you.** There will be times, particularly when you are starting up when it may be attractive to put time and effort into pursuing a role just because it's there, and pays. You've got experience in two of the ten fields they describe, so it's worth a go. No! If you've completed your charts, you know where your strengths, talents and skills lie. Stick to them.

- **Your work portfolio should be a good fit.** By the time you finish this book you'll have made the decision on how much of your life should be in the Paid Work category. Whatever that proportion is, it has to be a good fit with the rest of your life, or you've failed. If one of your goals is to spend more time seeing the world, then a part-time role which requires your presence 52 weeks a year is not a fit.

Generic Role Choices

We've established some of the principles behind the ideal portfolio role. But we've also emphasised that every portfolio is quite unique – this is your portfolio and nobody else's.

So, we now look briefly at some of what we can call the 'generic role choices' and their fit with a good portfolio.

The generic choices are part-time, temporary, interim, contract, secondment, non-executive, consultant, Jack-of-all-trades. You can seek assignments in the public, profit or not-for-profit sectors, or wherever else you can find the right combination of pay and enjoyment.

Part-time

Clearly, part-time work is a basis of many portfolios. A couple of days a week can be a very useful regular income, giving time for development of more interesting roles. Don't be afraid to look at the simple job areas necessary to keep income ticking over – these roles are unlikely to be for ever, so use them for what they are.

From your viewpoint, part-time work fits portfolios well – it can provide the flexibility and variety that create the new balance in your life. Bear in mind, also, that it's an easier sell to prospective employers. You have the talents they need, and you are willing to commit these on their behalf – but at less than a full-time employee would cost them. So part-time can be good for both sides.

Non-executive

Of course there are part-time roles that really can be major long-term elements in your portfolio – non-executive directorships (NEDs) being key amongst them. These are not only excellent in themselves but also open up doors to more directorships, seats on public bodies, and can be great for networking. 'Start early' is one of the clues to success here. If you are already on a Board, before making your portfolio move look to leverage your full-time position to gain a non-executive role. Employers are usually supportive, seeing this as a widening of your experience. With a fixed-term contract (non-executive directorships are usually a minimum of three years) you could even time your move so that the NED overlaps when you leave your corporate position and provides useful income in the early years of your portfolio life.

Remember that it is not just FTSE 100 companies that need NEDs. Many SMEs realize the benefits of having executive experience for their chairman. Spread your net widely and you will have a greater chance of success.

In deciding on a NED role, do bear in mind that non-executives now have the same legal responsibilities as executive directors. So make sure that you go in with your eyes open, and do the necessary research, particularly in the case of non-public and smaller organizations.

Like part-time, NED roles offer you flexibility – often a couple of contracted days per month plus some additional 'consulting' time if you play your cards right.

There are agencies, headhunters and websites specialising in filling NED positions. See our website for these and for further reading.

Consultant

A difficult role to define, as a very high proportion of executives being 'released' by their organization declare that they will become a 'consultant'. It has a better ring to it than 'selling my expertise' – but that's what it is.

Being a consultant can be a great fit for your portfolio. As the Paid Work element, it can be highly remunerative. Clients come and go, allowing you some scope for the flexibility for family or travel which you may want in your new life. With the appropriate expertise the new skills you will have to develop to be a successful consultant can also be useful for Gift Work in the charity or not-for-profit sectors.

If you choose to work on your own, then you will need to have, or quickly develop, selling skills. Start with the chapter on 'Selling' in Part 4. If you see this as a potential weakness, look for one of many consultancy agencies that employ freelance consultants but have specialist sales teams selling their services. The downside is that you won't 'own' the clients, but work can be more continual and it's easier to fit other elements of your portfolio if you are not the sole consultant available.

Interim Management

Interim management may have a place in some portfolios, especially in the early stages. In Chapter 8, we look in more detail at the various stages you may be at prior to 'crossing the bridge' to your new portfolio life. Timing is important, and if you can be in control of the timing of your departure from your corporate role you have a chance to prepare better.

On the other hand, for those for whom the end of their corporate life comes out of the blue, interim management may be a very useful half-way stage. It provides income, a useful entry on your cv, and hopefully some broader experience and contacts which will be beneficial for your portfolio life. Exercising some self-discipline, you should be in a position to limit your role to reasonable hours and devote time to building your portfolio future while performing the interim management role. Seen as a half-way house, an interval, but keeping your portfolio clearly in front of you, interim management has a part to play.

It may even be possible to construct a portfolio based around short-term interim roles. A series of three month contracts, interspersed by time on other projects, may be a possible different approach to portfolio-ing – if you can maintain the non-interim parts of the portfolio on the same on/off basis.

If you are seriously considering interim management as part of your portfolio, it is even more important that you have completed the exercises in the last few chapters and decided what you want out of life. Interim management could turn out to be a series of the kind of corporate role you have decided to leave behind. It can involve a weekly commute, living away from home for long periods, and potentially loss of the very life/work balance you have been seeking to improve.

So think and plan carefully if this is one of the options you are considering.

Gift Work

We saw earlier in the book how 'Gift Work' – putting something back – is an important chunk in many portfolios. There are a myriad of ways to do this, whether working through voluntary organizations or with the charities or non-profit bodies themselves.

You are clear about the skills and talents you have to offer and have the flexibility of time suitable for many of these organizations. More importantly, you are offering your talents free, or at a special lower fee level – having first ensured, of course, that your Paid Work chunk is bringing in sufficient income for your needs. You can also use this as an opportunity to do some work you find interesting and rewarding but which doesn't fit as paid work. For example, if your paid work involves mainly desk and brainpower, then a more practical hands-on role for a charity may bring its own particular reward.

Organisations such as Reach have expertise in placing available talent where it is most required in the charity and non-profit sectors. Look at the large national charities but also at your own local environment where your skillbase may be able to have an even greater proportional impact.

What are organisations willing to pay for?

The majority of Portfolio Professionals will set up their portfolio to sell services to organisations. At the top end, most of us would be delighted to become non-executive directors of some business, earning well for a couple of days a month. If you have the skills and, more importantly, the contacts, then this could be the foundation of a good portfolio. But there are good opportunities for part-time, project and contract working at all levels of organisations.

Organisations will buy in knowledge and skills. The world is changing so fast that the latest skills requirements are often absent internally and have to be either developed or bought in. There are opportunities for Portfolio Workers who have developed the required skills and are ahead of the market. Clearly they can sell their skills to cover the deficit. Alternatively, they can market themselves to develop the new required skills internally. If you have a skill, and the talent to communicate it, then training, coaching and mentoring are profitable areas you might want to consider.

In addition, organisations are now so focussed on their core activities that they choose to out-source non-core tasks; those out-sourcing contracts have taken over as the key revenue-earners for the international consultancy companies. Remember that for every international business which chooses outsourcing, there are hundreds of small businesses which would prefer to do the same. A creative approach and some enquiries will reveal what tasks businesses are still doing, which would be far more efficiently carried out by a portfolio worker selling his or her services.

It's a sad fact of life, but businesses have problems and an urgent need to get rid of them. They need problem-solvers. If you have the right skill-set, they need you. Problems exist at all levels of an organisation. At the top, chief executives lead lonely lives and may need the support of outside mentors. Throughout the organisation, objective and independent views are necessary to assist in identifying growth areas and strategic priorities. New ideas and new processes are vital to streamline and reduce cost. All organisations have peaks and overloads; the demands may be short-term, but it's a great way of getting inside and making an impression.

Keep an open mind in looking at organisations. Don't just think consultancy, coaching or customer relationships. Their problems are far more varied and hands-on (your hands hopefully). Organisations hold conferences using inexperienced speakers, need original ideas for hospitality events, care for the health of their staff, have employees who need relocating, etc. etc.

Do the organisations know they need you? Not necessarily. Can you express yourself in writing? Look at the average SME website, read the detail, observe the poor grammar and expression. Opportunities abound.

What are individuals willing to pay for?

In case you've forgotten, you're choosing a portfolio of roles and keeping an open mind. Why is it then that so many people starting a portfolio seem to forget that consumers, individuals, have cash too? Look at failures amongst Portfolio Workers and often they highlight an inability to see beyond the skills from their past life, and to miss the opportunities to develop talents and skills to market to individuals.

Significantly, individuals don't always spend their own money. More and more executives have personal training budgets. There's growing business for lifestyle management.

❋ *Whoever pays in the end, many of these opportunities can be termed 'a world of service to the limited by the unlimited'.*

Those who choose to stay in the stressful, all-hours corporate world deserve our support. They need personal trainers, coaching, chauffeurs, and gardeners. They have the money to spend; you have the flexibility to give of your time to increase your freedom.

Service jobs are in. Plumbers can name their price; dog walkers are in short supply; life coaches are the latest must-have; good electricians are discussed at dinner parties. A few years ago, Paul, a portfolio colleague, nearly threw it all in to become a pool-cleaner. A pool-cleaner? Yes, he'd been on holiday to California. The stars in Beverley Hills were absolutely desperate for reliable, trustworthy help, for which you could name your price.

In a world of home-delivery shopping, personal party planners and professional organisers, don't overlook the potential of consumers as elements in your portfolio.

Hobbies, interests ...

... dreams ... and passions. It's right to indulge yourself, that's one of the reasons you want to become a Portfolio Professional. If there was ever a time to develop your painting skills or get short stories published or design gardens, this is it.

In a recent report the think-tank, Demos, identified as 'Pro-ams' a growing category of people who 'work at their leisure ... and set professional standards to judge their amateur efforts.' Their work in organisations is controlled and scheduled by others but in their leisure time they take control back. What distinguishes them is the level of expertise they achieve.

We are not talking here of surfing the web for pleasure, but contributing to the writing of open-source programs; not digging their own garden, but designing gardens for others. Most do not see themselves as professionals, although that is the standard they reach. For many there is no intention of turning their interest into a business. But for those who appreciate how the mix of Portfolio Life works, there is a major opportunity.

✱ *This really is pursuing your passion and turning it into the basis of a business.*

So many of us have an interest or dream we would love to pursue but, knowing that it could never support a full-time business, we put it to one side or limit it to hobby status. Your portfolio offers you the chance to pursue your dream as one element of many in a varied portfolio.

Summary of principles of role choosing

The time for choosing your roles is getting close. Before you do, let's just summarise some of the principles we've covered.

- Your portfolio is unique.

- Consider your age, current employment, income requirements, family.
- You'll have time to plan your move so look ahead for your roles.
- Plan for a portfolio, not for a single role.
- Pick a 'no-brainer' as your starting focus.
- Aim to use the full range of the Wealth in Your Head.
- Make space in your portfolio for your dreams.

Charting your Portfolio: Completing the Planner

Have a look ahead to Figure 13 on page 137 and you can see where your data from the charts will be transferred under the eight headings from 'Experience' to 'Other Factors' in the left hand column, and where the Roles will go on the top axis.

There's a line at the bottom for feasibility that we'll come to later.

Figure 13 is a shortened version of the Planner; if you've visited our website you'll already have your own full copy.

Three points about the Planner before we start:

- It's not a decision-maker, that's you! It is a decision facilitator, allowing you to see the options clearer before you decide.

- There are no right answers! It's more art than science; the boxes and headings are a guide not a rule and you can find your own way to completing the grid.

- Different people complete the evaluation in different ways. Those mathematically inclined, might use a rating scale like 1-5, or %s, or +/−. Artistic types might use colours, such as traffic light system, or you might want to use ticks and crosses.

Filling in your role options

With the notes you've made, you'll be ready to list the roles you want to evaluate on the Portfolio Planner.

Remember this is your list and you can put anything in you want to explore. You can always extend the top row, or change it later; many PPs do!

You may want to organise your list by type of work: in profit and not for profit sectors, in paid or unpaid roles, in part-time or interim work, in consultancy or non-executive roles.

You'll want to think holistic: no work/leisure boundaries in the future balance! Think about Charles Handy's definitions of paid work, home work, study work and gift work ... and time for you.

Be outrageous, enjoy the imagining. Let your list include your dreams, your passions, anything you ever wanted to be.

Don't worry about being crazy; this is between you and the book.

If you dreamed of playing in an orchestra, put it in ... and also put in working in the music industry; if you wanted to be a Wimbledon tennis player, put it in to see how it fits ... but also put in sports management

Remember your Best Job Yet and put that in.

Include your current role, it's great as a control to measure against and see where it matches and where and why it doesn't.

When you've refined your list, put the roles across the top axis.

Roles

Experience

Special talents

Interests

Values

Needs

Want more of

Want less of

Other factors

Feasibility

Figure 13. Portfolio Planner

Assembling all your data for the left hand column

This is the time when having all the charts from the models in your 'Portfolio Plan' file will help.

We're going to transfer the data into the rows under the headings in the left hand column. Where it fits can be self-explanatory: special talents, guiding values, skills and experience

Other headings are more flexible:

We used Lifetime Circles to explore 'Want more of/less of' but other data may fit there too (from your Top 10 Hits for example). Successes and Disappointments raised data for 'Interests' but so did other models. Check your Last Big Birthday Party to capture the needs and values you want in the future.

You get the picture. Assemble your data where you think it appropriate for you and for your decision. Add in anything else that's important to you under 'Other factors'.

You might not have space for your entire list; it's good to prioritise!

Before you transfer to the grid, make a long list, then a short list, then go for the top 10, pick out the key criteria and focus on those.

So, you're ready to fill in that column under the eight headings. When the axes are complete, you can do some evaluation in whatever way and mode you wish; ratings, colours, symbols whatever works for you, as we said before.

One Portfolio Explorer converted the Planner into her own spread sheet and devised a multicoloured picture of her future, like painting by numbers!

The feasibility line at the bottom is there in case the realist and critic in you needs feeding!

It allows you to put a qualifier on 'how likely is it I can get this role in the time span I'm expecting'. If you're adding up your columns, you can weight your totals with a percentage for feasibility.

One we prepared earlier

In case further clarification is needed, here's one we .....!

	Roles				
	Current role	*Non Exec*	*Consultant*	*Charity*	*Coach*
Experience					
Marketing	8	7	8	4	4
Project leadership	7	7	6	8	3
Food industry	10	8	7	0	2
Special talents					
People	8	6	4	7	9
Writing	3	5	5	3	6
Empathy	5	5	5	7	10
Interests					
Sport	4	6	7	6	6
Astronomy	0	2	4	3	3
Phtography	1	2	4	4	4
Values					
Integrity	5	5	3	8	9
People not profit	4	6	4	8	9
Listening	3	5	5	7	10
Needs					
Solitude	4	6	7	3	8
Spiritual	3	3	3	7	7
Income as now	10	8	7	1	6
Want more of					
Flexible timing	3	8	8	6	8
Study work	4	7	8	6	8
Time for family	4	7	8	7	7
Want less of					
Travel	2	5	4	7	7
Weekend work	2	7	3	7	7
Politics	2	7	7	4	7
Other factors					
More open air	3	5	6	6	7
Parents' health	3	7	7	7	7
Feasibility					

Figure 14. Portfolio Planner

In figure 14, Robert has measured his role options against criteria in the left hand column; he's decided to use score 1-10, 10 being high.

He has rated how well the criteria are met by each of the Role Options.

His Current Role scores high for use of experience and income. However, he is giving more weight in the future to his talents with people, flexibility of working, open air and health; he wants time for his interests, family and study work with less time spent in travel and weekend working.

Adding up his totals, the Roles of Coach, Consultant and Non-Executive seem to meet his new criteria best; they are significantly higher than his current role.

The scores from the 'Portfolio Jury' are:

- Current job 98
- Non-Exec 134
- Consultant 130
- Charity 126
- Coach 154

This could be an important reinforcement for his 'gut-feel' about his new direction, even before he looks at feasibility!

This bit of analysis supports the 'head' in following where the 'heart' is leading!

And, as we've said before, the great thing about a portfolio is that it's a blend and our planner can blend any of the ones he's analysed.

Looking at your results

How does your Portfolio Planner look to you now?

Or more relevant, how does it FEEL?

The Planner does not give you the answer: it helps you know where your instinct takes you. It's an aid to your judgement.

This is your analysis of where you are and what you want – so they're your scores – and it helps show what's right for you/

You may be disappointed by the roles that score best.

We know Portfolio Explorers who look at the highest rated options and say, *'Oh no, I didn't want that one to win!'*

There's the sign! It's your gut-feel telling you which way to go. Go with your heart and revisit the grid to examine why the ones you don't want to follow seem to win.

More important, look at the ones you feel are right and see why the scores in the cells marked them lower ... and what has to change to get the rating where your heart tells you it should be.

Are there talents your chosen roles need you to develop?

Do you need to compromise on some of the needs?

It may well be that the roles you want overlap or merge. Are they looking like a combination of roles rather than individual roles, dare we suggest a portfolio?!

Themes for your portfolio

Charles Handy saw the Portfolio Life as 'a collection of different items ... which has a theme to it'.

Our experience is that themes emerge and in the early stages of developing your portfolio it is best to keep as open and flexible as possible. In the longer term, a combination of talents and interests will determine a theme.

James Alexander, our first editor, talks of his portfolio 'expanding and contracting until eventually the range became focused on writing and publishing, speaking and editing – all 'word' things.'

For Caroline, photography became a theme. She wants to publish books of her photographs, but meantime, a part-time role with a distributor of photographic equipment keeps her close to the trade and reduces her costs for her other role as wedding and portrait photographer.

So themes may be clear from the start or may emerge over time. Our message is not to get hung up on them. It's more important to keep a varied portfolio, using a mix of skills with a mix of clients.

Creating your own portfolio

So now you can select the roles that feel best off the Planner and put them on a new sheet of paper.

Consider how they can fit together, relish their diversity and their common themes, enjoy the way they fit your talents, interests and needs.

Picture yourself in the ideal week, filling your life this way.

Hear yourself talking about 'this is what I do now' to your friends and colleagues.

Does that feel good?

Now that you've seen that the freedom and flexibility that can be reached ... and how your future career roles fit into the context of your total life. You can take the you you now know so well, and develop into a Portfolio Professional. You've made a special decision, one that will change all of your life, personal and professional.

Time for a glass of bubbly, and why not!?

A *toast:* To you and your new Portfolio.

You've made a great step towards designing that portfolio, to drawing up your own 'job specification' for what's the right portfolio for you.

You might want to plunge in straight away and get swimming.

Gamblers and good swimmers can try ...but there is a better way, a way that keeps you in control of the when and the how and gets you to the other side dry, balanced and ready for business.

Chapter 8 will introduce you to the **Portfolio Bridge**. This makes sure that leaving the river bank you're on now doesn't have to be a leap into the unknown.

The Portfolio Bridge gives you a planned crossing with support against the risks, and the chance to enjoy the journey.

Chapter 7 gets you prepared for your portfolio and the Bridge by covering some of the questions that all Portfolio Professionals face as they approach this point in the journey.

To summarise ...

- You have explored the role options for your portfolio.

- You have brought together all your data from Chapters 4 and 5.

- You have evaluated the best portfolio for you.

- You have considered themes.

- You have made the decision on the career that's right for the rest of your life.

You're ready to move into Part 3: Implementing your Portfolio, which will guide you across the joys, avoiding the pitfalls, of setting yourself up for your Portfolio Life.

PART 3

IMPLEMENTING YOUR PORTFOLIO

7

APPROACHING THE TRANSITION

The longest part of the journey is said to be the passing of the gate.
Marcus Terentius Varro (116 BC – 27 BC)

In this chapter we look at the type of questions that all Portfolio Explorers face at the transition stage of the journey, and suggest some approaches to answering them.

Big change

Making the transition from fully employed life to Portfolio Life is a big change – for you and everyone close to you. Do not underestimate it.

It's up there in the top ten stressful events of your life, together with divorce, having children, moving house ... but hopefully not all at the same time!

Another top stressor in the list is bereavement, and it's not too fanciful to equate the breaking of ties with your old employed life with bereavement.

You may have worked for organisations for many years and that culture will have invaded all your life: being at work more waking hours than being at home tends to do that to you. Your social life may revolve around people you work with, and, even if you've kept that separate, your conversations at home (and your head when staring vacantly at the TV) will be full of it. The values that you are asked to espouse for 8-14 hours a day are not easily shed in the car park, tube, bus or train on the way home.

So it's no surprise that making the change is a major severance, with a real sense of loss. We're potentially losing friends, colleagues, status, security, money and however well we're planned and prepared it makes a great impact. And you never quite know when or where!

A number of Portfolio Professionals have successfully managed the handover to their successor, the leaving drinks and speeches, the pension and package arrangements, only to be caught vulnerable to the feelings when clearing the files.

It's a lot to say goodbye to, the unfinished projects, those great ideas, the hard work; a lot to dump in the bin as if worthless (apart from those boxes of papers that you'll take home to store in the loft for 5 years and open perhaps three times!). So don't expect to feel unmoved, it's a big step you're taking!

You can expect to be taken up by changes in mood in the course of a week, or a day: from euphoria to fear to fulfilment to worry, and back again!

As we open ourselves to be more aware of what's going on around us, the feelings come through the windows. You can be reassured that they're a sign of progress and something that affects everyone making the transition.

The emotions of the change are well covered in Max Comfort's *Portfolio People*, a very useful book, unfortunately now hard to find as a new copy.

> *'You say goodbye and I say hello.'*
> **The Beatles**

This chapter is all about managing the transition, dealing with the change.

The great opportunity is to look at your life again; not just repeat what you've been doing for the last decade/s. You have the chance to carry forward what you want from the past and merge it with the new things you want from the future, acknowledging the losses and celebrating the gains.

You'll find a lot of practical experience from Portfolio Professionals of what to try, where to find help and how to take the first steps with confidence, trust and belief.

Everybody makes changes their own way, but we all tend to follow a pattern.

It goes from denial (it can't be true) to resistance (I can't change) to exploration (let's see what happens) and then to commitment (I want to do it).

Shedding the onion skins

Making the change is like peeling away the onion skins that have been built up through the habits of years past.

For Portfolio Peelers who have been in the corporate world, there's one skin for the lure of status, a title, a bigger office, a taller pot plant, an extra initial on the back of the car ...

- *Okay, I can peel that one off, I think.*

  Another for the buzz of busyness and excitement in the office, the coffee machine chats, the competitiveness ...

- *Okay, been there, done that, can find replacements for that I think.*

  Another skin for the comradeship, the smiling face round the corner, the praise, the appreciation, the applause ...

- *Right, but I remember the rivalry, the scowling face, the put-downs, the criticism as well, so I think I can leave that behind.*

  How about the financial security, the regular income, the unseen reward dropping into the bank at the end of the month?

- *Ah – now you're talking, when do I peel that skin and how raw am I going to feel then? When can I replace it with the real belief that someone will pay me for my talents when I'm not carrying the title and the badge I have now!*

As they say about recovery from injury: feel the pain and go with it, don't fight it! Recognise and value what's happening to you, relish the sharp edge of new experiences, and witness the growth it is giving you.

Many Portfolio Professionals find it helpful to keep a journal of the transition, noting the feelings of leaving, the severance negotiations, the handing over of responsibilities, the new network contacts; see how many days of old work are ones you'd want to live again and how many just make you glad it'll be over soon!

Enjoy listening to the traffic reports and smile at the prospect of travelling outside the rush hour. Hear the weather forecast and imagine seeing how the day changes season by season.

Freedom and paranoia

In answer to the question 'What are the key words to describe Portfolio Life?' one Portfolio Professional says: 'Freedom and paranoia'.

Freedom to decide your own time, location and priorities; freedom to work with people you like; freedom to fit your work pattern around your best work cycles; freedom to work at home; freedom to balance the other fs, family, fitness, finances, faith.

And paranoia?

Paranoia that you've over-committed your time and are working harder than ever, or that no-one wants to work with you (like them or not), that your work cycles disappear entirely when not prompted by others, that home isn't 'big enough for the two of us all day', and that balance is actually the pivot of a seesaw and you're not in the middle but going up and down on the end!

An outbreak of hardening of the 'oughteries' can occur with lots of high expectations; 'should' be working harder, 'should' be enjoying it more, 'should' be working with charities. And who's doing the 'shoulding'? Usually ourselves when we stop and think about it; so we know who it is who can reduce the pressure and loosen up the flow!

Fear of making mistakes is another strong emotion; now I'm more on my own, no-one else can correct me ... and I can't blame anyone else either!

Good judgement comes from experience;
experience comes from bad mistakes;
mistakes come from bad judgement.

If you're inclined to worry, Portfolio Life gives ample opportunity; if you're determined to pursue opportunity and be positive, the world opens up with choices and freedom.

Big questions

The big questions have been faced and solved by Portfolio Professionals before you ... which doesn't make them any less cogent and real.

> **?** What am I going to call myself?
> **?** When they say 'what do you do' what do I say?
> **?** Will I be motivated to get up?
> **?** What happens when there are no calls/emails?
> **?** Will there be enough income?
> **?** What if no one values what I can do?
> **?** Who does what, now I'm home more often?
> **?** What does my partner think of the change?
> **?** How will we plan our extra time together?
> **?** Do I have to learn new office/admin skills?
> **?** Where do I find the support when my computer crashes?
> **?** How can I develop an external network; why would anyone take a cold call from me?
> **?** What happens if the body starts to run down and I haven't got the energy?

Those who found the answers have discovered they can get support, and many have put their experience into this book in their specialist contributions and their Portfolio Journeys.

All of them found the transition to be a major life change; many reflect the well-known phrase: *'wish I'd done it years ago.'*

Identity crisis ... what crisis!

What do you call yourself when you no longer have your company's card that says Chairman, Managing Director, Director of ..., Executive in charge of ..., Head of ..., ... Manager.

Well of course, as a Portfolio Person running your own company, you can be whichever you wish … and admin clerk, and facilities manager, and chauffeur to boot if you want!

But how do you describe all the parts of your portfolio in a distinctive way? Consultant, actor, adviser, director, gardener, tennis coach all sound too loose and unlinked. You need one word or a word and a tagline that captures all these activities in one easy phrase… don't you?

But do you? If all your clients are in the same industry and you're providing the same service to them all, perhaps you do. However, if like most portfolios, you are working in different guises in different areas, why try to catch all that in one catch-all statement?

The only common factor across all your portfolio is you, and you know who you are. Each of your contacts knows a different aspect of you and what you offer, so why not tell them just what they need to know.

Play the five-card trick! If you're an actor, have a business card for theatres, agents and casting directors; if you're also a writer, have a card for publishers; if you also design clay ovens for garden barbecues, put your name and your product on a card for garden centres and wholesalers; and so on. Cards and websites are economic ways of creating that new identity.

And when you're asked, 'what do you do?' you have a choice of answers depending on the questioner. Or of course you can happily announce your freedom from badgehood and your great pride in your new profession with:

- I do what I enjoy and get paid for it.
- I use what I'm best at to meet what the client wants.
- I'm an Independent Director, a charity worker, writer, husband, father, brother.
- I'm a Portfolio Professional ('I've read the book!').

The great thing is that you are your own person and not stamped with the brand of an organisation with all the associations that brings.

How might it go:

'Let's introduce ourselves around the table, shall we?'

(Oh no – what shall I say, I can't use Nemis Oil's name any more. There's four before me – think, think.)

'Managing Director of Lombard Glass, came up through Sales and Commercial, been there 15 years.'

(Oh hell!)

'President of Independent Cinemas USA, over here looking for blue-sky opportunities.'

(Oh heavens!)

'Chief Executive, MOCFO International, made CBE last year.'

(Oh my God!)

'Bishop of Wessex, Church of England for 25 years, member of Synod.'

(Even closer to God! Oh it's my turn)

'Ah well, er, I used to be.........' – No hold on, forget that.

'I am, I'm proud to say, a Portfolio Professional, that is I'm into a number of activities that fit what I enjoy, I'm a coach, a mentor, a lecturer, an adviser, and a fundraiser, some paid some unpaid... oh and a husband for 30 years, a son and a brother, and a father and hotel-keeper for three children. All of those unpaid! Keeps me busy.'

(What a relief! Sounded okay and they all seemed to smile, sounded pretty human too. And now, hey, I can say what I really think, what I believe in without worrying about the party line. I'm not speaking with the company in my mouth, but with me in my head – and no defensive words about ecology, oil reserves, Third world ... I'm going to enjoy this!)

Presenting yourself as a Portfolio Professional needs a different speech.

You'll be refining that '30-second lift conversation', and that two liner for networking events, with every contact you have, until it feels clear and relaxed – and that's how you'll look too!

The sections on Marketing, Selling, Presenting and Networking in Part 4 will help present 'Brand You' the way you want.

Ruth Ball's
Portfolio Journey

I've just finished burning 32 years of pay slips and it has kept the family warm all evening. I'm still not sure why I kept them. What I do know, is that it has taken me almost two years since I left corporate life to let them go.

Corporate life can be a funny old world. For me, it's where:

- *I grew up and became the seasoned professional that I am today*
- *I thought I worked in a risk-taking environment but in reality, the boundaries kept me safe*
- *I met some of my closest friends providing me with a great social as well as a professional life*
- *I was part of a community where I knew my place, played by the rules and had great fun.*

Now it's history. Of course it has taken time to build a new life and it has not always been easy.

However, for the first time, I feel grown up. My corporate responsibilities are gone to be replaced by my own. This has meant everything from:

- *deciding what I wanted to do with my time,*
- *supporting myself as my secretary went with my last day at the office,*
- *revisiting relationships as I have changed lifestyle,*
- *finding ways to stay with a different pace of life.*

I was lucky when I left as I was able to carry on with coaching the senior team and this gave me a springboard for my current coaching work. It also gave me a revenue stream.

I now had time to complete my MBA and was delighted to be one of the oldest students to graduate. I started a diploma and took up voluntary work in a local primary school. Working with young children was a welcome change to some of the canny senior managers I was more used to who have learned to keep their cards close to their chests. Kids are different. They live in the moment. If they are happy, it shows on their faces. However, if they are bored, that shows too. It can be challenging as well as hugely rewarding. It also gives me structure and a community missing since I left corporate life.

In my original plan, I had time set aside for getting fit but beyond joining a local gym, nothing much happened. I realised that unless I got off my backside – literally in this case – nothing would happen. The same happened with learning Spanish and I took the same approach. I want to visit Spain but was originally reluctant to book in case other work came along. My freedom to holiday when I wanted was becoming a myth and I had to give myself a good talking to.

I enjoy my professional work although it can be double edged at times. I am paid to do a job. I do not get involved in the politics, which is great. When I first started, I wanted to do more but it was not always welcomed. Treading the fine line between involvement and interference is an art that needs to be quickly learned.

It can be the same at home where my involvement was not always seen as helpful. Learning to dance around a partner with a routine, which works for them, is as tricky a skill to perfect as any professional one.

Originally, I thought I would decide how to structure my portfolio life and it would stay rigid but life is not like that. Opportunities come from the most unexpected places and that's how I got involved as a keynote speaker at a strategic HR conference in Malta leading to more conferences, project work and executive coaching.

Looking back over the last couple of years, I have learned to:

- *trust in myself more*
- *lighten up*
- *not worry where the next piece of work is coming from – miracles do happen*
- *keep networking*
- *have fun.*

My one regret is that I could not let go of my past quicker although the family would not have been as cosy as they were if I had burned those pay slips earlier!

> **Ruth Ball is a Director of Talkchange (www.talkchange.co.uk), an international consultancy specializing in 1:1 change coaching including executives working outside their home culture and team development/ transition.**

The time of your life

What will get me up in the morning when I haven't got to get in to work?

A familiar question ... and a familiar fear.

The allure of that extra hour in bed, then the chance to read the paper for once, then the extra cup of coffee, bit of toast before I get up, read the mail – hey, this is good – Hell! it's 11.30!

And why not, once in a while! When you can choose when your weekend is, why not listen to the neighbours scraping the ice off their windscreens, revving their reluctant vehicles, sliding away into the smoking traffic jam that calls itself commuting.

However, the odd thing (or not so odd) is that Portfolio Professionals don't do that often. They get up and about, not because the office deadlines await, but because they WANT to begin their activities whatever they may be; the day can hold promise of paid work, study work, gift work, home work or a combination. How good to be able to see how you feel (creative, practical, dreaming, organising, solo or with people), and fit your time around that feeling.

So, a better way to start your day, as the Breakfast Shows have it.

Which is not to say time management doesn't have its moments later!

'Time flies like an arrow, fruit flies like a banana.'
Groucho Marx

Managing your time and life

Michael Frayn amused radio listeners with a tale of getting out of the door to the station. With too much time on his hands, he'd get up late, breakfast on the move, and run to the station looking frantically at his watch. Determined for once to avoid lunging for the train in heated sweat, he gets up earlier, shaves at leisure, eats a calm breakfast and is ready at his front door with ten minutes extra to spare. You can imagine how many things he finds the need to check, recheck, worry about and go back for: to ensure that the ten minutes are more than taken up and normal missed service is restored.

In the home worker's case: have I got business cards in my bag, did I leave the printer running? Yes I did but I forgot to pick up the map, there's a new email, just open it, oh no – there's a virus, delete and delete, there goes the phone, just answer it, might be a client, it's the bank, another query...

Where was the PA when you needed him?

Working for yourself takes organisation and self-discipline. Organisation and control of the diary, freedom to switch time between paid work and others, and the risk of double-booking or forgetting an appointment! It's all down to you.

Switching off

There's a log-off and an off switch on your device and a door to the office. They're all the equivalent of the drive back from the office and the turning off.

It's too easy when the journey from the office to evening is just down the stairs, to just peep in later to finish off something.

At the end of the day, get your routine set: empty briefcase, file papers, log day in diary, gather material for tomorrow ... log off, switch off.

Trust the brain to sort out the unfinished business; it's the best computer you've got and can't work well when overloaded.

Taking time out

You're in charge of your own holiday roster. If you want to have three weeks off, or a month or a year … you can … it just needs planning in advance. You control that income-time balance.

Portfolio Professionals know that you do need to take the time off; when you're enjoying what you're doing you may think you don't need a break. You do.

You can't keep your energy levels on the ceiling if you're on the floor. Even doing what you enjoy gets tiring when you do it too long. You owe it to yourself, your colleagues and paying customers (not to mention the family) to give yourself a break with time to think, reflect, and revive. So do lock the work door, in your head as well, back up and leave the computer, and post a creative and polite out-of-office email reply.

Normal work can wait until you're ready. If you must be available in case of urgent contacts or emergencies, do it on your time terms. Instead of leaving the device on, tell everyone where they can leave a message.

The messages get left without disturbing your sleep (people forget time differences), your swim or your lazing on the beach. You can pick up the messages, sort the urgent ones and respond if you really have to.

Chunking the time

Some Portfolio Professionals find that the start of the day is hard without the 'Hello, good mornings' and the 'How are yous?' that never got a true answer.

One solved the problem by walking the dog at a different time to punctuate the day's start with a different routine.

Another used the 'Morning Pages' concept of Julia Cameron from *The Artist's Way*, where you begin the day writing any thought that comes into your head, flowing onto sheets of A4 – after 3 pages, all becomes clearer, gems of insight suddenly appear and you can start the day with clear focus and priorities.

And as the day progresses, a day where no paid work was planned, what happens when there are no phone calls, no emails dinging their arrival on the screen, no interruptions from people saying 'have you got a minute' (didn't you used to hate that).

What happens inside you? Panic? A feeling that no-one wants to know you? All very understandable and natural reactions when we've been conditioned by constant time pressure, overload of information technology, and a 'collusion of busyness'.

Remember that you now have the chance to break the conditioning.

What about all those other things you always promised yourself ... if only I had the time, if only I wasn't always interrupted – the walk in the park, that book you half-started to read, the photos that need sorting, the quotations you wanted to look up, the filing (oh yes the filing) that is going to reveal new ideas and leads under the debris, mowing the lawn since the sun's shining – the list is endless. You probably made a list when you were time-strapped in corporate life 'Things I really want to do when I retire'. Well now that you know retirement is an outmoded concept ...

✳ **NOW is the time and the time is yours.**

We've already mentioned diaries; Portfolio Professionals and their diaries (whether electronic, digital or paper) are joined at the hip.

Remember when setting the diary plan that you'll need to allow client hours, admin hours, preparation hours, break between meeting hours ... and a few meetings with yourself to regroup, recover, meetings that are just as unchangeable as your most important client meeting.

As well as logging forward timings, the diary can be a vital record of where the past time has gone.

It's clearly important to know where the time that's billable went, so your clients have the benefit of an invoice.

But it's also useful to check that you're using your time the way you planned.

Take those circles you created in Chapter 5 and put the targets of time into your diary – for the year, for the month, for the week. Monitor how the real use of time fits with the chunking you wanted for work (paid, gift, study, home) and the time you craved for you and family and friends.

A pat on the back

Another tip to keep freedom and spirits high and to avoid the paranoia spiral is to look back on that diary, or your action lists, for two months or more ago.

Portfolio Professionals by their nature are looking for the next opportunity, heading towards the next goal and the next challenge – and might give themselves little credit for the progress they're making.

> *'The difference between a pat on the back and a kick up the bum is about 9 inches.'*

Give yourself a pat higher up now and again: did I really achieve all that that week? Were those actions really such a priority at that time? I could do that so much more easily now, look at how that network contact brought that business in without my really trying.

Don't forget to reward yourself now and again. Take one of those two-hour 'treats for you' to reward yourself for a new success, or for having just done that something you'd been putting off for weeks.

Set yourself small incentives; take a break every two hours to listen to that music track, practise putting on the carpet, just stare at some trees, have an indulgent biscuit ... or chocolate coated for a large incentive !

Finances: how much is enough?

We've talked about the psychological issues of value and worth and how we're conditioned to measure ourselves by money. How's it going to flow, and how do I cope with feast and famine are common concerns for the transition.

Let's start with how much we really need rather than expect or want.

How much is enough? 'About 10% more than we have'?!

Or is it, as Brian Palmer puts it: *'Enough is that amount that causes you least anxiety.'*

Whose values are we reacting to when we think of money and worth – our own or the view of others; our memory of what we believed to be real and valuable when we were 'on the way up' or the view of all those looking down on us?

When did we last really check our forecast of outgoings; how's that going to change in the next five years? Many Portfolio Explorers find that their income from their corporate role is at its height, just as the outgoings (children leaving home, mortgage paid) are reducing.

Yes, there's opportunity to earn more staying in corporate life, and to enhance the final pension, but do you NEED that money more than you need the time, the health, the new experiences?

'Most of the people living on earth were unhappy for pretty much of the time. Many solutions were suggested for this problem, but most of these were largely concerned with the movements of small green pieces of paper, which is odd because on the whole it wasn't the small green pieces of paper that were unhappy.'
Douglas Adams

Your personal financial forecast

Annual income twenty pounds, annual expenditure nineteen and six, result happiness. Annual income twenty pounds, annual expenditure twenty pounds and six, result misery.
Charles Dickens

The question of 'how will I afford to make the change' arises with every Portfolio Explorer at this stage. It's all about Income and Expenses, and particularly how both will change with your move to Portfolio Life. You need to assess each carefully, discuss with an Independent Financial Adviser or use the 'Setting up your own business' services available from the banks. The best we can do here is to offer some thoughts that will enable you to check your assumptions and do some 'ballpark' sums as preparation for the fuller assessment.

Let's look at the two sides of your personal Profit & Loss account separately.

Income

Your starting-point is all-important here. If you have the luxury of time, you'll have some years in which to prepare and to assess the potential income from your portfolio roles. In other words, your employability, how marketable you are, and what price your product or services can be sold for. It's a gradual introduction to your Portfolio Life where success and the sweet click of transfers into your bank account can help you decide to make the move earlier than planned. If the income's more difficult to achieve, you may defer for a while longer.

Of course, if you're currently out of a job, you won't have this 'trial period' and your income estimates will have to be more of a stab in the dark.

What you earn from your portfolio roles will depend on the time you choose to chunk to Paid Work. The book has given you guidance on how to make your income/time decision. Bear in mind that it isn't set in stone. You may be prepared to give more time to earning income now, and to having holidays or gapping in future years.

That's income from your portfolio roles – in effect, the profits from your new business. But there are other forms of income. If you took a pension, or gained a lump sum then these are also very useful changes on the income side of your forecast. Lump sums can provide a breathing-space to get your business going, and pensions can give you regular income to help the at times variable cash flow.

If you have investment income, project this. There's no reason for it to change as you change your role, except that you may have more time to plan and maximise it.

Expenses

Your move to portfolio-ing can have effects on your expenses in both directions. Working from home can save on travelling costs to your former place of work, and even on lunches. On the other side, you'll have the expenses and set-up costs of your new role, many of which are tax-deductible.

Rather than trying to calculate every tiny part of your expenses budget, concentrate on the major changes.

Savings and investments

If you have savings for a rainy day, then you have to decide whether these can assist your move. Is your new life important enough for you to use some of your investments to get it off the ground? Perhaps the money you were saving for a conservatory may have a far better short-term use, resulting in greater long-term advantage.

Many PPs are reaching the stage where their mortgage is becoming a smaller element in their expenses, or will soon be paid off.

If you've been in a position to increase your investments annually, then you need to look at what you are saving for, what the money will be used for.

Look well ahead

You have to calculate the immediate effect, in order to satisfy yourself and those around you that your new life is a viable option. But it's also important as part of the same exercise to look further ahead, to 3, 10, and 15 years. Your mortgage may be paid off, the school fees may finish, the children support themselves. All these are elements to be taken into consideration in your decision and the timing of your move.

Again, look at the big changes you can foresee.

Ups and downs

The simple table in figure 15 gives you some indicators on how to approach your financial forecast, and some of the items to be considered. These will be different for each of us. Take some time, gather the facts, and ensure that your assumptions are realistic.

That simple title 'Profit from portfolio paid work' will be the difficult one, which is where some investigation and, even better, some on-the-job experience will help.

Finally, when you put it all together, you calculate the 'Difference'.

If it's a positive, an increase from now, then you're either a born optimist or you've got great portfolio plans.

If it's a negative then all is not lost. Are you going into Portfolio Life for the money? Check your list of what else you intend to get out of your move.

How much time have you chunked to Paid Work? Can you increase that, at least for the first couple of years, in order to give you more income?

Are you prepared to use some of your savings, investments or severance pay to contribute to the Difference, either short-term or even longer-term?

There are no absolutes to any of these questions. It's your decision. Just be sure that, after all the recalculations, when you have the final copy, it's as accurate as you can make it.

	Now	Year 1	Year 3	Year 7
Income: – current job – pension – severance pay – investment income Profit from Port folio Paid Work				
Total income				
Expenditure – mortgage – healthcare – insurances – housing costs – school/university – vehicle costs – general expenditure – other				
Total expenditure				
Difference				

Figure 15. Financial forecast table

There is advice on negotiating the best severance deal from your current employer in Part 4. Think about the benefits you currently receive as part of your employment; can you get a good deal for buying your company car, your laptop, the gym membership; more important, can the company arrangement with the Private Healthcare provider be extended – healthcare is one of the big expenditures that is risky to remove, and which can accelerate outside the original terms of agreement.

Of course, a big factor in all this forecast is tax, especially if you are looking at corporate tax and personal tax. You need to seek professional expert advice for your particular circumstances. There are software packages available, as well as the Tax Adviser and IFA contact points, not forgetting HMRC themselves who can be seen as gate-openers as well as gatekeepers!

Developing this rough checklist into a real financial plan will reassure you on your decision, and add substance to the emerging faith that you can cover your costs doing what you enjoy.

Richard Jones's
Portfolio Journey

There I was, trundling along in the pressured but 'secure' corporate fold, knowing that this wasn't really the right thing to continue but ducking the scary alternatives. Then it happened. Corporate re-organisation came along, and so did the reward for jobs well done. I was asked to do a job that I really did not want to do – another one of those times where you have done something well so the organisation motivates you by sending you back in time/career to do it all over again!

It was the best thing that could have happened. I had the example of a friend whom I had helped to leave corporate life not long before who was successfully carving his own portfolio professional niche. Not only did he provide helpful guidance and encouragement, he was invaluable in providing a 'disinterested' sounding board. Not least to underline that it is never too late to make a start. I made it aged 58 and have found that grey hairs in a portfolio professional can even be very helpful! And it is so true that however difficult the issue we face, someone else has been there before.

Of course, when you write it down like that it all sounds straight-forward and simple. Not so. Before jumping, I spent time thinking of my life goals and how they would fit with a major career change. I also, rather obviously, looked very carefully at the financial situation including, in particular, what the impact would be on pension. There were also detailed discussions with the family, which raised lots of issues.

All these debates were paralleled by the discussions with the company on the scale and nature of the exit package.

So, having negotiated what I felt was the best deal the company were going to offer, the final deliberations went on and the decision was taken to jump. It was not a unanimous verdict by all the family but, in the end, I told myself that the only person who could and should take my decisions was me.

I negotiated a leaving date with a cushion of time to prepare myself for the future. During this interim period, the most important and valuable activity proved to be networking. Those who had been there before me said that 90% of opportunities come through people you know. For me, all the clients I have had over the last three years, I have either known or have been introduced to by someone I know.

So that, in brief, is how I did it. Where am I now? Well, in the nearly 10 years I spent working for myself I secured several good clients in a variety of sectors. They all had very different demands but the common theme, apart from HR which is my specialism, is that I was not involved or sidetracked by company politics and was able to get on to deliver what I was best at. I am now 'retired' but am still able to put some of my experience and skills to good use in the voluntary sector.

When asked what the key reflections from my experience are, I have come up with a top five:

1. *We are usually pretty good at understanding how important it is to align our corporate activities with the corporate goals, yet we ignore that essential principle when it comes to the far more important issue of our (and our family's) life.*

2. *'Life is not a rehearsal.'*

3. *Do not fall into the trap of thinking 'it is much easier for them; their skills are much more marketable than mine'. You have skills that you can only appreciate when you sit down and analyse what you have done over the past few years and the individual skills you have used to be successful.*

4. *If it still feels right when you have considered all the angles, even though it is a scary prospect, do follow the advice of the book 'feel the fear and do it anyway'.*

5. *Network, network, network ... ...*

Richard Jones has been a successful Portfolio Professional for over 10 years. An experienced HR Director, equally at home in the private and public sector, he is now retired and helping in the voluntary sector.

Home on the range

But whose range?

'I married you for richer, for poorer, for better, for worse, in sickness and in health … but not for lunch!' is a familiar refrain from portfolio couples, now adjusting to many more hours together per day.

'Yes, I know I always asked to see more of you at home, but since you weren't, I got on with my own routine; that's why the photo albums go where I say they go!'

The impact on partners and families can be missed by a Portfolio Professional, understandably deep into planning his or her own lifestyle change.

But the change of the eldest child's bedroom into an office is not just an economic decision, it's a signal that he's not there any more, it's bringing work into home, it's replacing the drumbeat of his CDs for the ringing of the office phone.

The routine of someone disappearing for the day to the mysteries of work that brings in a steady monthly sum may have lasted for most if not all of the family's lifetimes. Now it's changed.

The smallest symbols can mark the change.

'I've got to go out, can you empty the washing machine when it's finished.'

'I'm working! It's just as if I'm out at the office, so I can't.'

'No, you're not, you're here, and it's a small thing to do.'

'I've got important calls to make. I won't hear it stopping. Can't tell my clients I've just been hanging out the clothes.'

'I've got important shopping to do if you want to eat, and it takes longer to find it cheaper now there's no regular money.'

'Yes, there is, it just comes in fees instead of salary.'

'Well, the bank balance doesn't show it.'

From washing to financial security in one heated conversation, a conversation that reflects the deeper concerns of making the change.

It's important to find the time to dialogue about the change, the hopes, the fears, the feelings beneath, how it fits into all the other life changes at the same time.

Otherwise, false assumptions and misunderstandings leap in to turn a great opportunity for new beginnings into potential for conflict. One person's freedom is another's paranoia.

Decide where the territories are in the house, physical areas and tasks; keep a joint calendar of where you'll be in the next week, find time to share some of those hours which couldn't have been there before. Talk about how much the portfolio can be worked on together; will it be Yourco & Partner or will you keep the parts independent; if you're both directors, is there a chance for a regular 'company outing' as well as the Board meetings around the kitchen table; how does the financial planning look now from all sources.

How can you both make best use of the extra time there is now to share?

That 'wish we were both home sometimes to go to the gym' becomes 'can we take an hour now for the gym?' The trip to the stately home that was rained off on Sunday can happen when it's dry on Monday. The visits abroad can be planned around paid work and time together in a more flexible way.

Who's using the phone and the web device is another fine transitional game!

Install Wifi and as many links as you need to differentiate home from office.

And, thinking of admin and secretarial help, how about a PA for the business, for the family, for all those things that the PA can do better than you and yours?

Using your special talents

A frequent mistake Portfolio Professionals can make is to think,

'I can replace all those back-up services myself.'

'Always wanted to learn Excel, PowerPoint; can do my own accounts; I'll work through that Tutorial and speed up my word processing ...'

The answer, as many have discovered, is just the same as with plumbing, car maintenance or building work. Earn enough to pay others what they're good at!

Get your hourly rate above theirs and make best use of everyone's special talents!

Spending your day on clerical admin may feel like a saving, but is it best use of your time? Many Portfolio Professionals find that skills like PowerPoint presentations get developed if and when a client needs them. Building skills in isolation in case they will be needed is not a motivator; building them to add value to clients is.

Your support team

? So where do I find the people to replace the back-up services I had in my organisation?

? What happens when my electronics crash and I automatically reach for the phone to ring IT Hotline?

? Or when Companies House sends a reminder about the Annual Report?

? Or I want to book a flight to New Zealand stopping off for a night in Hong Kong (or LA?)?

? Or a client wants a 3,000 word document from my notes by midday tomorrow?

The answer is twofold.

- Look around you and think local!
- Develop your own personal support team!

With the growth in people taking the portfolio route, a whole infrastructure of small businesses has sprung up to provide the services.

With a few phone calls, you'll find that the man round the corner who's an IT expert knows someone who prints stationery who knows someone who does word processing who knows someone who's an accountant ... a wondrous network of small businesses just like yours, great for contacts as well as the services you need.

Get a local word of mouth recommendation, get to know them and treat them as your personal team; introduce them to each other, let them know what's happening in your business, what you need, and listen to what they need too.

Get behind the roles and get to know your team as people; it leads to better teamwork and to much more interesting conversations!

So who's in your team?

❋ *Your partner, your children, your extended family are 'shoe-ins' for key support roles.*

And then there's your accountant, IT expert, PA/Secretary (on remote?). Don't forget the bank, tax inspector (yes, better the devil you know!), travel agent – and what about the local gym (a personal trainer?!), and your doctor and dentist.

Not to mention the colleagues you see in all your different activities and of course your clients who hopefully support in all sorts of ways! Other members of your support team are the Portfolio Professionals you'll be networking with: exchanging experiences, mistakes, break-throughs, and contacts. The power of networking is covered in Part 4 and there are more ways to keep contacts with your fellow PPs in Chapter 9.

So, to replace the organisational back-up services you had, there's a hand-picked team of people to support you.

And to replace the office facilities, you'll be surprised how many 'free or low cost' meeting rooms you can use: from societies and clubs, such as the Institute of Directors, to coffee bars to hotel foyers to libraries to parks (yes, why not meet, talk and breathe the air!).

....and finally

Three last points on transition.

Firstly, keep taking the compliments. There will be times when you need a pick-me-up. Don't open the bottle – open your compliments file. My what?

From the moment you start your Portfolio Journey, start a file for all those good things that people say about you. The appraisals, the evaluations, the letters, the snippets from emails, the words from your leaving do, the photos of successes; put them all in there and, when you need to, get them out and believe – that's you and that's what people think of you, and why they'll want to work with you.

Be your own best complimenter too; when you have a great day, record what you're pleased about, why you've succeeded – put it all in the file!

Why not create your own selection of your favourite uplifting music, music that celebrates where you are as a Portfolio Professional ('Watching the wheels go round and round' as John Lennon had it ... or 'I Feel Free' by Cream? or 'All right now' by Free? or 'Freebird' by Lynyrd Skynyrd)

Second, be aware of your assets you're building. At the start, it may seem vital to keep in touch with your industry and the old knowledge base, the websites, the trade journals, the conferences – after all, we have the time now. Can we keep it up?

No we can't! However hard you try, you can't be as on the ball as you were when you were living it 14 hours a day. And why try? Your asset base is changing.

Your asset in knowledge and information will reduce, don't fight it. Something else is rising – your asset in experience, wisdom, contacts, relationships, all the people-based things that are timeless and which will be the basis of your new life.

Finally, make time for yourself. You are your product, your brand and your future business; make sure you're not wearing out before expiry date. If you want to be on top of the game for your clients, put yourself first. Invest in keeping your assets primed.

Invest wisely in three ways.

- Invest time in customers.
- Invest time in networking.
- Invest time in yourself.

To summarise …

- In this chapter we've explored a lot of the issues that can concern an unplanned Portfolio Professional….not one like you!

- We've covered transition issues, emotional and practical, and approaches that Portfolio Professionals have to them, and the resources that are already there to help.

Part 4 will deal in greater detail with the hardware side of setting up your own business and organising your life as a Portfolio Professional.

We're ready to move to Chapter 8 where we will introduce the concept of The Portfolio Bridge as a basis for our action plan.

8

CROSSING THE BRIDGE TO PORTFOLIO LIFE

Sometimes, if you stand on the bottom rail of a bridge and lean over to watch the river slipping slowly away beneath you, you will suddenly know everything there is to be known.
Pooh's Little Instruction Book, inspired by A. A. Milne

You're nearly there!

It's been a long, but necessary journey. Let's look back at what's been done and where we've got to.

- You've identified and assessed your skills and talents.
- You've set your long-term goals.
- You've selected suitable roles for your portfolio.
- You've checked the alignment between those roles, and your talents, skills and goals.
- You've analysed your finances.
- You've considered the implications for your family, and yourself.

But you're still on the portfolio journey, and with all this input you should feel confident about making the move. Now's the time to turn theory into reality and step onto the bridge – the bridge to your portfolio life.

This is a big move you're making. It helps to know that thousands of others have made it before. To help you make the move you need good advice, a plan for your portfolio, and some 12-month objectives. That's what this chapter is about.

How long is your bridge?

Bridges come in every length. They're rather like the portfolio itself; your bridge is as unique to you as your portfolio. Just how long you take to make the move depends on your personal and job circumstances and your commitment to your new life.

You've made the decision to become a Portfolio Professional. Your move can involve one or all of these potential scenarios.

- **The Inside Job.** You're in a job and want to take your time, develop your portfolio while still earning, and choose your own timing for departure.
- **The Soft Landing.** Whether you're in control of timing or not, there's a major plus in having a continuing role with your employer.
- **The Planned Departure.** Whether or not you can control the timing, if you're well prepared you can influence the financial terms.
- **The Short Bridge.** If you've already left the limited life without time to plan your portfolio future, the Bridge can still help you launch your Portfolio Life.

We'll now consider each of these.

The Inside Job

Your current job may not be the exciting place where you want to spend the rest of your life, but it is a wonderful launch-pad. You've taken your decision, completed the Portfolio Planner and you have a clear picture of what you're going to do in your portfolio. In other words you've tackled the Why? & What? and you're left with the How? & When?

We haven't pulled any punches in telling you that it's a big move and can be a cold world out there for the unprepared. Here you are in your job, surrounded by all the benefits, the cushions of employed life. Make the most of it.

✳ *Take time to plan your escape.*

You're on the long bridge; regard it as that every day, continually seeing yourself on the bridge, or you'll go backwards and commitment to your new balanced life will fade. It's easy to follow old ways, being driven by your job, losing your purpose and following old habits. It's up to you to ensure you don't. Some simple reminders may help you. A reminder at the start of each day; a post-it note on the dashboard of your car; a daily alarm on your mobile. They just need to say the one word – **Bridge**. They'll catch your eye to remind you that your priority today is your future.

Remember the harsh realities of the modern workplace: organisations will downsize you without batting an eyelid. The old loyalties have gone. Your loyalty is to yourself and your future. That doesn't mean not doing the work for which you're being paid, and certainly doesn't mean being disloyal; you very much want to keep the organisation on your side. But it does mean that you limit your excess hours, that you plan your time around your future, and know where your priorities lie.

We'll come back later in the chapter to what you can most usefully do with that time.

The Soft Landing

When you considered your potential portfolio roles in Chapter 6, you would have asked yourself: which is the easiest assignment/project/ role for me to get? The answer is staring you in your face: it's with your current employer. This really is the soft but highly sensible option, and applies whether or not you are determining the timing of your departure.

As you get into your new life, you'll discover that potential customers all ask the same questions: What's your track record? Have you done this before? Who have you done it for? They know the difference between working on the inside versus working from the outside. So picking up your first part-time or temporary assignment from your existing employer can be a big plus.

You leave on Friday and arrive back in on Monday. The salary and benefits have gone, but hopefully the daily rate looks good (just make sure you cover your costs). But you're there in a totally new guise. You have a business card which is about you, not them; you have confirmed the contractual arrangements on your new letterhead; you record the time you spend, because you'll be invoicing it on your new invoices.

Suddenly you're in business, and you can look at the income as contributing to the set-up costs of your Portfolio Life.

In recessionary times this 'ideal' scenario becomes an attractive proposition for both employee and employer. Employers need to reduce their payroll costs but are reluctant to lose the associated skills and talents. So a part-time solution is a good move for both, and one you should actively pursue.

It takes lateral thinking and a bold approach. The most direct opportunity is to perform some element of your old job, on a part-time basis. This may be the prime role for the early days of your portfolio. But that might not be on. Don't give up there. What about an element of your old role in another department? What about another role from your portfolio? Your employer may lift the eyebrows, but if you're going to sell your skills to anybody they're the most open. If it's in a learning area of your portfolio using evolving skills, then your daily rate may be lower, but just as valuable. What about another location, another part of the group?

There you are, home office set up, brand running, first payment awaited, your portfolio life on the way, and a story to tell to your next prospect.

The Planned Departure

Departures can be set in motion by yourself or by your employer. Either way, if you're prepared, you can set the agenda – you have the better hand.

There's something very satisfying about having anticipated and as a result being prepared. It doesn't soften the blow, but it does put you in the driving seat. It's important that even if you can't control the timing, you have as much control as possible over the terms of your departure. Leaving the limited life should, wherever possible, become a springboard to your new Portfolio Life.

Imagine the scenario for our Portfolio Explorer:

Employer: *'I'm sorry, but we're going to have to let you go.'* (...and starts on long list of platitudes)

Explorer: (interrupting) *'That's OK. Now here's what I want. And this is why I expect to get it.'*

You have two key objectives: the best possible financial package, and a soft landing role to kick off your portfolio. It's a negotiation; keep your cards close, play them at the right time, know when you should give way and when you should hold firm. Your employer doesn't hold all the cards. Offer them an easy option, a win-win situation and they are likely to accept it gratefully.

If you've been able to follow our Inside Job route then, when the time for your departure arrives, you will have your future life well mapped out and be clear about your departure objectives.

In Part 4, you'll find some good advice on planned departures from one of our specialist contributors. Richard Jones is a Portfolio Professional who knows about planned departures from both sides of the negotiating table.

The Short Bridge

You may be reading this book because you currently have no job. We all know that we're only one job away from redundancy, our face not fitting, etc – and it got you. If this catches you unawares, it is invariably a shock to the system and a blow to your confidence. A number of books are available to give advice and support; but what you want most of all is to see a future ... and some income.

You haven't had an opportunity to enjoy inside jobs, soft landings or planned departures. But there's still a great portfolio future ahead of you. If you've worked through the earlier models, then you will be feeling considerably better about yourself, your talents and skills. You will have appreciated that you can market yourself and get all the pluses of life-work balance that go with it. Negatives may become positives as you view the lump-sum not as a diminishing resource but as a source of investment in your new life. If you were of an age to be able to get an enhanced early pension, then you're feeling even better.

You may feel like rushing in but, if you're to be successful in the Portfolio Life, you still need to use the bridge and take it step-by-step. For financial reasons you may have to move through the steps more quickly, but at least you have the time to devote to them.

John Ayres's
Portfolio Journey

I had promised myself that, if feasible financially, I would step back from corporate life at 55, draw a reduced pension and set out on my own as a training consultant.

It would be a great opportunity to do more of what I really enjoyed in my corporate life while leaving some of the other parts behind. I had been a Divisional Director of an international perfumery company and had developed an enduring interest in training and education from the early 1980s. I retained a love of teaching and passing on my passion for fragrances. My plan was to continue and expand this interest.

Fortunately, it happened even better than I planned. My company supported me and offered me a job as an internal training consultant for nine months, providing a soft landing into my self-employed status. Then reality struck. For the first time in 24 years I had to buy my own car, mobile phone and computer system, set up a home office, register my company, register with Inland Revenue and establish some sort of business plan.

The first key decision was whether to have a website. The advice I received through my network of colleagues was very helpful. A website provides a convenient and professional reference point for all the background information, rather than a primary source of new business opportunities. I spent the first few months 'waving' at potential clients by telephone, email and meetings. Fortunately, I had a couple of projects to work on in the meantime, and my first positive responses came through, while relaxing on holiday in Portugal. My June mobile phone bill was three times higher than average, and the villa veranda became my office for a couple of mornings.

My portfolio currently comprises assignments with academic institutions as associate university lecturer and external examiner, together with corporate training projects and opportunities for freelance journalism, unpaid charity work and chairmanship of professional bodies, as well as time to pursue my interests in choral singing and geology. To provide the training service, I joined two colleagues to start a limited company. Although there are now three times as many people to support financially, the increased strength of our offering provides enormous added value for our clients; projects are starting to be converted into contracts.

I feel an enormous sense of support and relief in having two co-directors to share the workload and to help provide creative solutions. Overall, in my journey, there have been surprises and there are still difficult challenges:

- *Working alone and being home-office based, I miss the companionship of colleagues. My office companions are two West Highland Terriers who often bark while I'm in the middle of a business call. One of them reflects my state of stress and acts as a Phillip Pullman-style 'daemon'. Working alone requires strong self-motivation through difficult times as well as good times.*
- *The amount of time needed to do everything including all the admin.*
- *Flexibility to change plans for time off. Real holidays have to be taken away from home and office.*
- *The presence of the office at home is surprisingly invasive.*

Ideally it should be sited well away from living areas so that the door can be firmly closed and work mentally 'filed away'.

The advantages, however, far outweigh the challenges:

- *Independence and flexibility*
- *Knowing that the work I do is 100% for the development of the business, and not corporate justification for the shareholders' benefit*
- *Being able largely to control my own timetable and diary*
- *Networking with supportive colleagues*
- *Unexpected opportunities for travel and new business contacts*
- *Freedom to become involved more effectively in charity work and in professional organizations*

- *Personal recognition as one of a very few independent specialists in my field of work*
- *Opportunities to contribute to press articles and to write as a freelance journalist, without constantly having to refer to a central PR department for company clearance*
- *Access to a far broader body of information and range of contacts than I had in corporate life.*

John Ayres is a Director of Pandora Limited who offer training courses and consultancy in all aspects of perfumery and the fragrance industry.

The rest of this chapter gives you sound practical advice on the moves you should make as you cross from limited to Unlimited, from employment to portfolio.

As we've said, the timing is up to you, so the priority you give to each of these and the time you allocate is for you to decide. But each is important for your future.

Researching your Portfolio

You've used the Portfolio Planner to select your ideal roles. They're a good match for your experience, interests, values and needs; they reflect what you want more of and less of in your life. As you read the advice in Chapter 6 and completed the Planner, you also considered how feasible, how viable they are, and took this into consideration on the bottom line of the Portfolio Planner grid.

You should take this process further now with some market research.

For each of the roles you are planning, you should look at these points.

- **What do customers want?** Is your proposition well-designed to meet their needs? Are there gaps in what the market currently offers them? What would they ideally like?
- **Ease of entry.** How easy for a newcomer to get business? Are qualifications necessary?
- **Market Size.** Is there plenty for everybody, including you? Is it growing or declining?
- **Competition.** What form is it — one-man businesses or corporates? How entrenched is it? How good is it? What can you learn from them … and improve on?

The best form of research is to talk to potential customers. Use your current position, career background, or networking skills to get the appointment. Explain your portfolio plans; they'll be supportive. Assure them they're not going to be sold to. Ask questions and, above all, listen. Don't just hear what you want to hear.

By not selling, you will listen more and project yourself less. By not selling, you may very well be learning the important lesson that in selling, listening is more important than talking.

✷ *By not selling, you may just have won your first customer.*

Having talked to some potential customers, are your expectations still realistic? Could the role fill two days per week of your portfolio? Do you need to change your thinking? Do you need to acquire more knowledge and skills?

If you're considering new markets for some of your roles, do your research. The internet is a great killjoy, bringing us down to earth. But if you have a good idea and if you can't find a mention of it after much searching, then maybe you really are onto something. If you're not involved in a particular market now, immerse yourself in it, via the internet, trade press, and as many people as you can contact. Don't set out without research.

Choosing customers

If your portfolio roles are a mix of what you're good at and what you enjoy, then your proficiency will vary from role to role. Take the example of an HR professional confident she can get temporary assignments in the Human Resources field. But how easy will it be to find customers for the Life Coaching she really gets a kick from?

Experience and skillbase have to be taken into consideration, and customers chosen accordingly. For this, we can put customers into three categories:

Income customers

This is the income any portfolio needs to sustain itself. It comes from customers who need your services. The work may not be particularly new and exciting, but your skills fit the requirement. You could call it the 'commodity' end of the market.

Learning customers

Your portfolio will only be successful if you're constantly developing your skills. Study Work is a key part of the successful portfolio. But you also need to practice new skills. Customers who offer opportunities for learning on the job are a valuable part of any portfolio, giving you vital experience. Payment may be minimal, or based purely on results.

Our HR professional needs some history, and the chance to learn on the job. Before setting out her prospectus for wealthy individuals, running an evening class or offering her services free to a charity would be good learning processes.

Volunteering is a great way of opening the door for opportunities, as well as fulfilling your Gift Work chunk. You'll be in a quite different arena from much of the rest of your life, meeting many new faces, often volunteers themselves. In this medley of different backgrounds and different industries lie great opportunities.

Specialist customers

This is where your developed skillbase really counts. The customers have a compelling need and you have the skills to meet it. The price reflects the fact that demand exceeds supply, even if only temporarily. Our HR professional has foreseen the next generation of legislation and set herself up to train customers in it. Others will catch up, but being ahead of the game pays better and establishes reputation.

Knowledge and skills

While Study Work is an important part of your on-going portfolio, it should be a really major element of your time on the bridge. There's so much to learn and so many new skills to acquire. Some of these may be mundane and administrative, such as how to backup your files. Others are vital parts of your armoury – cold-calling, making presentations, networking (more knowledge on all of these later).

But we're looking particularly here at the knowledge and skills you will seek to sell. Do not think that just because you're about to leave your employment as a Defaults Underwriting Manager (a DUM) that there are customers out there just waiting for you to become available. Your assessments were good; your skillset was sufficient for the role you had; but that doesn't mean it will be sufficient for other organisations. And is 'sufficient' the same as 'marketable'? We're talking here of an industry you were in, so what about the roles you would like to perform but have no history in?

Will the professional orchestra welcome you just because you have a trumpet tucked under your arm and once played in the school band?

If you thought that your career involved considerable acquisition of skills and knowledge, you ain't seen nothing yet! And it starts on the bridge. You may need to invest money in formal training (a trumpet coach). You need to have the widest possible industry knowledge, even of the industry you were in. If you worked in a large organisation, you need to understand small business thinking; and vice versa.

The industry par is not enough; you must be up with the latest concepts and the blue sky thinking. You may not sell this per se, but the impression such knowledge will give when you're performing the assignment will help in building your future reputation.

Finally, read, read, read. There's a good book available on almost every subject you will need (although only one on the subject of being a Portfolio Professional) and the internet is an amazingly good resource.

Parallel lives

If you're still working, you are about to begin a second life. You have time to set up the nitty-gritty, the equipment and processes. This phase starts with you developing a thinking separate from your day role, that of an independent. There's advice in Part 4 about setting up your home office and your business.

Your parallel thinking is important if any of your portfolio roles continue elements of your paid role, or is in the same industry sector. Keeping in touch with the industry will be a high priority; but the trade magazines are all at your workplace. Are your email newsletters delivered to your work email? How many of your contacts know you through your work email address? What does it say on your various memberships and subscriptions? These are just some of the many ways that you are tied in to your employed role. Your parallel life starts here.

In taking these steps, in setting up your office in the spare bedroom or designing your logo, you increase your commitment to your future role and lessen the sudden impact when the day comes to say goodbye to your work job. You are then not 'stopping working', but rather moving to the Portfolio Role already well-established at your home.

Open mind and open eyes

We've all experienced the way in which you meet somebody from a company you've never heard of and the following day you spot their wagons on every motorway, their adverts in every publication. Your eyes have been opened.

Portfolio Professionals have a particular need for open eyes. We have the flexibility, all we need is the opportunity, and opportunities present themselves in all manner of different ways – if you're looking for them. If, on the other hand, you have your old work blinkers on, and think only about your prime portfolio role and its surrounds, then you won't see them.

The *Six O'Clock News* is a good start (you should have a better chance of seeing this now). What new initiative is the government coming up with today? What are they demanding that businesses do next? Rather than getting on your high horse regarding red tape stifling businesses, think of how you could contribute to easing its impact. Be the first to read the draft legislation. Set up a website to establish yourself as the authority on the subject. Offer to help businesses understand its impact. Set up training courses for staff. Thanks, BBC.

Getting together

'Joint ventures' may be a rather highfalutin' term to apply to it, but it makes the point that being a Portfolio Professional doesn't have to be a solitary life. In your employed life, you will probably have worked in project teams, brought together to fulfil a specific purpose and then disbanded. If you develop your portfolio friends and community, forming temporary project teams can be a most enjoyable part of your portfolio, with a different set of values and satisfaction criteria. The writers of this book are an example, as you will see from reading about their separate lives at the end of Chapter 9.

Management guru Tom Peters calls it 'organising around enthusiasms', and you'll see from that term that it's probably best suited to the lower-paid and more interest-driven parts of your portfolio. Virtual organisations are so easy to set up. Domain names can be purchased for a few pounds; basic websites can be hosted for the cost of a good book, and you have a business. If it goes nowhere, you've had fun out of the association with your peers and developed some new networks. If it succeeds ... Wow!

Networking

We've left the most important until last. Through the book you've read the Portfolio Journeys and you will have seen many references to the importance of networking. Networking is the foundation which will underpin your Portfolio Life and the bridge is your opportunity to develop that network.

You're still working for your employer, but you've always been head-down at the tasks in hand and never gave time for wider networking. Now's the time. Develop your campaign through social networking, attend every industry function, accept every hospitality invitation, join every professional association. But you've got wider needs than just the industry you're in. Look at the other roles you've chosen for your portfolio. The same applies – join the professional bodies, etc. As you haven't yet launched your portfolio, the networking will be more effective because you won't be selling anything, apart from yourself.

As you develop your portfolio, look to become a mover in your chosen areas. Join committees, write articles, anything to establish yourself as an authority in your field.

Paul McCrudden and Heather White are just such authorities and their specialist advice on social media and networking is in Part 4.

Crossing the bridge

You have all you need now to get started across the bridge to the opposite bank.

The Portfolio Bridge is your plan to get to the other side dry, safe and at the pace you choose, depending on opportunities, on finance needs, on emotional needs.

It's an opportunity to try out your portfolio in practice and build confidence in your new way of living. You can experiment in new roles, through secondments or interim; you can network with people already in those roles; you can research and study the new areas. You can start a role for two days a week and see if you want it to grow.

It's a path of exploration as you juggle your income and time balance. You can confirm your choices for the portfolio by actual experience.

As you travel across the bridge to your new life, your progress will be marked by the changes in:

- the phasing of your income stream
- the acquisition of skills and experience
- widening horizons through study work and research
- growing relationships via networking
- balancing your time.

First decide how long a bridge you want: 6 months, 1 year, 5 years? Then assess the key decisions.

How much money do you need at different points: when can you begin to reduce the 'guaranteed monthly salary' of current employment and increase the income from 'unpredictable fees'?

How long will it take to research your new roles – can this be done 'on the job'?

Get out your networking targets and invest in the time with them.

How long do you want for the emotional changes of leaving the current way of work?

Have another look at the Portfolio Journeys of those who've been over the bridge and see how they phased the crossing.

Your bridge plan

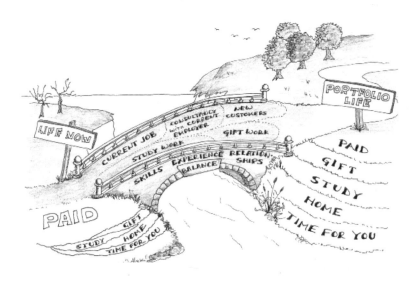

Above is a Bridge picture that might help you to plan the journey to the other side. By now you'll be well used to charts, maps and models. You can be creative with your own picture. You might want to draw your Bridge and keep it in front of you at the desk or on the mirror to remind yourself of the steps.

Plan your Bridge length with the time you want from now to Portfolio Life. Put on the other bank the changes to your time-chunking (remember your Wheel of Life from Chapter 4). Include the other things you wanted 'more of' from the **Lifetime Circles Model**.

Look at the skills, experience and relationships that make up the fabric of the Bridge.

Check the support team you chose in Chapter 7 and imagine how and when this will take over from your current back-ups as you meet new people on the Bridge.

Put in the paid work that may stretch from the current bank to give security until your new income begins. Phase in the experiences to explore; when might the first role move from research to actual, where will time open up to pursue the things you love doing, when will the skills be transferred to new areas.

When will so much have changed that you'll be on the other bank?

❋ *Enjoy the planning, enjoy the journey, no-one needs to ask 'are they waving or drowning'!*

The basic principles for bridge crossing

- Talk to those most affected by your decisions.
- Use the time to explore the options in practice and narrow your choices through experience.
- Don't leap at the first roles you're offered; they're likely to be close to where you are now and not a step to where you want to be.
- Don't commit all your time in the first weeks; leave some flexibility for the opportunities that will come later on the Bridge.
- Don't try to change too much too soon.

To illustrate the last point, take a Marketing Director in a multinational who wants to be a consultant for small businesses in totally new industries from where he has been. It's a big leap for him, and for any prospective clients.

Will they buy *two* new things: he's starting as a consultant and in a new industry? Would it be better to make one change at a time: consultant in current industry or director in new industry?

Putting your feet onto the Bridge, you need to use the contacts and reputation you've already got to open the doors and then break into new areas once you've grown in experience and credibility.

Getting into action in the next 12 months

And finally, let's celebrate our timetable planning with just one more chart!

If your new Portfolio Life is really going to happen, and you're going to cross the Bridge, the next year is a wonderful time of change.

Whatever your time scale, the next twelve months are vital.

They're so important that they warrant setting goals and giving yourself a measure to monitor your success.

This is not a complicated chart – by now you don't need much help in what to do!

First, think about your Bridge Plan and explode it into the actions you need to take. You'll be well used to this process by now!

What are the biggest changes from your life today; what are the biggest challenges you have to overcome?

It's helpful to look at them in smaller chunks, in the steps as you pass the milestones on the Bridge.

Then go for the top ten Goals in figure 16 and make the measures **SMART**!

- **S**pecific
- **M**easurable
- **A**chievable
- **R**elevant
- **T**imed

My Top Ten Goals for the Year Ahead

Using all that you have learnt about:

- Your Portfolio Life
- The Bridge Plan

... choose your Top Ten Goals for the year ahead.

For each goal, think through what the SMART success measure will be.

Goal	Success Measure
1.	
2.	
3.	
4.	
5.	
6.	
7.	
8.	
9.	
10.	

Figure 16. My top ten goals

To summarise ...

- You've learned about the Bridge which leads you to your Portfolio Life.

- The timing is up to you, but there are advantages from taking time to plan, prepare, and take the first steps.

- You've determined the small steps, which will keep you on track on your bridge crossing.

- You've confirmed your goals for the next 12 months, keeping you focused on your future.

Clearly there's a lot to do and you're going to have many new things to deal with over the next weeks and months. You may need more specific guidance, and there's a lot of this in Part 4 where our specialist contributors offer their advice.

Before that, Chapter 9 shares some of the realities of making the Portfolio Life the rest of your life.

Clive Morton's
Portfolio Journey

After 36 years of corporate life, I took the plunge and became self employed, feeling grateful to Charles Handy to be able to use the label 'portfolio' reflecting that 20 years beforehand, we would have called it 'casual work'! Shortly after starting, I was speaking to an ex-corporate colleague and his reaction was 'I always thought you did have a portfolio career!' His comment was flippant of course but apt since looking back, I had prepared, probably subconsciously, for that day.

I guess the thought started with my parents' expression, 'always have more than one string to your bow'. My father had a chequered employment career being made redundant 3 times in one year at age 15, owing to fluctuations of business. He then stuck, through thick and thin in the 1920s and 1930s to a steady but low paid boring job. Graduating in the 1960s, I found the then conventional wisdom of job-for-life distinctly unattractive.

Hence, ahead of today's generation, I changed employers relatively frequently, and started post-graduate studies part-time whilst holding down a full-time career job, and supporting a growing family towards a potential career in behavioural science and people issues a mile away from my civil engineering genre. Also, the 'portfolio' diversions started early with interests outside the employer's business, but often loosely connected with it.

My interests were and are associated with the role of business in society; social justice issues such as industrial relations, employment of those with disabilities, and impact of unemployment on communities. The interest was not academic, but rather what could and should employers do about it and how in the long term it can help their business.

When I was asked by Komatsu of Japan to help establish a new factory in the North East in an area of high unemployment, it was an opportunity too good to miss. They encouraged me to get involved with the community to set up a joint venture with the public sector for a centre to help people with disabilities to find work. Subsequently I became a non-executive in the NHS which has continued now for 15 years. After a sumptuous dinner and much champagne, North East bred entrepreneur Karl Watkin pushed an Apple Mac into my hands and said, 'go and write the story!' Never having written anything readable before, I was not full of confidence.

This was a turning point and four successful books have followed, together with part-time academic roles.

All these interesting diversions alongside intense jobs as director of blue chip organisations, I guess gave my waggish colleague the accurate jibe!

I can't say the launch into portfolio was without its angst. As I read one ex-CEO's account of becoming self-employed, it rang a bell: 'You find out where the Post Office is!' However, such losses of corporate support are educational to say the least and give more variety to the day. It also gets you alongside others who cope in different walks of life.

The biggest fear is, of course, continuity of work. Looking back, this has never been a problem – the work varies, clients come and go, there are fallow months and frenetic months and crucial times of going from sublime to ridiculous – the contrast between high level networking, 'putting bread on the waters' and planning to pay the tax bill and VAT return at appropriate months!

Another quotable quote came from a fellow traveller on the portfolio road who said 'the one great thing about a portfolio is that at any one time something, somewhere must be going right!'

With my variety of consulting, coaching, non-executive roles, academic work, writing, balanced between paid and unpaid activity, I do find one part of the portfolio is often needing more attention than another. The real problem comes when many need the same available time to be applied.

My last reflection relates to the hoary question of work-life balance. Many are wary of working from home – I think it's wonderful. To me it's work-life integration, it's holistic but balanced because you are on hand to be involved with family issues. Forget dividing up the day into water-tight compartments – for me that doesn't work, because with *being involved in global businesses, 9-to-5 has no significance. On the other hand, I can go to the gym at 11 am, go on leave (and still write while I'm away), and do family things mid week! However, sometimes weekends are not sacrosanct! For me, this is the life!*

Clive Morton advises and coaches on world-class strategy and Board development. His experience covers Non-Executive and executive Directorships, former Chair of NHS Trusts, and the role of Associate Professor at Middlesex University.

9

LIVING THE PORTFOLIO LIFE

*Every day you may make progress. Every step may be fruitful.
Yet there will stretch out before you an ever-lengthening, ever-
ascending, ever-improving path. You know you will never get to
the end of the journey. But this, so far from discouraging, only
adds to the joy and glory of the climb.*
Sir Winston Churchill (1874–1965)

Congratulations! You've arrived ... at the final chapter in Part 3 and at the first step on the bridge to your Portfolio Future.

A moment of celebration, take a while to drink in the atmosphere of where you are now (a glass of something cold and bubbly might be good too!)

Think about how you're feeling compared to when you started the book and the journey. You've taken on a lot of extra weight in terms of knowledge about yourself and your options and your planning ... but does it feel somewhat lighter?

You've narrowed your focus more on the sort of life you want to lead ... but does it feel broader?

You've arrived at your destination ... but does that feel like the end of a journey or just the beginning of the next one?

As Churchill indicates, we're always on the way to somewhere, and this particular part of your overall journey has set you firmly in a new direction.

Remember how far you've travelled from the 'where are you now', which has become 'where were you then'.

Making a change may have seemed a big leap in the dark, that's why it's often avoided or postponed. You've had the courage to look the change in the face and take the right path for you, discovering all the support that turns leaps into stepping stones. And that support is of course there for good as you start your Portfolio Life: the skills you have built, especially in networking, the confidence you have established by knowing yourself better.

So, cheers and here's a toast to you and all Portfolio Professionals.

While you enjoy that feeling of celebration (and the rest of whatever you fancy), let's pick up some final steps on the path and some first steps on where it leads next.

The Portfolio Day

So what's really going to change now that you'll be living the Portfolio Life?

What will a typical day look and feel like?

Perhaps there's no such thing as a typical portfolio day, but ... the alarm rings at 0800 ... that's new!

Time for tea and the paper in bed ... ditto.

The things to do today pierce their way through the fug of sleep (well yes, some things don't change!), but instead of looking like 'just-get-through-those', they look like 'forthcoming attractions'.

Today, at an office not far from your sitting room:

- planning the week and day into work chunks
- fixing the time for sport and exercise
- arranging the evenings out
- sending some invoices (always uplifting!)
- playing some music in the background
- priming the network
- reading that article ...
- ... and all before breakfast, or even getting dressed!

When the days go well, you're in the flow, network clicking, business rolling, finding those wonderful synchronicities that lead to people you want to work with and who want to work with you.

Instead of rushing with indigestion from meeting into meeting, there's time to digest the one before and savour the one to come.

Of course, to keep the analogy going, there's feast and famine to be managed; work and cash flow have a way of bunching up and defying the laws of averages and smoothing. You can try to regularise it, but many successful Portfolio Professionals have failed to do this; the trick is to manage it, in your mind (expectations), in your finances (budgeting), and in your use of time (that admin and study work that fills the gaps productively).

And sometimes the days don't go well and you're down.

What? Down? When I'm doing what I really enjoy? When I have all this choice?

Yes, it happens, when you least expect it and for no apparent accountable reason. As we move outside our comfort zone and give ourselves space to feel, some old demons surface like lethargy, self-doubt, painful memories and everything in between.

The worst thing to do is to beat ourselves up about it.

'How can I be miserable when I've got what I want?' 'How can I waste so much time sitting here when I'm free to be creative?'

Yes, you've got the freedom – the freedom to be miserable if that's how it is today, the freedom to accept and recognise where low is, so that high will feel good when it comes again.

Get out that compliments file if it helps; take a walk with those 'freedom' anthems in your ears; or just be peaceful and listen for the reason that has taken you down – it'll come. All better than burying the feeling and racing to the next meeting with the mask on as you might have had to before!

Best practices

You've seen lots of other best practices of Portfolio Life throughout these pages. Where else to look? How about the mirror?

You'll be amazed how many people look to you as a role model for the life they've always wondered about.

Everybody has their 'if only I didn't have to work at this place' moments; you probably remember them well.

Some just like complaining and don't really mean it, and certainly aren't going to do anything about it. They may watch your new life with curiosity and try to disparage it at every opportunity. Others watch with greater interest and think 'Could that be me?' and quite possibly, 'Well, if they can do it, I must be able to as well.'

When they say, 'You're looking so much more relaxed, less stressed' (and yes, those frown lines have decreased along with the stomach upsets), they're thinking, 'I could have some of that!'

Your role modelling gives a glimpse of what might be, a hope that there is another way ... sometimes envy doesn't find a tongue to congratulate but it will find a voice to question and an ear to listen.

Time for the most important things

> *Until you value yourself, you will not value your time.*
> **Thomas Paine**

Many PPs are astonished how quickly the time they had for work is filled.

'Don't know how I had time to do the normal job', is a familiar cry.

And often it's because unforeseen and unpredictable – and pretty major – events have occurred.

Family illnesses, bereavements, friends' problems, children's difficulties have an uncanny way of knowing that the PP now has more flexibility in his or her schedule!

'How could I have helped there if I'd been working 14 hours every day?' Well, truth is, perhaps you couldn't.

'How can I get on with my Portfolio Life when I have to give time to all these unplanned things?'

Well, perhaps you are!

Whether you believe it was fate that gave you the time to help, or people who knew they could call on your freer time, or it's just that time of life, or just bad luck, something has thrown the problem and the opportunity in your path.

Remember the Last Big Birthday Party and that speech about you that someone makes.

In 'old life' it might have said, *'unfortunately his brother died while he was abroad opening up new markets in China for the company.'*

Or now, *'he was able to be there with the family when his brother died, as he'd left the company and started his own portfolio business just three months before.'*

We each make our own decision, but at least now you have the choice.

Keeping on track

When you're running your Portfolio Life and enjoying the feeling, it's easy to get taken over by the pleasure and the pace.

So it's good to visit your own checklist on a regular basis to make sure all parts are in good working order and that you're not losing focus on what you really want to do.

Here are some thoughts for starters.

- Make an annual stocktaking of where you are emotionally, physically, mentally. Keep up the annual health checks with the doctor.

- Give your business a regular service and MOT; make the annual accounts more useful by reassessing the Business Plan.

- Talk to other PPs, keep in touch with latest developments.

- Make time for marketing and selling at the same time as delivering; you'll soon notice the gap if you don't.

- Use your Portfolio Planner and the Bridge Plan as monitors for how far you've travelled and for keeping on the path.

- You need training and development: assess your personal development plan and invest in your future assets.

Regular checking makes us very aware that Portfolio Life is an evolving journey – what we thought was good keeps getting better!

Special talents grow further with being challenged in new roles; new areas of skill open up as confidence grows; we find ourselves doing things we never thought we could. The river bank where we started is getting lost in the far distance. As we change, it's good to reflect that in the Plan. A new Plan every three years makes sure we're reviewing where we are now and where we want to be – you'll know where to look for the framework!

Where the journey takes us

You've read the Portfolio Journeys dotted throughout the book and now you have your own story. We hope you can tell us about it sometime in the future.

Meanwhile, what about the authors, who crossed their Portfolio Bridges a while ago? We thought you might like to hear where our journeys have taken us so far.

Adrian's Portfolio Journey so far

My great opportunity to explore a portfolio career came after 30 years of working for multinational corporations.

I'm an inveterate planner, so I enjoyed the path through the exercises, the Portfolio Planner, the Bridge. When I left corporate life, I had my plan that in four years time I'd be a coach, non-executive director, charity worker, lecturer and writer and I set out on my bridge – well, in fact, past and under the bridge, because my daily walk at that time took me along the Thames just where the Millennium Bridge was gradually rising from the water. It was a good place to dream and reflect on the future. The hopes and fears of a new Portfolio Life, the questions without answer yet.

The day of the bridge opening should have coincided with the start of my new business but of course it was late ... and then wobbly!

ATB Directions Ltd was on time but had its wobbly moments! Across the next four years, things wobbled, and like the bridge, became sound. A succession of bereavements and severe illness in the extended family needed time (where would that have come from when I was 6 days a week in corporate life?). The business with its new company number, domain site, and business cards first saw life in an 'office' piled with cardboard boxes and luggage, the property of eldest son returning temporarily to his bedroom!

In the middle of it all, the plan and the bridge got firmer; I became Non-Executive Chairman of a food business helping the MBO team to double shareholder value in four years, Non-Executive of a corporate social responsibility organisation, guest lecturer at University, adviser to homeless charities, and I trained to be an Executive Coach with The Success Group.

A lot of good things happened too with time to enjoy them: family anniversaries celebrated; Maureen returned to teaching and our life took on a different pattern; our three children were becoming more financially independent and into relationships of their own; I walked the North Downs Way.....including bridges over motorways and rivers.

Now when I pass the Millennium Bridge, it's amazing to reflect how the portfolio came to fruition, and that income can be as much when doing what I enjoy as it was in corporate life.

And the plan to be a writer? Well, here's this one, which started its travels as an idea over a table at a golf course and a series of conversations at the IOD!

Like all portfolios, mine evolves and requires an updated forward plan every three years. The balance changes as my needs and drivers change; more time now for sport, health and home and for celebrating milestones with the growing family and friends. My paid work increasingly focuses on what I love doing and what can fit with the other priorities.

The current forward plan concentrates on Coaching and of course on sharing experiences of portfolio life through seminars and meeting people who are on the journey, or thinking about it.

Christopher's Portfolio Journey so far

With hindsight the initial planning for my portfolio career started in 1976. My first major responsibility for my then employer Abbey National was to co-ordinate the redrafting of the company pension scheme. A scheme that won awards, and the eternal gratitude of many employees with its generous early retirement provisions. I remember thinking then those provisions would be useful one day.

As my career progressed upwards and through personnel, operations, finance and banking, much was learned though times of great change and seismic shifts in the industry. I learned to cope with all the usual things, frustration, long hours, etc., but work was fun. I also discovered many things of value, particularly networking, together with a sense of knowing when time was up as many respected colleagues fell by the wayside. Sooner or later employment with my preferred partner would end.

As my late 40s progressed, the foreboding sense of what the next 25 years held became stronger. The early signs of the company starting to lose its way were all too apparent. Importation of external resource, rather than home-grown talent, became the order of the day and political manoeuvring overtook productive work. The incentive to plan the future elsewhere grew by the day. I quietly extended my network of contacts, sought advice, proactively chased external facing corporate activities and obtained a Masters Degree in Strategic Finance.

When the opportunity arose, it came quickly and timing was everything. A handsome job offer coincided with yet another corporate reorganisation so it was off to see the Personnel Director, rechecking the letter in my inside pocket. Yes someone was going to pay me triple what I had been earning. At least someone placed value on the Masters degree expensively funded by the company. The Personnel Director was exemplary. Well used to running onto the field of battle to tend the wounded. Half an hour of negotiations saw my exit plan complete.

As it turned out, I had escaped the ensuing years of carnage in what had been a well run, energetic, commercial organisation in which the employees were highly valued. My next two years on the executive board of an asset management and banking entity were a period of transition, setting down firm foundations for a future portfolio life. Networking and contacts were key during this period and the initial stages of constructing my first portfolio. Setting it up took time and I chose to have themes of strategic planning, governance and finance at the core whilst playing to my historical strengths of banking, finance and new ventures. My current portfolio is founded on three main areas comprising non-executive directorships, consulting assignments and specialist advice on foreign exchange and corporate transactions.

Since taking the plunge the range of business problems and issues I have been involved in have been intellectually stimulating and far beyond that which I could have imagined. They have ranged from setting up project finance arrangements to operate in Nigeria and Iraq, through to directing the renegotiation of borrowing requirements in a large complex organisation, and recently advising NHS England on the establishment a number of commissioning entities throughout the UK. The portfolio has grown in size, widened in interest and reinvented itself with interest.

I now Chair the Board of an AIM listed company having recently Chaired the Board of two regulated organizations. I lecture at both Durham and Kingston Business School and have served on the Board of the world's leading international maritime consultancy and a charity.

It is a rich and varied portfolio deriving much satisfaction and time to do things I enjoy even finding time to rediscover golf, long train journeys and interesting walks such as the Thames path. Again that sense of timing has arrived. With this edition of the book put to bed I shall now turn my attention to a series of home and lifestyle improvements.

Colin's Portfolio Journey

After the strictures and demands of running businesses for almost twenty years I was ready for the freedom, the choice and the flexibility offered by the portfolio life. Ready ... but unprepared; there was no book to help – a gap that I'm proud to say that I've since contributed to filling.

So my portfolio was one which evolved rather than being tightly planned.

My talents led naturally to consultancy, strategic advice, running board workshops, and I complemented these with Study Work pursuing my interest in emerging fields such as eBusiness (yes, back then I had to persuade apparently intelligent business leaders that ecommerce was going to be important for them). One of my clients invited me to become their Non-Executive Chairman, providing a solid foundation for my portfolio and giving me an involvement in results, one of the elements of my chief executive role that I'd missed.

When I say my portfolio evolved, it was a case of gradually feeling the need to be doing other things, and incorporating these. The 'time running out' awareness hit me and with it a conscious decision to err on the time side of the time-income equilibrium.

So, despite a busy portfolio I decided to pursue some non-earning interests. Prime among these was my passion for wine and I set myself the challenge of studying for the full professional qualifications. A long haul, but great fun and tremendous satisfaction. I've since taken the first steps towards turning this interest into a paying proposition hoping that one day it could even fund my cellar.

Wine and an extended family in Australia have been great pretexts for travel, not always possible in my employed days. Since setting out on the Portfolio Life, I've visited every major wine country and region in the world.

Having spent my school years intent on becoming a journalist, I always had the writing bug. So when the three of us came up with the idea of writing this book, to help other would-be portfoli-ers, it fitted that particular gap in my experience, and provided not only another element in my portfolio but a real case of doing what you enjoy, with people you enjoy working with.

Time and flexibility came to their greatest importance when my wife, Lyn, became seriously ill. For three years I was able to juggle the various demands of my portfolio, maintaining some income and some interests, but fitting them to give priority to her needs and to the realisation that our time together might be short. At least I am now able to look back in the knowledge that she and I spent really special time together that would not have been available to us had I still been in corporate life.

So over a period of more than ten years, my portfolio has been a varying blend of Paid Work, Study Work, Gift Work, Home Work ... and making the most of that most precious resource of all, Time.

These foolish things ….

There are some words you hear often from new Portfolio Professionals: freedom, liberation, flexibility, balance, independence … you'll have your own to add. And there are some new things they experience which bring the words to life.

In Chapter 2 we mentioned that you don't see PPs standing out in a crowd very often, perhaps because they're travelling outside rush hours.

What a joy to have room for legs, elbows, even a seat, and not to have your nose in someone else's armpit … and a train that leaves and arrives on time!

One of the little pleasures to savour. Here's some more:

- Christmas lunch of a Turkey and stuffing sandwich (oh OK a doughnut too) at Prêt a Manger with someone you want to be with, instead of the Company Christmas Do making false fun with people you have to work with.

- The Company Day out that isn't the Disneyland extravaganza but is the two Directors (who happen to be sleeping partners in all senses) walking to the pub together.

- The Company AGM at the kitchen table, resolutions passed over the cheeseboard and minutes on the back of the wine bottle.

- Company hospitality days replaced with real events – midweek golf with fellow PPs, test matches, trips to Glyndebourne – where you choose who you play/watch/listen with.

- Enjoying the fruits of your own customer relation policy instead of defending the inadequacies of your employer's.

- Developing and exploiting your own ideas rather than having them sidelined in the company suggestion scheme.

- Looking up at the architecture in town, that bit above the shopfronts, the bit that's been unchanged for centuries and speaks of history and has looked down on all the rushing, stressed people below since before you were born.

- Stopping to smell the flowers; why not? You'll get into the most surprising conversations!

- Setting yourself a treat just for you. Two hours a week to do something off the wall (who else has to know); something you've not done since schooldays, something you wouldn't put in your CV, why not!

- Granting yourself permission (after much probing, of course) for a sabbatical; three months off to re-find yourself and see more of this big world which we have only a short time to experience.

You'll have many moments to savour like these; capture them and put them in that Compliments file, for a rainy or tearful day.

Fare well ... until we meet again!

This book began as a dream around tables and over drinks at golf clubs and the Institute of Directors. It has been a pleasure to realise the dream!

The authors were guided by the philosophy of Charles Handy's books and inspired by our direct discussions with him and his wife Liz.

Our motivation was to guide prospective Portfolio Professionals through the decisions and the transition to portfolio life based on our own experiences. We wanted to share what worked for us on the trip, and to help people see that it is not a leap in the dark over a dangerous river but a well paced walk across a bridge of their own choosing.

The tide has risen since our first book *You...Unlimited* was published, and in recent years the water has become much more choppy! More and more individuals are reviewing their real options and making a choice: the lifebelt and cling on to the big ship, or the lifeboat and share the smaller boat with others, or paddle your own canoe, or build your own bridge!

We've been excited to see the growth in portfolio working and especially to hear the results from our readers like these:

"Finally I know what I want to do and what I can do best. It would not have been possible for me to work it out on my own. I am sure that this will change my life, for the better"

"I have made a career shift that I couldn't have imagined without the book"

"I have to say it has proven to have had a profound impact on both my personal life and my business already"

Rising tide of awareness

Blogs witness the rise in Portfolio Professionals and the forums they have found to speak to each other:

"This time round, people have become more tolerant of risk in their income streams (or perhaps just more aware that the risk profile of the old paradigm has changed), and I believe more will be prepared to take that jump away from the traditional corporate career, if the payoff is living their life with spirit and passion."

The renowned journalist Mary Ann Sieghart published an article saying:

"There is only one phrase that sums it all up: "portfolio woman".......
Increasing numbers of women my age have given up working full-time for one employer to lead a life that is more varied and more flexible.
"I had spent 19 years of my life commuting from West London

to Wapping and back, and most weekdays I was also doing a round trip from Wapping to the West End for lunch with politicians. By giving that up, I have gained two-and-a-half hours a day at a stroke. If I want to go to a school event during working hours, I simply put it in my diary. And in August, when my family decamped to Wiltshire for the month, I could join them without any arguments about whether working from home was acceptable. Freedom! With freedom, though, comes insecurity. Where is the money to come from? I immediately started to live a lot more frugally. I now go everywhere by bus or Tube and wouldn't dream of taking a taxi. Funnily enough, I quite enjoy the challenge of saving money and anyway, in these straitened times, I am hardly alone in doing it.

"........It isn't for the faint-hearted. If you fall sick, no one will pay your wages. On the other hand, in these recessionary times, at least we aren't worrying about being laid off. The great advantages are variety and flexibility. For the easily bored, it's as bracing as jumping into the sea. That fantastic tingle you feel afterwards is with me still, more than a year after I first took the plunge. My husband loves seeing more of me, as do my children"

The word is spreading – and we keep on learning!

Across over ten years since the book's first publication, we've learnt that:

- portfolio life is a growing trend across many countries of the world

- while it began as a new opportunity for over 40s, it is now being taken up by people at every stage of their life, giving a 'life of careers' not a 'career for life'

- people are taking their futures into their own hands, rather than relying on others

- many consultants and agencies in the career advice business have yet to adapt to the change; they still look on the 'employer' as the client and funder, instead of focusing on the individual

- home life and work life are harmonising in a dramatic new way; one Portfolio Professional develops into a Portfolio Couple, achieving a new life-work balance for themselves individually and together

We'd like to hear your experiences so you can share with others what's worked for you and what we've missed; and we're able to offer coaching and advice to individuals or groups to support transitions or just spread the word about how portfolio life works in practice.

Please contact us at the addresses shown on the contacts page at the back of the book.

We like to keep Portfolio Professionals in touch with each other and ensure the joy of networking keeps off the fear of remoteness.

This helps to:

- ensure Portfolio People are recognised and appreciated for the professional qualities of their employed and unemployed lives

- give support, as more and more become 'masters of their own careers', to nurture their talents and guide their career.

- facilitate the sharing of experience and promote best practice

- enable the community of Portfolio Professionals to know each others' talents and mobilise into working groups around specific business initiatives

Let us know who or what could help you in your explorations. We'll be happy to help make the connections. Visit our website and contribute.

When we talk to people in evenings at business schools, seminar events or special industry gatherings, we emphasise the three key points of success in making the transition to portfolio life:

- PLAN for the future for all parts of your life
- ASSESS your transferable talents and experience to broaden your options
- EXPLORE as you step confidently across the bridge

Wherever your own journey takes you, we hope this book has been a stepping stone on the way.

In Part 4 there is a wealth of practical knowledge and expertise from our specialist contributors. They advise on running your own business, selling, marketing and living the portfolio life. You will find it helpful to dip in here now... and again and again... as your journey evolves.

Farewell and have a good trip. Enjoy.

PART 4

RUNNING YOUR PORTFOLIO LIFE

Leaving the Corporate Fold
by Richard Jones

The Business of Portfolio Working
by Christopher P Lyons

IT for the Portfolio Lifestyle
by Chris Meggs

Presenting You
by Chris Collingbourne

Networking
by Heather White

Marketing You and Your Portfolio
by Barnaby Wynter

Selling
by Colin McCrudden

The Power of Social Media and How to Harness It
by Paul McCrudden

Smart Moves for Exercise and Health
by Maggie Humphreys and Les Snowdon

LEAVING THE CORPORATE FOLD
BY RICHARD JONES

You have decided to leave. You may have no choice about the manner of leaving – e.g. being made redundant – or you may be in a position to take early retirement or to negotiate an exit. Whatever the circumstances, the most important thing to remember is, regardless of how you leave, the package that you take with you is almost invariably something you can influence. To maximise the package, you will need both knowledge and negotiating skills to match that of the employer. You may be equipped to do it all yourself or you may need to benefit from some more expert advice.

The following notes are designed to be a guide to the main things you need to think about and research. Some of them will be obvious but they are so important that they are worth stating anyway.

So where do you start?

The first important thing is to remember that the rules have changed. However good a relationship you've had before, you are now negotiating for the best deal for you, and the company is on the opposite side of the table. So, as any successful negotiation starts with knowing your position, you need to do your research and it is vital that you do not have any formal communication with the company about finance until you have established:

- your contractual position – read your employment contract and the relevant parts of any accompanying employment handbook
- your financial position – the parameters of (a) what you will need financially in your new portfolio life and (b) what you would want to aim for

- the legal position – there are specific employment and tax laws which deal with redundancy and retirement.

When the actual negotiations start, remember that while it is personal for you it is impersonal for the person you are dealing with even if it is a boss who has been a great colleague. They are representing the company and as any agreement is with the company not the individual, you cannot afford to trust verbal assurances.

The contractual position

Your contract will have details of your notice period – both from and to the company – but bear in mind that when you leave at their behest, you will not automatically receive pay for that whole period. The amount you will get is a negotiation. For example, the wording of the contract in respect of notice period has a direct impact on the tax position in cases of forced exit.

The employment handbook will have details of the processes that have to be gone through by you and the company, certainly in the case of redundancy. It is important that you ensure these are followed. Employment law demands good processes and success in any contest demands that these are followed – by you, so as not to give the company an advantage, and by the company so as not to give you one.

The financial position

You will have your own ideas about the minimum cushion you think you need in order to get the portfolio career up and running. The maximum is best thought of in terms of what you believe would be a fair settlement, albeit erring on the generous side (to you!).

Particular issues you will need to consider are:

- current and future commitments
- pension:

- if you can take it immediately, is that the best thing to do in the longer term
- bear in mind that you can use part of any settlement package – with the company's agreement – to boost the value of your pension
- putting money into the pension is tax efficient – it is not taxed
- if you decide to take your pension, it is normally best to maximise the lump sum since that is not taxed while continuing income is taxed
- savings and how sacrosanct they are – or not
- what is a realistic estimate of future earnings and how long from start-up before that level is realistically reached.

The legal position

The minefield! This ranges from the law of mitigation (the reason many do not get payment of the notice period specified in their contract) through redundancy processes to tax treatment of redundancy payments, pay in lieu of notice and limits on the amounts that can be used to boost pension. Others include the ins and outs of compromise agreements – what undertakings it is reasonable for the company to ask for and what are unreasonable. Particularly difficult issues here can be confidentiality clauses and clauses requiring you not to compete with the company for a period of time.

So, what are the key things to remember?

Redundancy or forced exit

If it appears that the company may be looking to change things such that you may no longer have a position, assume that they will not do so to your best advantage! To tackle that, make sure that you get them to set out the position, even in draft form, at an early stage. Ideally, get advice as soon as they have indicated that your exit is on the cards even if that is just in conversation – asking the right questions is important to ensure you put yourself in the best position.

A key question is what opportunities exist for you in the new structure/ venture and how those compare with your current position and responsibilities. An alternative job needs not only to be comparable in terms of remuneration but also in terms of levels of responsibility and, sometimes even, career prospects. If there is any doubt about comparability, it can put you in a strong position in negotiating your exit.

These first exchanges are likely to be fairly general but they will set not only the tone but the framework for what follows. And once you have got something from them in writing, get advice on how best to frame your response. This is an area where wording is crucial. What you say in your response, how it is framed and the exact words that are used have to fit within the legal framework that applies to redundancy and to dismissal for other reasons – and different types of dismissal have different processes and different legal considerations. What is said now will have a major impact on the final outcome.

It may be that the company will seek to avoid redundancy by offering you an alternative role that they claim is, or will become, just as good as the present job. In these circumstances, it is important to protect your position so that you do not lose the possibility of being made redundant. Careful crafting of correspondence is needed.

You will also want to give thought to the timing of the exit. Very often the company will have strong views on this and for some roles, an early exit is unavoidable. But even in these cases, the length of time you spend on gardening leave as opposed to receiving pay in lieu of notice is an issue, and can have taxation implications.

A forced exit also means that the company should make arrangements to help you find your next role. You have already decided what that is going to be, but help is still extremely valuable. So, always try to negotiate an outplacement package, ideally including finance and career advice. These 'experts' can provide real help in the early days by facilitating your research into the markets you want to aim at, commenting on your early efforts at self PR, giving constructive criticism on your plans and, above all, helping you to network. And you never know who you will meet who is also going through the same process with the outplacement consultants! But make sure that the money that you negotiate for outplacement fees and such like is kept very separate from the settlement for losing your job.

This is a complex subject and, for most people, not one in which they have had previous experience. Expert advice to fill the gaps in your own knowledge and expertise is essential. You should look for an advisor who is able and prepared to provide a tailored service that just fills those gaps that exist in your own expertise rather than one who only offers a standard full service – unless a full service is what you think you need. So, before you commit yourself or put anything in writing, find your adviser. An HR expert with experience of this area (redundancy, termination of contract, pensions) will probably be better than a lawyer in helping the negotiation of terms although a lawyer will be essential if there is a compromise agreement.

Unforced exit

If you have not had any indications that the company might wish to say goodbye and have just decided to go, don't burn your boats by resigning before you have explored with the company the opportunities for an agreed exit with a package. And do get advice on what the options might be before jumping – good advice can be worth thousands!

Pensions

Whatever the basis of the exit, you will need to give careful thought to the pension position. If you are going well before being able to take it early then the decision will depend on what type of pension you have. If you happen to be lucky enough to be in a final salary scheme, then freezing it is the answer. If you are in a defined contribution scheme, then you will want to ensure that you can continue paying in.

If, on the other hand, you are in a position to take the pension early then you need to decide whether that would be the right course. Taking a pension early usually means that the amount you would have received at normal retirement age is actuarially reduced. The simple rule of thumb to help decide what is best is as follows.

1. Get details of what would be payable if the pension was frozen and taken at normal retirement age and the comparable figure for taking it early.
2. Work out the total gross amount you would be paid in the years before normal retirement age if you took the pension early.
3. Divide the amount from 2 above by the annual difference in pensions (1 above) and you get a result in years.
4. Add the figure from 3 above to your normal retirement age and the answer is the age at which you will start to be better off (all things being equal) if you freeze the pension. If this looks like 80-plus, then it suggests that enjoying the money by taking it early may well be the right answer. Less than that and, subject to your views of personal longevity, it might not.

From March 2014, pension arrangements became more flexible with new rules creating greater choice and opportunities for financial planning. Further announcements are expected and it is important that you consider both the taxation and future income implications by taking professional advice. A useful start would be to seek free and impartial information from the Pensions Advisory Service.

Of course there are other important considerations such as family and whether you think you need a cushion so as to ease the pressure of having to become a successful Portfolio Professional quickly before savings are too diminished.

This is a very brief guide to some of the issues that you will need to consider and some of the complexities that surround them. It can all seem pretty fearsome and off-putting. But don't be put off. With a good advisor, you can make it work so that your start as a budding Portfolio Professional is a sound one.

Richard Jones has been a successful Portfolio Professional for over 10 years. His successful career in 'paid work' as HR Director in major corporations, has evolved into a portfolio of 'gift work' in the voluntary sector with more time for family, leisure and 'home work'.

THE BUSINESS OF PORTFOLIO WORKING

BY CHRISTOPHER P LYONS

Time for reflection

So, you've decided to take the plunge, explore further and seek to join the ranks of the Portfolio Professionals. Or have you? If you have been in employment and you are "going it alone", what about all those questions around being self-employed, running your own business or perhaps acquiring one. There are important issues which you must address or potentially sleepwalk into this new environment.

The purpose of this chapter is threefold:

- to give a clear view of reality before channelling effort into operating as a business, as you are the business
- to identify issues worth considering before buying a business or establishing yourself as a portfolio business
- to offer guidance on the route to take.

Many readers will have spent most of their formative career in paid employment. Adopting a portfolio approach to work brings with it potentially significant change in employment status. The reality is that whilst you and your family are the main beneficiaries of your endeavours, you must consider your status with the others wanting a share of the spoils. Correct, the State and its agencies such as HMRC will want their cut.

Business on your own account?

Being in business on your own account brings its responsibilities. Take time to consider these before the requirements to earn cash overtakes your thinking. Unless you are very lucky to live off an inheritance, win the lottery, or retire on a very healthy pension, it is likely that you will need some form of income from your portfolio.

It is at this point you should consider the following questions:

- How will you generate your income?
- How will you gather it in?
- What will be the easiest and most efficient vehicle through which to conduct your business affairs?

This may involve becoming self-employed or in many instances forming a business. Alternatively you may wish to consider buying a business and acting either as owner/manager, or getting others to do the work whilst you take the risk and the dividends. These options raise a number of questions. Sadly there is no well tried formula which provides the answers. Seeking advice from various sources will be helpful and in doing so you should ask four questions. A no answer to any of the questions demands a rethink.

The right person?

First, are you the right person to run your own business? Are you the right person to own a business and delegate control to others? Or do you want to be hands on? Be honest with yourself, seek a second opinion from somebody whose judgement you trust and ideally from somebody who already runs a business. You will have just finished evaluating your most important asset, which is you. However, there are issues which will hit you on day one of your new life. Your ability to withstand being rebuffed for work whilst the bureaucrats at the bank, tax office and customs chase you for payments will all weigh heavily upon the spirit. You will face disappointment. People will pay late, others will try to steal your ideas AND clients. Falling foul of regulations brings with it fines and charges the like of which irritate you.

What are you selling and who will pay?

Second, what is your product or service? Before answering that, imagine receiving your first payment. Who will give you money for something that you are offering? People often have great ideas for a business but many of these ideas rarely see the light of day. Businesses fail in all industries on a daily basis. The odds are stacked against you. Can your service be supplied commercially and will somebody buy what you offer rather than what somebody else is offering?

Can you finance the business?

Third, and most importantly, this question needs careful assessment. You need to have sufficient funds to cover your initial outlay be they start up costs or buying an existing business.

How are you going to market your goods or services?

This last question is dealt with in different parts of this book, not least in the chapters on Marketing and The Power of Social Media. However, you should remember that your unique selling point – your USP – may not be the product or service itself; it is you and a poor idea professionally marketed is exponentially more valuable than a good idea not marketed at all! Essentially you have two options, firstly to acquire a business and act as owner receiving dividends or salary as an owner/manager. Secondly, as a result of your change in employment status to form your own business. The rest of this chapter examines these options and the issues associated with being involved in your own business even on a self employed basis.

Acquiring a business

Ultimately the only reason for making an acquisition is to add value over time. The important thing to remember is that any acquisition should be a means to an end, not an end in itself. Empirical research shows that around half of all corporate acquisitions fail to meet expectations, with a considerable proportion deemed to be failures. Why is this and how can such problems be avoided? There are a number of key factors that influence the success, collectively or individually.

Before embarking on the acquisition trail you should examine your motives and be very clear about your future role in a business and its relationship to a portfolio lifestyle. Questions such as are you happy to be an investor/shareholder or olderpreneur, how much of an active role do you wish to play, what sort of time commitment are you prepared to give, do you want to be an owner manager are key to your decision.

At this point three main points must be made.

- **Firstly, the importance of planning cannot be over estimated.** Planning and assessment are a primary theme of this book, but in this case it really is crucial. A random or opportunistic acquisition will rarely be successful. If you want to acquire a business then you must understand the prime objectives from the acquisition and stick to them.

- **Secondly finding the right business at the right time at the right price is not easy.** Rather like entering an auction, the acquisition parameters should be set out clearly from the start, including type, size, location and price.

- **Thirdly one of the most consistent research findings is that professional help can make a material difference to the success of an acquisition.** Specialist organisations dealing in the small to medium (SME) business sector such as the Beer Mergers, www.beermerger.com are always willing to talk informally and without obligation or cost to prospective clients about their acquisition plans. Follow the link on our website or contact the author by email.

Forming your own business formally

So which is the best form of business for you? It depends on your circumstances and personality – however, you should consider the following questions.

- **?** Are you going into this venture alone?
- **?** If you do not go into this business alone, who will go into it with you, and how active will the other participants be?

? How long can you carry your business and finance it before it starts to break even, let alone make a profit?

? How much liability are you and your family prepared to accept?

? What degree of control do you wish to retain over your business?

? How much regulation are you willing to tolerate?

Set yourself a clear objective. Why you are establishing this business? Do you want a structure for trading on your own volition, or are you building a business which has inherent value? One may generate value now, the other may generate value in the future.

When setting up in business, you will need to decide its legal form. You have broadly three main choices:

- Sole Trader, also known as being self-employed
- Partnership or limited liability partnership (LLP)
- Limited Company

The main differences are set out in figure 17 on page 230.

If you intend working on your own, your choice is likely to be between sole trader and limited company. Other entities do exist, such the limited liability partnership, which is mainly used for specialist purposes.

If you have a pressing need to work with others, the choice will be between partnership, limited company or co-operative. You can of course work as a sole trader and employ others as opposed to working with them. Many choose to set up a company, in order to limit their liability. However, there is no advantage if there is no liability to limit. In the early days of a new start up, the two likeliest creditors are the bank and possibly a landlord. It is likely that they will ask for personal guarantees, which negates the value of limited liability.

When the time comes to make a decision, it is worth consulting a lawyer or accountant. Remember they bill you for chargeable time, rather than give consultations like your GP. Have your objectives ready and your questions. Remember that there is no requirement for you to fix your decision in concrete – you can always change the legal form. There is no reason why you should not have different business structures for the different business aspects of your portfolio.

Main differences in trading entities

	Sole trader	Partnership	Limited Company
Formalities	• Simple arrangement • No legal entity • No need to register • Pay class 2 NI	• Not a legal entity in England • Advisable to have an agreement	• A legal entity • Needs registration • Accounts required • Formal governance
Risk	• Potentially everything you own • Business debt is a personal debt	• Potentially everything you own • Your partners can also lose it as well	• Shareholder liability limited • Company liability unlimited
Taxation	• Taxed on trading income • Tax paid up to 12 months after earnings	• Payable by you as an individual	• Corporation tax • Payable by the company • Some timing tax advantages
Suitability	• For simple business	• Must be based upon trust • Loose association has risks	• Limited liability to shareholders • Has own identity
Advantages	• Easy to start • Least work • Few formalities • No audit of accounts • Cash flow advantages on tax payments under self-assessment • Lower NI rates • Offset losses against profits of same trade	• Easy to form • No audit of accounts • Some cash flow advantages • Lower NI rates • Perceived more credible as a larger entity	• Possible credibility issued with banks • Liability limited • Wider capital raising choice • Company can make pension contributions
Disadvantages	• You are liable for all funds owed by the business • If you pay higher rate tax, your business profits will be taxed at that rate • Raising funds is difficult • Cannot receive some DSS benefits	• You are liable for your partner's debts • Difficult to dissolve or sell unless previously agreed • If you pay higher rate tax your business profits will be assessed at that rate	• Bureaucracy • Legal requirements • Must produce accounts • Directors can be liable in law • Personal liability for company debt when giving personal guarantee

Figure 17

The practicalities

The best piece of advice given to me was to spend time getting the basics correct even if you delay business activities. Failure to put the basics in place from Day One results in playing catch-up and they become more complicated over time.

Set out below are a series of very short checklists and they represent the minimum you should establish. Take your time to work through them – it will pay you in the long run.

The basic necessities

- Decide on what business form suits your purposes. If in doubt start as self employed.
- Register as self-employed by notifying the tax authorities.
- Ensure NI continuity and arrange to pay nominal Class 2 contributions.
- Decide on a name to trade under, and avoid infringing other businesses.
- Design a letter head and get it printed.
- Produce business cards with email, mobile and land line numbers.
- Portfolio workers carry many cards, and pick up many! Buy a business card holder.

Setting up a company

- Decide on your timing; you will have to submit accounts 12 months from incorporation.
- Decide on the name.
- Decide on the registered address – either your home or your accountant.
- Decide on the shareholders and get their consent.
- Decide on a company secretary and get his or her consent. This can be you.
- Decide on the initial capital. Most companies are set up with 100 £1 shares. You do not have to issue all the shares. If you are going

into business with others, consider establishing the company with 1000 £1 shares, and issue 100. You can always issue more later.

- Decide on the directors. You will need their consent, full name, address, and date of birth.
- Call a corporate services provider, or company set-up agent in Yellow Pages. Nationwide Corporate Services www.anewbusiness.co.uk are very helpful. You can set up the company over the telephone for about £100 to £150 which is cheaper than your accountant who will ask you all the above, ring the same firm and charge you double!
- Wait for the certificate of incorporation and the company documents.

The financial aspects

- Estimate your start up costs.
- Estimate your normal overheads when the business is operating.
- Do a cash flow forecast over 12 months.
- Be very pessimistic, establish when it generates cash.
- Can you generate enough cash on a monthly basis?
- Work out a pricing strategy for your services and products.
- Work out some simple metrics, such as fixed costs, breakeven, turnover and profit forecasts.
- Assess your own salary requirements.
- Develop a business plan including the financial element.
- Discuss your plan with a mentor and your accountant.
- Will you need to borrow money to start up the business?
- Open up a business bank account, or designate a separate account. If you have more than one credit card, allocate one for all business expenditure.
- Keep all invoices and make a note of everything that you spend; include paperclips, stamps and so on – they all add up.
- In year 1 as a sole trader, you can claim set-up expenditure incurred in the previous 7 years.
- Record all your business mileage. You can use the Revenue approved rate to get tax relief.

- Ensure that all journeys you make have a business element in them, such as research, networking, cold calling. Don't get greedy or put your holidays in here. The penalties outweigh the benefits.
- If your business is trading in goods, seriously look at the VAT implications on cash flow and pricing, and register with Customs. You should be prepared as if expecting a visit from them at anytime.
- Set up an accounting system and manage it ruthlessly. Record payments as they occur.
- Remember to save money as you trade to pay for tax, National Insurance and VAT. Both these authorities have very efficient billing and follow up systems.
- Regularly reappraise your budgets, cash flows and tax position.
- Consult your accountant, or tax advisor regularly if you change the nature of your portfolio.

In addition you should hold detailed discussions with your advisor on matters such as personal and corporation tax, VAT registration and the provisions of IR35 for people acting in a consultancy capacity.

If you believe that your new venture will involve trading overseas you will have added a further degree of complexity. Entry to foreign markets needs careful research. Internet and Social Media use has made exporting so much easier. For product sales, Amazon has a fulfillment service and it also translates your product into the language of the main European markets. Useful sources of advice are UKTI and their website www.greatbusiness.gov.uk and if you are looking to sell to a global market, then look at www.thegreatbritishstore.com who have great expertise in promoting products and services worldwide.

Lastly, your new venture will be faced with a Foreign Exchange issue if you trade offshore. This can be complex and potentially value destroying if you get it wrong. The service provided by a number of institutions is often opaque, expensive and worth a book in its own right. The author is willing to provide pointers, advice and introductions based upon his own experiences , so please make contact with me through e mail.

Insurances

? Have you told your insurers, including motor insurer about your new career?

? Do you need to take out new life insurance to replace the one you had in employment?

? Do you need to set up permanent health insurance for sick pay?

? Is your pension provision sufficient – consult a financial advisor?

? Do you need professional indemnity insurance?

? Do you require directors' liability insurance?

? Do you require public liability or product liability insurance?

? Do you require employee liability insurance?

? Are you covered for foreign markets?

Business documentation

- Design and print your letterheads.
- Design and produce an invoice.
- Ensure that you have a draft confidentiality agreement.
- Design a proforma proposal, for services or goods to be supplied covering:
  - a response to the client's stated requirements
  - a marketing document which sells your services
  - an unambiguous definition of the scope of the tasks to be undertaken, and by whom
  - a timetable of events to delivery
  - a schedule of costs and the terms of payment
  - a place for the client to sign indicating that it is contractually binding.
- Employment contracts if you are going to hire people.
- Any sub-contract documentation.
- Are there any licences, trademarks or designs which you need to organise?

Time and space precludes covering every eventuality. The above checklists should give you a flavour of the sorts of items you are likely to have to tackle if you are establishing a business for the first time. Do spend time planning and getting the basic infrastructure in order. The list looks daunting, but tackled in a systematic and careful manner, you should be able to start trading almost immediately.

Shareholder agreements

If you are going to establish a limited company with other participants as part of your business interests, it is advisable to consider a shareholder agreement for the company. Whilst your business will be governed by company law, a shareholders' agreement will regulate the manner in which the company is to be run and certain aspects of their relationships with each other.

Without an agreement, each shareholder typically holds his or her shares without any restriction on transfer. Whether you like it or not, things happen, events occur, people change their attitude and before long what seemed like a cosy arrangement can turn into a nightmare. You should seriously consider events such as death or bankruptcy of a shareholder, which can all too easily occur to a company shareholder in everyday life.

A carefully drafted agreement will make provision for all of these events to be settled amicably by the shareholders.

Running the business portfolio

Running the business involves a series of transactions. It is important that some form of contract defines the nature of the agreement and these may be contracts orally, in writing or by implication. The golden rule of thumb is that it is always safer to put matters in writing and record everything.

Many people reading this book will have been in full-time employment, usually where others have kept all the basic records of the business. Supplies get ordered, payments get made, invoices are issued, cash is collected, bills are paid. Now you have to do it your way.

There is no need for this to be an arduous task; however the sooner that you recognise that you are going to have to take responsibility and that keeping books and records is essential, the easier the task will become. There are plenty of books and publications that will give guidance on what to record, but at its simplest, you should build your business interest around a cash book and recording sales and purchase invoices.

How much to charge?

Deciding how to price your services is the area which causes more difficulty than any other. There are however a few basic rules.

- **What the market will stand.** This depends on what people are used to paying. If there is a recognised rate for the job, there is not much you can do to change it – establish what it is, what others are paid and what they do for the money. Try to differentiate your services to charge higher than the market norm but ensure you are adding value in some way.

- **Be aware of perceived value.** If you are asked by a multi-national to quote a day rate, then £100 is unlikely to impress them. Go too low and you will be seen as lightweight and low profile. The rule is to match their expectation and reassure them of value. Employing someone who is too cheap is potentially bad for the image and raises questions about the quality of work – your client may be presenting your proposal to someone you will never meet. It is important to know the culture you're pitching to, its habits and its attitudes regarding money.

- **Your personal needs.** You should spend time calculating these carefully. Establish your requirements over the year that deliver a good lifestyle for you and your family. Planning for mere survival will only generate resentment and deplete your drive and enthusiasm. Work out how much gross income you need to generate per year including all your business operating costs. You should calculate on the basis of 45 weeks per year to give an average weekly rate. Remember it's a minimum. Remember you are in business and you need to deal with administration, planning, your training etc. Do not establish your minimum daily rate by dividing by 7 or 5 – be realistic and divide by 2 or 3.

Generally there are also three rules around what to charge.

- **First, always quote more than you think.** If you go in high you can always come down if you have to. You don't want the client to feel undervalued so talk about repeat business, regular consultancy and long term relationships as reasons for reducing rates. If you go in too low, you will be stuck with it!

- **Second, freebies are a danger zone.** Avoid them unless you know the person well enough to be certain that their intentions are honourable and you can get something in return. The rule is, if a prospective client wants you to do speculative work, simply say you don't work that way.

- **The third rule is no negotiating.** People who are 'needy' will be prepared to negotiate and give in to demands for rates that will not serve them. Don't be tempted to say 'yes, anything' as this may be a temporary state of neediness. You don't want to be lumbered with time committed to loss-making projects. On the other hand if there is nothing else on the horizon, come down with dignity and treat it as an introductory rate. Above all, don't allow your rates to be pushed so low that the client ends up not respecting you. This is not a comfortable dilemma. Don't give away your assets before you start getting paid; don't overdo the proposal meetings!

In pricing your services you should ask yourself several questions.

- **?** Should I charge everyone the same rate? You may have different rates for different roles.
- **?** Should I charge a daily or hourly rate?
- **?** Is travel time included in the charge structure?
- **?** How do I calculate expenses? Always include them in your proposals.
- **?** How do I estimate the timetable for the project? Quote both a day rate and project rate.

Terms of business

You should aim to have a simple set of terms and conditions. Design them to inform, rather than confuse, and to spell out clearly what you will do for the client, and what you won't. It is worth listing the range of services to be provided. State clearly that you accept no responsibility for decisions affecting the assignment taken without your knowledge or out of your control. Any variations to the specification should be between you and the client, confirmed in writing and only executed when signed off by the client. All terms and conditions should be agreed early on, and in writing, whether in a proposal, contract or letter. Specific terms of business should explicitly cover the following:

- Payment of invoices
- Method of payment
- Chargeable expenses
- Travelling
- Hotel and subsistence
- Printing, copying, courier and other expenses
- Cancellation and postponement fees
- Pre-contract development work

Managing the cash

Managing cash flow is the key issue. Cash is the lifeblood of any business and getting paid promptly is a top priority. Always remember that your objective is to generate regular income. The reality is that you will be faced with either feast or famine. Be prudent in managing cash and start with getting paid.

There are four important aspects to getting paid promptly.

1. Ensure that your sales documents, goods and services are satisfactory.
2. Understand your customers' payment systems.
    - Find out what information is required before an invoice is accepted and processed.
    - Establish who deals with your account. Make friends with accounts payable.

- Establish when businesses pay their suppliers. Remember they manage their cash too.
3. Chase payments if they are overdue.
   - Make clients aware of your credit terms.
   - Chase up using the phone, email, letter or in person.
   - Keep up the pressure.
   - Charge interest on outstanding debts.
4. Structure your payment terms. Get paid an engagement fee and monthly payments.

Legal services

In corporate life, we had a love-hate relationship with the lawyers. Hate might come to mind first. They were the people who told you what you couldn't do, what was wrong with what you had done or how many years in jail were possible.

So where does a Portfolio Professional go for the expertise, and what are the key issues that an independent business has to worry about in legal terms? The short answer is don't try and do it yourself, closely followed by don't go to costly lawyers too early. Whoever looks after your legal affairs must be a specialist with an understanding of the particular issues affecting advisors, consultants and the like. Whatever the commercial activity you are engaged in, you need to be aware of the legal issues involved. While the full range of business law is vast, the key points the owner of a start-up business needs to know are relatively straightforward. Understanding the basics of business law will help you to avoid any legal difficulties.

Which laws affect you?

At the heart of business law are two specific areas. First, contracts between yourself and your suppliers and customers, and second, those relating to trade covering how you are allowed to sell and what restrictions apply.

Other major areas of business law are:

- forming a business
- tax and NI
- premises
- employment law.

You may not need to use a lawyer's services in setting up as a sole trader, however it would be wise to employ one if you are drawing up any form of contract. If you form a company, it is important to avoid the potential pitfalls of commercial law. Whoever looks after your legal affairs must be a specialist in small businesses. Should you become involved in drafting contracts for clients, you should have them drawn up or checked by someone who specialises in contract law.

Dispute handling

Finally, what happens if you get in to a dispute? Remember these can be time-consuming, expensive and damaging. Time taken in sorting it out is the lost opportunity cost of doing business elsewhere. The cost of further action can often be greater than the value of the disputed transaction. Try to keep it out of the hands of lawyers if at all possible and endeavour to resolve it on an informal basis. Consider the following issues.

- Always keep calm, being polite and sympathetic. It may help pacify the customer and reduce your stress.
- Are your goods or services wholly or partly at fault?
- Seek a third party opinion.
- Can you reach a compromise?
- Is your reputation at risk or just your pride?
- Is the dispute with a valued customer?
- Are your records and documents up to date?

Keep a comprehensive record of the dispute. It's invaluable if you wish to take further action. Consider when entering into a contract to add a no lawyer clause, or alternatively a clause on how disputes might be handled and resolved without recourse to legal action. Consider the use of arbitration or mediation in a dispute. The Centre for

Effective Dispute Resolution (CEDR) can be found at www.cedr.com and its library provides a number of contractual clauses which may be useful. CEDR's mission is to encourage and develop mediation and other cost-effective dispute resolution and prevention techniques in commercial and public-sector disputes.

Further reading and advice

Much can be written about the above subject and space demands that this chapter can only scratch the surface. Wherever possible, or if you are in doubt you should always consult a professional advisor, particularly in areas such as legal matters and finance. In addition HMRC provide very helpful guides for the layman starting in business. They are free. Also any of the large clearing banks will willingly provide business planning documentation, and cash flow planning software which are invaluable. Just ask to see the new business advisor.

In addition you will find that a number of specialist books are published on each and every area discussed above. I would particularly recommend four as additional reading. They are *Running Your Own Business* by Robert Leach and John Dore, *Running a Home Based Business* by Diane Baker, *Going it Alone* by Sally Garratt, and *Taxation Simplified* edited by Tony Jones.

Happy reading ... and good business.

Christopher Lyons has developed a portfolio of interests advising a wide range of companies, and the public sector clients, on strategic and financial matters following his extensive career in banking and finance. He has served on the board of a number of domestic and international companies and currently chairs the Board of an AIM listed Health and Social Care Infrastructure business. Additionally, Christopher provides specialist mergers and acquisitions services to corporate clients through his work with Beer Mergers Limited and Foreign Exchange service advice to clients. He is a visiting Fellow of Kingston Business School and on the MBA advisory Board of Durham Business School.

IT FOR THE PORTFOLIO LIFESTYLE

BY CHRIS MEGGS

You may have chosen the PP path, it may have chosen you (a stroke three years ago provided me with the opportunity to consider PP as an alternative to the 'norm' I had been pursuing all my life.)

We are all different when it comes to IT needs and IT skills. The subject is vast and complex. In writing this chapter, we will have to make some assumptions. As a Portfolio Professional in using IT you will have some fairly simple goals. For example, you may want to:

- Work productively
- Appear professional to your client base and prospective clients
- Remain on the right side of the law
- Remain in touch.

Work productively

You don't want to spend weeks learning how to code technology as a career. Technology is a means to an end, not the end in itself. Besides, there are many very competent technologists out there. You are now an entrepreneur and as such will have to make daily decisions about whether to commit your time and effort to some aspect of your assignment or to delegate it to others under your control, provided your client or the security regime will allow it. Check the sub-contractor section of your client contract: check your ISO20007 compliance guidelines. One aspect that we will be covering later is the rise of acceptable out-sourcing agents, who will perform less skilled work with cheaper talents than your own.

The object of your creation, the item the client has engaged with you to produce, is only a part of the deliverable. Part of the product as the client sees it, and an item you will be involved in, is delivery.

Your aim should be to make the delivery, reception and understanding of your product as frictionless as possible for the client. You must take into account their word processor, its version and level number, the security they impose on documents or products entering their operation, the standards of document layout, fonts and so on. These seem small when iterated like this, but any deviation will cost days in turn round and may actually affect one's contracted delivery date.

Appear professional to the client

Whatever your charge rate, even if the work you are undertaking is **pro bono**, your client and its staff will expect certain standards from you. Here I do not seek to offer you advice on how to be a successful consultant, there are other places for such guidance, but professionalism will apply to your product and the delivery of it. As such, the details in the latter part of the previous paragraph apply.

Remain on the right side of the law

Your choice of actions are outside the scope of this book, but what you produce and how you do it is not. Most of the following advice needs to be read and accepted only once, it should remain with you for the balance of your life as a PP. It mostly concerns using other people's work, and is divided into three escalating levels of importance and complexity. The three levels are:

- **Copyright** – a fairly simple law to understand and to practise. Copyright is defined as a legal right created by the law of a country that grants the creator of an original work exclusive rights to its use and distribution, usually for a limited time. The *exclusive rights* are not absolute, they are limited by *limitations and exceptions to copyright law*, including fair use. www. copyrightservice.co.uk contains details on how to copyright your work and how to avoid using other peoples copyrighted products.

- **Trademark** – a trademark is a recognisable sign, design or expression which identifies products or services of a particular source from those of others. It would be unusual for you to come across this, but details on how to apply (it costs!) can be found at: www.gov.uk/register-a-trademark.

- **Patent** – a set of rights assigned to an inventor or assignee for a limited time in a specific geography covering a product or process. Patent law is long and complex. As such, there are a myriad of firms who claim to expedite the process for you.

A general piece of advice here: usually, by contacting the author of the piece to be copied, authority to publish will usually be granted, providing you attribute the author. It will also expand your network – no bad thing. It is generally better to publish your idea as soon as possible, despite patent and copyright law. The downside is that the idea may be copied, rushed to market and even maybe patented. It is this author's opinion that early publication is preferable to waiting for someone else to move ahead. At least, in the former case, you may be retained as a consultant for the implementation of the idea. You could always come to some arrangement with the publisher of the idea; people who invent things are rarely in a position to exploit them, whereas that is potentially your prime mission.

Remain in touch

We are all familiar now with the concept of 6 degrees of separation, Bacon or the Erdős number theory. It's time to play your part. **Networking** has begun to gain a slightly distasteful aura, but probably because of the crass way some practitioners go about their craft. One can network passively simply by NOT discarding contact information that comes into your possession. There are several software products on the market to support the avid contact collector, indexed by almost any attribute you care to mention. *My belief* is that maintenance of these databases becomes costly and ineffective. Better to follow the guidance of Heather White in her chapter on Networking.

Are you IT literate?

This section is primarily aimed at those who believe that they are. The cobbler's children go unshod.

As an ex-It consultant, even I have difficulty in keeping up with technology and maintaining a full range of IT resources. The speed with which technology changes makes it difficult to keep up to date. However by taking a small amount of time to learn and refresh the basics then your productivity can soar.

One can always benefit from a refresher course. Consider taking the European Computer Driving Licence. It does the same job as a driving test, except it's for computers. The basic rules are:

- Understand what your client expects
- Increase your productivity
- Avoid simple security errors
- Keep software up to date
- Plan your handling of intellectual property
- The known unknowns (à la Donald Rumsfield)

Understand what your client expects

It's not just about the commissioned product (report, research or whatever) but also about its usability in the client environment. So, can he receive it? Is it readable by his software, including version and level? Do his firewalls prevent Word documents passing through? Is it named according to convention, and version control? Is the document formatted? Does it have to go through a review cycle?

As mentioned before, the client will expect the service delivered in a consumable format. Does delivery include a presentation? Does the review cycle have a sign-off? These things are important and can adversely affect the true delivery date. To protect yourself and to get a better idea of cost, these things should be detailed in the contract, or at least in the schedule of the contract covering the deliverable.

Increase your productivity

This certainly does not mean do everything yourself. Is it really useful coding up the mainline of the program in c++ if this means going on a course, albeit a 'Dummies' one? Effective use of your time may be to delegate this piece of work to an expert – there are plenty around. This will also test your entrepreneurial skills.

Avoid simple security errors

Learn your basic IT operations. Backing up is all well and good. Have you tried to restore from the backup? Practice on a cold bare machine until it works flawlessly. I have used Western Digital's Passport for some time and have no complaints. That A4 pad you cart round with you to jot down important notes or to create part of your report in an airport lounge? What would happen if you lost it, think of the inability of recalling those exact pithy words and phrases, think of what the contents may give to your competitors!

Keep software up to date

Some hackers hack for a living, they are working while you sleep. As a matter of policy, keep all software up to date. Errors caused by back-levelled software are guaranteed to bite only at the worst possible time. It's also no fun to run out of licence for a key piece of your delivery machine. All these expenses are tax-deductible. They also need to be factored into the cost of doing business when you quote for a job.

Plan your handling of intellectual property

You should also establish how you are going to handle intellectual property, both up and down the chain. What can you legitimately use from your previous employment? Have you at any point signed the Official Secrets Act? Does your contract with your client cover IPR? It's no fun to cover it in a court room afterwards with expensive lawyers champing at the bit. Get hold of a pro forma Non-Disclosure Agreement, downloadable from the web. Incidentally, if this document contains the word 'copyright' anywhere, usually in the footer, then an eagle-eyed operative will not photocopy it for you. I speak from experience!

When we are talking about security, are you cleared at any level? SC (Security Clearance) or the dreaded DV (Developed Vetting)? Get professional advice, talk with the Security Officer at your employers or clients, they are much nicer than painted.

The known unknowns

Get a feel for knowing what you don't know – most of us are unconsciously incompetent when it comes to IT. Compose a list of your core competencies and a similar list of incompetencies. Make it a background task to cover the latter list with a list of trusted people who can cover the gaps for you. Understand what they would charge for such a piece of work, their availability and so on. Smooth the path with them so that nothing goes wrong halfway down the slipway.

Where do you intend to make an office?

Even in today's Internet age, and maybe all the more because of it, it is possible to operate from a variety of locations and types of location. Consistency of operation will be the key. Understand that there are key differences between working from a stable location and working on the move. Despite all claims to the contrary, mobile devices, while excelling at connectivity and consuming material, are still not a good tool for creating material. Using the same tool for the same material at different locations can also ease the pain. Never before has the acronym KISS held stronger meaning.

Small offices

Small shared space offices often provide limited IT support. It may require you to conform to some guidelines and practices that seem foreign, but it will be worth the effort to conform for the level of service you will get back. Beware of becoming the office IT go-to expert yourself; you will often end up in an unpaid, unproductive, pressurised position helping others at your own expense. Not to mention the liability issues. If using a shared machine, be sure to delete all cookies and auto-complete data from the machine each time you leave. This applies to machines found in the lobby areas of hotels as well. Once bitten, author.

Working from home

This is probably the most often chosen method, the spare bedroom or garage turned into your office-at-home. It may not work for everyone with interruptions, background noise and babysitting being potentially intrusive. However develop good working habits and reduce stress by reading the chapter on 'Smart Moves' later in the book

If you can do it, then fine, and there are some tax advantages too but discuss these with your friendly HMRC representative and beware traps such as Capital Gains Tax and the like. At home, you will still need to access the internet, partly for your own purposes, partly to remain in contact with your client base and potential clients. Do you need a PC? Probably and the range of solid, reliable PCs is growing every day. Buy one with a good repair/return policy and keep it simple.

Similarly with printers: many exist now, most will operate wifi. Whether this mode of operation will be reliable in your house is up to a suck-it-and-see approach, the backup is to use a cable connection (then at least no one else can jump on and use all your paper and ink!) The ability to scan is also very useful these days, my advice would be to invest in a printer/scanner all in one device with a document feed option. Depending on usage you have a cost-benefit analysis to do in relation to the cost of your machine and consumables such as ink.

Mobile technology and working

Mobile technology is exactly what the name implies – technology that is portable. Examples of mobile IT devices include: laptop, tablets and netbook computers, smart phones, global positioning system (GPS) devices and wireless debit/credit card payment terminals.

Mobile devices can be enabled to use a variety of communications technologies such as:

- **wireless fidelity** (Wifi) – a type of wireless local area network technology
- **bluetooth** – connects mobile devices wirelessly
- **'third generation'** (3G), 'fourth generation' (4G), **global system for mobile communications** (GSM) and **general packet radio service** (GPRS) data services – data networking services for mobile phones
- **dial-up services** – data networking services using modems and telephone lines
- **virtual private networks** – secure access to a private network

It is therefore possible to network the mobile device to a home office or the internet while travelling. Mobile computing can improve the service you offer your customers. For example, when meeting with customers you could access your customer relationship management system via the internet – allowing you to update customer details whilst away from the office.

More powerful solutions can link you directly into the office network while working off site, for instance to access your database or accounting systems.

This leads to great flexibility in working – for example, enabling home working, or working while travelling. Increasingly, networking 'hot spots' are being provided in public areas that allow connection back to the office network or the internet. The growth of cloud computing has also impacted positively on the use of mobile devices, supporting more flexible working practices by providing services over the internet.

There are costs involved in setting up the equipment and training required to make use of mobile devices. Mobile IT devices can expose valuable data to unauthorised people if the proper precautions are not taken to ensure that the devices, and the data they can access, are kept safe. My earlier comments refer.

Cloud computing

Cloud computing offers businesses a way of managing their data, hardware and software requirements online. Documents, emails, customer information, business applications and other assets can all be stored externally – 'in the cloud' – to be accessed using a computer, laptop or smartphone with an internet connection. You can use cloud computing as a stand-alone solution or in addition to your existing IT infrastructure.

Cloud computing can help you: reduce hardware and software costs, support more flexible working, practices, scale your IT systems, reduce your need for in-house IT support and access reliable and secure back-up for your business' data.

Cloud computing can provide a number of useful applications for the Portfolio Professional including, sales tools, office software, CRM software, HR software and payroll software. Many such applications are available on Software as a Service basis- where the software is maintained an upgraded by the provider and accessed through your web Browser. ,

You should consider firstly trialling any services with non-critical applications, or processes and before implementing cloud computing you need to consider the following:

- **data protection** – what measures are offered to protect and secure your information, and where do the liabilities reside in case of a breach. Establish if the provider's servers are outside of the EU and what jurisdiction rules apply.
- **business continuity** – what back up systems operate, what service guarantees apply and what happens with downtime, service loss or security breach?
- **service levels** – what support is offered free or otherwise? What financial compensation applies in the event of service loss?
- **pricing** – what are the costs and what are the deals?
- **flexibility** – what are the options to upgrade or downgrade services in the future?
- **contract terms** – what are your obligations with early termination or change of provider

And remember, in order to work effectively using the cloud you need a fast internet connection. Leased lines or superfast broadband internet connections are preferable to standard ADSL lines as they support faster upload and download speeds.

When configuring your mobile and at-home setup, the author believes in building in redundancy – have more than one phone provider, say a different supplier for your mobile and home, and have more than one route to the web, say a 3G or 4G main connection and a backup ADSL. At home, be careful with your phone package. Many suppliers now offer bundles ostensibly attractive to the small businessman. Other than those that route mobile to home or vice-versa, these offerings should be carefully examined.

Ask to see a demonstration and put yourself in place of an irate or busy potential client. Is it a frictionless experience? Do you eventually understand what he wants, when he called and how he wants you to react and in what timeframe? Cliff Russell, the previous author of this section, wholeheartedly recommends the **Vonage** phone setup. Details available at www.vonage.co.uk. I include Cliff's write-up verbatim:

Vonage plugs into your normal phone and broadband router. You use your PC to set up the Vonage box which provides very powerful call handling features. My personal setup is that a user rings me at my home office land line number, this rings 3 times, if it's not answered it checks to see if my mobile is available, and if it isn't it diverts to voicemail, turns voicemail into an email and then sends it to me. You will also find conference calling and other premium features included. There is no line rental as such, making it ideal. Once set up, you don't need the PC on. When you are abroad or away, you take your vonage adaptor with you and plug it in elsewhere, and it will ring. Nobody needs to know that you Surrey office is temporarily operating out of Uzbekistan. For a tenner a month and as many calls as you can make it represents excellent value for you and those who may call you internationally.

Sold me, Cliff!

Skype offer some phone call features, including picture communication. Seemed like a great deal at the time, but beware, Skype has been bought out by Microsoft. Make of that what you will.

0870-0845 – Initially a good idea and easy to install/order, but calling them can be prohibitively expensive. Some phone providers, including Vodafone (usual disclaimers) offer a small monthly fee to cover calls to these numbers. You can reference www.SayNoto0870.com to get an equivalent land number connection.

Remote access

For remote access to your main PC when you are away from home, two products offer the same basic service. These are www.gotomypc.com and www.logmein.com. These allow you to securely log in to your home PC from most corporate or café-type locations. There will be some latency in the connection. Remember though, you are essentially opening your PC, and storage connected to it, to the outside world, only protected by the password and security wrappings you put round it. It is likely there will be further technological advances beyond the time of this book.

Security

You simply MUST get on top of this issue. Even taking the first one or two steps will cut down your vulnerability significantly. Use strong passwords, use different ones for different services you sign up for, change passwords regularly and frequently. Install anti-virus and firewall products and keep them up to date. Most will update themselves, but it costs nothing to force them to check their currency and updates tend to fall within the package price.

Nothing is worse than turning on a PC that you haven't used for months and finding the security products you have installed are out of date. Bring them up to date before you go online, before you read your emails. Backup security is not just about securing data at rest, there is data in motion (email and the like): this is covered more in the email section later. Remember the trusted position that you have established with your clients – don't lose or corrupt his data as well as your own. And, how is your professional liability cover by the way? Which brings us on to.....

Backups

One in a hundred of us back up our data Of those, one in a thousand test the restore. To be fair, it's a pain to test out. Full restore, partial restore, bare metal restore. They all need testing regularly, perhaps not frequently. Consider staging your backup, with a total backup done, say once a year, and held offsite. More frequently accessed backups held in a more accessible medium and held more locally. You may be asked to describe your data security by your client, maybe even demonstrate it. Be prepared. I use Passport from Western Digital. Usual disclaimers apply.

They are on the web now for a reasonable cost, depending on data volumes. The software sits in the background of your PC and notices each time you modify a document. It then backs it up to its own USB-attached disk storage. Retrieval is by document, folder, document type, name, etc. It does not seem to take much power from the PC, but will spend some time at start-up indexing recently changed files. But still worth it, *in my opinion*.

Your presence on the Web – web hosting

You may at some point consider having a website. Be cautious, it's a big step and will take a great deal of your time. Will it significantly improve your chances of landing a client deal or expose you to a new client base? Would a typical client of yours go to the web to find out about you or the services he requires, or will he use more conventional means?

It may make you feel important. It will also, if it is effective, bring in a whole raft of near-miss enquiries that may well sap away your efforts and time. As Churchill once said "one will rarely achieve one's goal if one stops to throw stones at every dog that barks along the way." 20% of your clients will bring 80% of your revenue. Ditch the 80% and spend the energy on the 20%. Research by Russam GMS shows that about one third of total market assignments go through intermediaries, with the rest sourced directly. The smart thing to do is target your marketing effort directly at end-user clients – your website should be a key part of this, and content is the key. The chapter on *Presenting You* has useful tips on organising and presenting your content,in order to hold the reader's attention without compromising on quality.

A website is your advert to the outside world. Existing clients are unlikely to look at your website for anything other than basic contact details. You may have a discussion forum or a repository for technical papers but a website for a Portfolio Professional should primarily generate leads. If you are not clear about what you offer then you will give a confused message. Your main audiences are likely to be:

- Social contacts
- Previous employers
- Business contacts
- Alumni network
- Trade operators
- Headhunters
- Management consultancies.

Consider the above and ask – how could they get to do business with me? More to the point, isn't the majority of what you want to say and who you want to say it to manageable by a service like Linkedin (www.linkedin.co.uk)? Still not as chatty as Facebook, thank heavens, and useful, especially as a Premium User. It also allows you to upload adverts for your skills, thinly disguised as research papers. Discussion forums and contacts get you noticed. The basic service is free to join, give it a try.

Also advertising your offering/capabilities, and a place to source the word processing of your papers cheaply and effectively is a website called Elance (www.elance.com). It's your turn to be the entrepreneur! I suggest you test the market with one or two simple tasks that you need done. You will need to hone your specification skills.

If however you choose the website route then in order to improve website traffic, take the time and effort to explore ways to increase website search engine rankings. The most important thing is to create the website with interesting and desirable products, services and/or content. Some tips to do this are:

- **Use keywords** – place primary and secondary keywords in the first paragraph of articles and information, and then spread them evenly throughout the remainder of a web page. Be careful not to make the placement too dense in case it gets classified as spam.

- **Use market research** – perform market research to find target keywords to attract the most ideal customers. Put the keywords in the meta-tags, title, headings and sub-headings.

- **Employ a simple website design** – keep the website design simple. Customers must be able to easily navigate between the web pages to find what they are looking for. If it's too complicated or has too much flash, potential customers can get frustrated and then will not want to continue to find information, or buy products or services. Try not to clutter the web page with flashing advertisements or banners. If the website sells products, ensure that payment and shipping methods are simple. It is essential to have as simple a checkout process as possible, for the smoothest customer experience. Customers will be more likely to return to an easy to navigate website.

- **Search engine submission** – submitting web pages to popular search engines can be an effective method to increase web traffic. Submit them manually rather than use automated services, since some employ spam and scam tactics that search engines have policies against. Be aware of search engine news such as that offered by SEOmoz, which offers valuable tips and information about how to increase website rankings and on which sites to register, e.g. Google, Yahoo, Lycos and Alta Vista.

There are many online tools and utilities to keep track of how a website is performing. Be sure to use them.

- **Study competitor websites** – take a look at highly ranked websites. Study the website design, content, keywords and navigation. Web hosting operators should have available reports and logs to establish how web visitors find your site. Analyse visitor location, incoming sources and keywords being used to find your website.

- **Ensure the website is properly maintained** – hire professionals to handle the details effectively if you do not have the time. The money spent on maintenance may well worth the cost that a lack of visitors, traffic and less sales will ultimately cost.

Consider your website to be an ever evolving, dynamic sales tool – to be designed and monitored just as a traditional business relies upon customer relationships and new prospects.

Email – 'a great servant, a poor master'

There has been much written about email. It, perhaps more than any other application other than SMS text and Twitter has dominated the communication scene in the early part of this century. Here we will visit some of the handles we have on the product, seeing how we can modify it to be a productive part of our box of tricks.

Email requires a personal discipline to prevent it being a time wasting diversion. Fortunately we can tune it up, organise it. Many people only access their mail a certain number of times a day, say before breakfast and at the end of the working day. Even so, we must be wary of getting prematurely involved in conversations.

It is also useful to amend your signature – that piece of text that the email program appends to each of your outbound messages – to inform the person with whom you are holding a conversation that, while their input, contribution and opinion are of interest and of worth to you, in order to grant the message your full attention, you will only be looking at your mail at the following times.... Setting their expectations will reduce their disappointment at not getting an instant reply.

I also create a number of folders, by recipient, by topic, whatever, and during my initial scan of my Inbox, I file the inbound mail accordingly. This operation does several things at the same time:

- It satisfies my feeling that I may be missing something
- It allows me to dump spam
- It organises my mail so that I can prioritise the full attention I need to grant it at a later date.

Some email products allow one to create automatic rules based on several attributes of the incoming message to provide some degree of automated organisation on your behalf. Be wary of using these, as you are now essentially "coding" and thus your product will need testing and debugging. However Google Desktop and Live Search could be used which will index everything on your hard drive , including photos, videos, e mails, documents attachments and more.

Email will also end up as a document repository and a forensic audit trail of activity. If you find a large amount of your emails contain attachments which you use as reference or as a base for email conversation, perhaps you need to question whether email is a satisfactory mechanism and repository. Would you and your communication partners be better off using discussion forums as you would if they were working with you in-house? One can expose SharePoint sites among a community for example.

Equally, a number of services providing collaboration are emerging. They have the advantage of removing the need to develop and maintain the product, an offsite storage capability and access from wherever you are in your new, mobile world. This also removes the need for version management of all the attachments you have received. Steer clear of build-it-yourself products like Sharepoint or any of the IBM Lotus Notes derivatives at first. Practice on the smaller services. They probably reduce the number of choices you have but what you lack in flexibility you will more than make up for in clarity and ease of use.

Never allow yourself to allow the development of the tool take priority in your investment of time and money. Remember your primary mission, a tool is exactly that – a tool, not an end piece in its own right. From personal experience I can tell you how easy it is to fool yourself. "Well, I need this type of service. There must be hundreds like me. Maybe I could develop and sell the tool." Slippery slope.

Many Portfolio Professionals will have multiple identities (see the section on Social Media). It would be wise to support this with multiple email accounts. People are wise and can spot the commonality of email addresses between different persona. This will also allow you to separate email conversations into buckets so that you are not easily distracted.

Moving documents around with email is easy. Too easy. It is also prone to creating huge security gaps in your (and your client's) organisations. If you are going to password protect a document, remember to send the password via another channel. Sounds obvious doesn't it? An encrypted CD containing passport applications was found recently, the password was written on the face of the CD in permanent ink. Ho hum.

The way you treat document storage AND transmission will be monitored as part of your organisation's compliance to security standards and ISO accreditation. A popular, effective and relatively simple way of transmitting secure documents is a technique called PGP. Find out about it on Wikipedia, it is supplied by many companies, among whom is one you will already of heard of in security circles – www.symantec.com. Next to an open Internet connection, email is the obvious hackers' route into your company, so treat it with the respect it deserves.

Life with limited IT support

It is likely that you will soon discover that limited IT support with no in-house IT department will be limiting. So what are your strategies? The following are suggested:

1. Learn to set up your PC from scratch. It can be easier than you think.
2. If you don't want to learn how to reconfigure your PC – be ultra conservative. No special applications, no Games, no Music archives, and don't let the kids use it !
3. So steps 1 and 2 fail and your PC has crashed. Find a local IT professional , and befriend them. Explore working on a skills swap basis, e.g. business planning or good wine.
4. Go back to the maker. Dell and Acer will do a system rebuild, but you need to back up all your data.
5. Go to your local PC computer superstore. Many have reasonably priced fixed menu servicing.

This chapter aims to give you a taste of the complexity, range and issues surrounding IT and the Portfolio Professional. Included are some useful tips, hints and areas to exercise caution. Good luck and if in doubt consult an expert.

Chris Meggs is a seasoned serial career proponent, coming from a trainee IBM Systems Engineer in the middle 60s through various stages to the business side of IT. He now acts as a bridge between the Boardroom and the technical shopfloor.

Cliff Russell wrote the original text of this section and we are all indebted to him for his contribution. He is a model example of the description "polymath" and can turn his considerable mental talents to almost any subject. He currently acts as an advisor to a solution provider in the banking and financial services sector.

PRESENTING YOU

BY CHRIS COLLINGBOURNE

As a Portfolio Professional, you're on your own. You have to be your sales department, marketing department and publicity machine rolled into one. So you must look for any opportunity to get your message over, to project yourself, to spread the word about You. It's yourself you are selling, yourself you are presenting, and it's vital to present yourself professionally in every possible situation. Remember the golden rule: 'It's first impressions that count'.

This piece looks at a number of these situations:

- presenting you in public speaking
- presenting yourself in a lift speech
- presenting yourself through your CV
- presenting yourself in one-to-ones including telephone and email
- presenting yourself via websites and social media

Public speaking

What's the best way of presenting yourself in the most authoritative form to the most number of people?

It's getting up on your feet and talking to as many people as possible – about what you do, about your expertise, about your beliefs.

Giving a presentation is probably the best form of exposure. At the close, you'll be approached by many of your audience wanting to learn more and benefit from your advice.

We see in the Chapter on Networking how important it is to be active in professional and trade bodies and how useful it can be to project yourself as an authority in a niche area of your chosen markets.

So speaking is a fantastic opportunity. When did you last make use of it? When volunteers were requested, did you put yourself forward?

Public speaking ranks alongside illness, death and darkness as one of the top human fears. One of the most difficult transitions we face in life is the few feet between talking sitting down and talking standing up. It's a short step which demands a giant leap in confidence.

But with such potentially great rewards, it's one we, as Portfolio Professionals, have to overcome. It can be learned, just as any other skill, practised and developed. And with the rest of the world sitting on their hands and avoiding it, speaking offers an enormous opportunity to shine.

Developing the skill

This article will give you a few key tips and pointers, but if you don't currently have the confidence then the best outcome from this piece is to encourage you to develop your skills.

There are some great books out there on speaking; one strong recommendation is Granville Toogood's *The Articulate Executive*.

Reading can give you some theory and tips but you then need practice, honing your skills with low-risk audiences.

Evening classes in public speaking are widely available, but the best choice is to join a local speakers club, where you can practice the art, and receive constructive criticism from fellow members.

Planning

It is said that for each minute of presentation we will spend an hour in preparation – that's for thinking time, analysis, planning, writing and rehearsing.

- Know your audience – how much do they know already, why are they there, what are their expectations.
- Know your environment – where will you stand, how do any visual aids work.

Remember the initials AUDIENCE that sum up the preparation:

Analysis, Understanding, Demographics, Interest
Environment, Needs, Customised, Expectations.

Once we know something about our target audience, we can start to plan. You can try a personal brainstorm – a little self indulgent, perhaps but it works.

Put your topic into the middle of a piece of A4 paper (larger if you have it to hand) and in spider-like form get as many thoughts as you can down onto your 'mind map'. Here's an example:

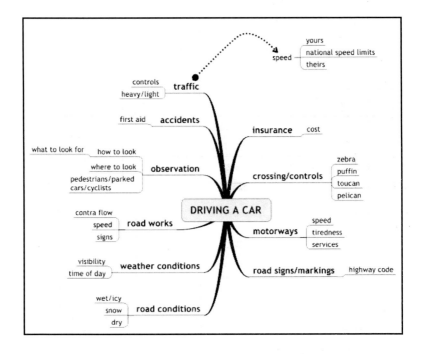

Figure 18

From the brain-storming, select your core message and a few key supporting themes. Cut out everything else.

- Be clear about what message you want to leave with your audience. What do you want them to remember a week later from your speech?
- Audience attention-spans are typically about 15 minutes. If you go over this, you are at risk. If your content doesn't fit

into 15 minutes, go back to your central message, cut out the excess and re-focus.

- Build a structure, and tell a story. Use the Three Tells:
  - Tell them what you are going to tell them.
  - Tell them.
  - Tell them what you have told them.
- Rehearse – not only for practice but to check your timing. Always plan to be under the allotted time.

Notes

For the few who can speak without notes, bask in the admiration from the rest of us.

If you need notes, try to keep them brief. Cards are the best form, containing just headings to keep you on track. Number the cards and ideally tag them together. Make the words big and few. If you prefer to start your preparation with a full script, gradually reduce it during rehearsing.

Visual aids

Do you need them? Do they add anything to your content or presentation?

If you have to use visual aids here are some rules to apply.

- Visuals can dominate. You're trying to sell yourself not the screen
- Never talk to the screen, it can't hear you.
- Don't start or end with slides
- Don't use screens with just script – they usually add very little. If you have to, don't read the words from the slide.
- Where slides can be useful is for charts, lists or quotations.
- Don't turn the lights down – it's you they've come to see.

Delivery

- Be conversational – short sentences, simple words, no buzzwords.

- Be yourself – behave naturally. Anything else will look and sound false.
- Make eye contact with a wide span of the audience. If you ignore them, they'll ignore you.
- Use stories to illustrate your theme.
- Silence is powerful. Deliver a key point and pause to let it sink in.
- Use tone of voice, pace and body language to enhance understanding of your message.
- Your body language reinforces your message. Keep an open posture at all times, spread rather than cross your arms. Use open hand gestures selectively to emphasise your message.

Start and finish

First impressions matter. You have about ten seconds to win over your listeners before they start mentally planning their next holiday or re-living their last game of golf.

These are the impact seconds. If you can use silence well (and it's an art in itself) then five seconds of silence will build anticipation. Then let them have it. A controversial statement, an apt quotation which focuses their minds. Learn your opening by heart; don't read it.

End strongly. It is the final impression that you leave in the minds of the audience that will linger the longest. Spend time working on this, combining pauses, intonation and alliteration to create a memorable closure. Encapsulate your presentation message in one or two sentences.

Short powerful sentences will hold the attention, emphasising key words. Deliver your summary where all can see you, come out from behind the lectern and stand authoritatively. Sit down with a bang, not a whimper. Don't expect a standing ovation, or confuse it with people leaving!

Beating nerves

All but the most experienced will feel nervous. Nervousness, such as butterflies, mouth dryness, sweaty palms etc. will prevent you from being natural. The chief cause of nervousness is fear. Preparation and rehearsal reduce the chances of this happening.

Laurence Olivier is reputed to have remarked, "When going on the stage, everyone has butterflies in the stomach. But the professionals have learnt to make them fly in formation."

Leave nothing to chance. If you feel tense beforehand, try to find a quiet place to relax and gather your thoughts. If you are aware of your nervousness, be positive about it. These feelings will soon become familiar, welcome their arrival as old friends, restyle them as anticipation and develop a calming ritual of deep breathing and exercises to eliminate tension. It will take your mind off things, and it's always comforting to have some undemanding repetitive actions prior to a stressful event.

- Being well-prepared controls nerves and builds confidence.
- Develop a calming routine to reduce tension before you speak.
- Remind yourself that the listeners are on your side, they want you to succeed.
- It helps to meet as many of your audience as you can beforehand.
- Remember they want to hear your message – that's why they turned up.

Passion

Hopefully you're speaking about something you're enthusiastic about. So let your enthusiasm show. Get the audience on your side by appealing to their emotions.

Feelings, not facts, move people. When you feel strongly about something, you tend to radiate energy.

In preparing, take time to discover why you care about what you are saying, and express those passions in a single sentence. Politicians call them sound bites!

Make yourself into a speaker

Developing your public speaking skills is one of the most important training recommendations for you as a Portfolio Professional. As well as the publicity and PR aspects, the skills you will learn and the confidence you will gain will impact on every aspect of your Portfolio Life.

Speaking can become enjoyable, can give you the kind of thrill that actors get on the stage – and it can boost your income.

Presenting you in a lift speech

There's an opportunity to present yourself to the right person when one of your target audience unexpectedly joins you in the lift at the ground floor and presses 22.

How can you explain in one sentence and 21 floors what it is you do? Here are the essential dos and don'ts:

Do:
- say what you offer and why it's better
- say who your target customer is and why they will buy from you.
- keep it simple
- use analogies, pictures so the message sticks in the mind.

Don't:
- get into the technology or the support team
- try to explain complex figures like the market size and shares
- use industry jargon.

It's just like presenting your own personal soundbite.

As you learn and refine your speech, it will come more naturally.

You'll find it useful in many different areas: the introduction to your Business Plan, your website home page, the start of your presentations and the top of your CV. Talking of which...

Presenting yourself through your CV

Portfolio Professionals are always looking to be contacted, and contracted so you'll often be asked for your latest CV.

PPs look at CVs in a special way. It's not a record of your history of jobs, but an opportunity to state who you are now and where you want to be in the future. Make sure it's continually updated to reflect your progress.

Make your CV stand out from the other chronological litanies of job titles and jargon. Don't just list your jobs, but highlight your skills and experience; remember 'the three past jobs' model from Chapter 4. Create a memorable sentence about where you're going from your Bridge Plan and put it at the top of the CV.

A resume that gets read shouldn't exceed two pages.

What do the readers want to know in what might be a 30-second sweep? Who did you work with, what real responsibilities did you have, what results did you achieve, what was it about you that made that happen? Why did you make the career moves you did and what did you learn along the way?

For style, use active words to describe skills, abilities, and achievements: promoted, delivered, achieved. Avoid the empty words like results-oriented, performance-led, added-value, and keep away from the subjective terms like surprisingly, incredibly, uniquely. Include statistics that add a context of size, but don't pepper the paper with too many.

In your CV, as in the lift, you have perhaps 30 seconds to make an impression; make sure you come off the page smiling, showing enough of your character to leave an enjoyable, memorable picture in the mind.

Presenting you in a one-to-one situation

All the advice given earlier regarding preparation work is just as valid for meeting people one-to-one. However, because you are sitting with a potential client, there are some more key points to use to your advantage.

Watch and listen to see how the other person likes to communicate.

Some of us have a leaning to being 'visual' communicators, some 'auditory', others 'kinaesthetic'.

- Visual people often keep their eyes up and breathe from the top of their lungs. They see pictures and say 'appears to me', 'how does that look', 'a bird's eye view'.

- Auditory communicators often move their eyes sideways and breathe from the middle of their chest. They learn by listening, like music, and memorise by steps, procedures and sequences. Their phone bill will be expensive! They say things like 'clear as a bell', 'let's hear your proposal', 'a word in your ear'.
- Kinaesthetics might be breathing from the bottom of the lungs and can move and talk quite slowly. They respond to physical things and touching and might use 'start from scratch', 'lay cards on the table', 'get to grips with', 'it feels to me like'.

Watching for their signals helps communications and lets you use the most underexploited art of listening: using your ears and mouth in the same 2:1 proportion. Establish good eye contact; it conveys genuine interest and self-confidence. Avoid nervous habits, e.g. tapping of pencils, rubbing your nose, etc. It is distracting. Be open minded and flexible. If you are too dogmatic, it will leave your host unconvinced as to your problem-solving capabilities

And if you can't see the person you're talking to, it's even more important to create the right impression; they'll be painting their own picture of you in their mind.

Here are some thoughts on presenting you by phone.

- If it's an important call, stand up to make it (you can hear the difference!).
- Treat the phone receptionist or PA as allies not barriers; genuine interest opens the lines and prompts future recognition.
- Check your messaging regularly; you don't call yourself often so callers will know before you if the tape's blurred, the message out of date, or reverted to the system's standard drawl.
- Make the messaging short and helpful; is there another number they can call? when are you back?
- When you leave a message, be sure to give your telephone number, slowly in order for the listener to write it down. Most people can remember about 7 digits in sequence, not the current 11 for national numbers. Repeat the number before you sign off.
- Taking a mobile call while paying for the taxi and running for the train may feel important to you, but incoherent to the caller; make the calls when you've time to give them full attention.

- Put your important callers in your list so you see their names when they call, they'll like to hear their name first not yours – 'oh, so I'm on his speed dials, am I?'

And what about email, another innovation that was to save so much time but has merely filled it a different way? Someone called it 'an electronic postcard' to signify its security and its transience. For Portfolio Professionals, it's great for speedy responses but can be either an opportunity or a danger to your image:

- Does a hotmail or yahoo address reflect your quality as a supplier or would your own domain name be a better option?
- Could you use your contact's actual name via the address book rather then just their email address?
- Make sure your 'out-of-office' message is on, is informative, and is off again when you're back.
- Do watch spelling and grammar as much as you would in a typed letter; the reader of your email will judge you on what she sees not on how quick you were.
- 'Please', 'thank you' and 'regards' take two seconds on the keyboard and may give you a distinctive stand-out in style!
- Every email is a contact opportunity, put your name and contacts in the sign-off – who knows who your email may be forwarded to?

Do evaluate your own performance, ask for feedback, and practice.

Remember 'the only way to discover the limits of the possible is to go beyond them to the impossible.'

Presenting your business

Image is important for your Portfolio Life. You must be professional and appear professional In everything you do Good presentation and communications can overcome the fact that you're working on your own. The issue is about promoting the image and value perception of You and your business.

Your opportunities to present what you do can come in many forms and Barnaby Wynter's chapter on Marketing will give you many pointers. What is crucial is that you are consistent across all the mediums you use . Here we explore some useful tips should you choose to use a virtual office, website, social media or video to promote who you are and what you do The subject matter is vast and punctuated with a language hitherto used by technology staff. It is worth researching the topic and getting knowledgeable advice.

The virtual office

Mail is now less important but you may still need to do bulk mailings. In addition your business card may do you no favours if it states "742 Evergreen Terrace" (the Simpsons' fictional address). Consider using a PO Box number or accommodation address, alternatively explore the use of a virtual office, from which you can hire a range of services to achieve the aims of promoting image and value perception

Virtual offices can offer the following whilst allowing you to work at the same time:

- A prestigious address
- A professional telephone answering service
- A reception and concierge service
- Response management to marketing and selling.
- Travel plan arrangements
- Resolution of IT infrastructure problems
- Managing mailings
- Production of presentations
- Web hosting and content

These are all necessary but time consuming distractions during which you should be building and managing your portfolio. Remember, the objective is to get a better work life balance not a worse one.

The website

If you are going to have your own website then it could be an invaluable aid as your advert to the world. However the key issue is content and it is something that has to be worked at continuously.

Content plays an important role in building a relationship with your readers and consequently, converting them into a buyer or a client. Along with good content writing, it's also quite a prerequisite to present content in an interesting and user friendly way. This goes a long way in improving and influencing your website's usability. Improving content means improving your website, and if you can, spend the money to get it done professionally.

Here are some useful tips on building, managing and presenting content on your website to hold the readers attention.

Headers – break up your content

Research has shown that internet users don't view content as a whole like reading a book, they view content in segments or blocks. Thus to hold their attention, it's important to present your content in blocks.

In addition, readers on the Web skim through content, skipping a great deal of material written in each article or block. Readers simply pick out what they are looking for. Hence, for a successful communication, it's absolutely necessary to make this task as easy as possible for the reader.

Easy-to-read content

The above point brings us to this requirement – content should be easy to skim through. Researchers have found out that people don't read in a straight manner, but rather in an F shaped structure.

Eye movement patterns are known to indicate movement from the left to the right and then skip content and go downwards, repeating the process. Hence, appropriate headers are good for online reading. Rather than bulk content, you can present your work with bullets and numbering, which improves readability.

Visually appealing content is easier to read than something that has no colour or flavour.

Search-engine-optimised content sections

The other advantage of having headers is using them as sections for inserting keywords. The best part about headers is that it satisfies your reader's desire to acquire information and makes the search engine spiders happy because they can crawl and index the right keywords.

Sequential importance of information

Readers like content to be simplified; place the most important information at the beginning. Sequential importance means putting the most crucial part on top and decreasing in importance or relevance the further you go down.

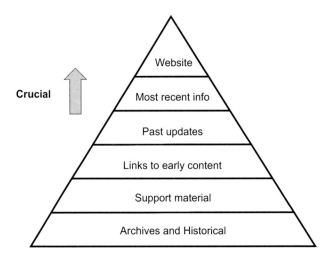

Figure 19. Progressive importance of information

Use images and strategic display

Research shows that...

- People pay attention to images well synchronised in content
- People also ignore images used for decoration or padding

So, as a Portfolio Professional, trying to improve the content of your website, you should be using images that are displayed smartly across your website. Content with images are appreciated by readers for visual appeal as well as relevance. Ensure that images are not too heavy and don't affect the page speed as this will have a negative influence on your website.

However above all it is what you write. Your website usability should be improved by keeping content and presentation in mind and at the same time, without compromising on quality.

Blogging

Blogs, or Web logs, are online journals. They are updated frequently. The updates or posts are usually a few sentences, and readers can respond to an entry online. They are a conversation but essentially an open postcard for anyone to read. While blogs are a great way to keep an audience up to date, as a professional you may wish to exercise discretion in this area. Writers often scorn bloggers, because their informal online writing rarely benefits from a good editor. Blogs are known for their casual writing and unpredictable subject material. The best blogs have proven that – regardless of punctuation and spelling – even "novice" writers can be entertaining enough to attract a broad audience.

Bloggers with an engaging subject have the advantage of inherently interesting material, but even mundane material can attract an audience if you have an engaging style and voice. There are three guiding principles to writing a successful blog. Firstly develop a style and tone appropriate to your subject material. Secondly, post often, even if they are short. Lastly allow or invite your readers to comment. For further advice on blog-writing see the chapter 'Writing a Good Blog' in Janine Warner's book *Creating Family Web Sites For Dummies.* Note that you need to be mindful of the impression you create and your audience and avoid publishing matter which may be sensitive, or that you wouldn't tell your mother or a vicar.

The content is the relatively simple part. Getting started and avoiding pitfalls is a little more complex and which technology to use is not within the scope of this chapter. There are plenty of Technologists and Bloggers offering step by step guides, but remember that for many this is a moneyspinner. Research the issues and understand them, as they could have a huge effect on your future blog.

The important decision to make is to select a domain name and it is advisable to using a .com, .net or .org name. Secondly, you will need a host platform. The internet is littered with adverts for free blogging service platforms like Blogger.com, Typepad.com and WordPress.com. If you choose this route they will host your blog for you on their own domain. You will get a "subdomain" and your website link will look something like http://mycookingblog.blogger.com. However, be warned they may be free – but as we know there is never a free lunch! The catch is you do not own the Blog, or its contents. You have no control over presentation, what adverts appear next to it and if they don't like you, you will get evicted with little recourse. All the content, backlinks and traffic gone in an instant.

Find a Webhost that provides the online storage that allows visitors to access your blog. Find a host you can trust with your baby (your blog), so you won't end up paying someone to repair or reboot your blog after your really cheap host lets you down. Read the reviews, and be prepared to pay for the service. In this game, it's service that counts so ensure you choose a quality customer service with 24/7 support through chat, email or phone.

Presenting on video

The camera lens can be likened to an intense robotic stare .However, you also need to remember that your viewing audience sees you through that eye – so what it captures is very important when it comes to compiling your web videos.

Presenting on video requires a completely different skill set from live presenting. Being able to speak to a live audience does not necessarily mean you will come across well on-screen.

When members of an audience are watching a presenter on stage, they have choices about where to look. They can look at the speaker, the stage, the PowerPoint presentation, other audience members, or more often their cell phones and laptops. The level of scrutiny an audience has towards the stage presenter is greatly reduced due to the distance the audience is from the speaker.

Presenting to camera is like having your viewer standing 4 feet away from you – you are under a microscope! The camera shows everything, tension, nervousness, bulging eyes, reading an autocue. And is that a real smile or a fake? In creating your video, it is about preparation and knowing what to do at the right time. To produce good quality videos it is about what to say, how to say it, eye contact, how to speak on camera, making yourself get used to the camera. Here are a number of suggestions:

Dressing appropriately

Dress to look the part. Dress appropriately as it creates an impression. Prior to a video shoot, consider:

- What is your role in the video?
- What is your position in the video?
- What is the purpose of the video?

If your role is to demonstrate something in the video, dress in a way that will enhance the performance itself. If you want to demonstrate ship security precautions at sea, wearing the appropriate gear in your video is more appropriate rather than wearing a suit. For purposes of position, dress appropriately to reflect the position you are holding in your organization or business.

Consider the following when deciding what to wear for a video:

- Plain clothing is better than tightly-patterned ones. Pin stripes and checks can easily create optical illusions on video.
- Avoid shiny and stripped outfits. Striped clothing can introduce shimmers and waving patterns in your video. .
- When wearing a tie, keep it simple. Avoid thin lines, complex patterns, bright oranges and reds as they will create some shimmers in the video.

- Wear makeup that will add value to the final video. Concealing blemishes and any spots that may attract the attention of the viewers.
- Avoid jewellery that reflects light, makes distractive noise or prevents you to perform your role appropriately in the video.
- Opt for solid colours when choosing shirts. Blue, and beige work well. Avoid bright white because it will disturb the contrast of the video.

Don't look scripted

Unless you are a natural, appearing for the first time on camera may be like a rabbit in the headlamps. To avoid looking nervous and stiff, you need to practice. Practice helps most actors avoid looking scripted. When being filmed, ensure that you are relaxed and smile.

1. Practice enough to shed the look of being scripted and stiff. Project confidence and a deep understanding of the subject you are presenting on video.
2. If you opt to use a script go over it until you are comfortable. Choose a familiar subject matter and be clear when presenting.
3. If possible, do retakes and watch them on real television or a computer monitor to get the impression of the exact output.

Confidence and relevance

Viewers of your video must have confidence in you, so when creating the video, it is important to be relevant to the needs of the viewer and to instil confidence. Confidence can be brought about using examples, tonal variations and mere facts. Some customers are already aware of you, so don't gloss over the truth; put it out there instead and do it confidently. Do the same for any shortcomings or a different side you are presenting in the video. In a nutshell, follow these tips:

1. Be audible enough, but don't shout.
2. Highlight the main facts of your video and explain them clearly.
3. Give relevant examples and demonstrations.

4. Connect with your audience using your eyes, so expressions on your face should be appropriate and friendly.

The purpose of adding video to your website is to ensure that you communicate and engage your audience viewers. Remember videos are a way through which your audience will virtually meet you. Therefore, make them look professional.

Chris Collingbourne's experience across financial services, retailing, wholesaling and manufacturing has given a unique perspective on Presenting in many different guises. A Portfolio Professional for 18 years, Chris is now putting theory into practice in the hospitality, sport and leisure markets.

NETWORKING

BY HEATHER WHITE

To be a successful business owner or portfolio worker you need to be a great networker, it is your prime route to market.

Readers will include those of you who love networking, who get it and just need to hone their skills, and those who have tried it, hate it and need to be convinced of the need to do it. Whoever you are, this chapter sets out clear steps to help you build this important skill.

To get started we have to address a number of key questions...

What is networking?

There are many definitions of networking with the most commonly used expression being:

'Developing long-term relationships for mutual gain.'

Although a reasonable definition it has two problems, firstly, it's not exactly very exciting and secondly, the very essence of networking is somehow lost. So let's look at what makes networking happen. By addressing this question we add a practical dimension to the definition. To understand what makes networking happen, reflect for a minute and ask yourself:

- Why would you refer a contact to someone?
- Why do you trust certain people? What have they done to earn your trust?
- Why do you want to stay in touch with some people and not others?

The answers transform the definition of networking into:

'Leaving a positive residual energy with others which inspires mutually beneficial behaviours and actions'

.....using these definitions:

- Residual = ongoing or lasting for a long time or re-creating
- Energy = my essence, my personality and my values

Networking can only happen when you have met the right people, created the right impact and built rapport and trust. All too often people turn up to an event or meeting to see what they can get out of it. The moment they do this they send out signals and, in the same way that a dog can smell fear, business people can instantly sense the pursuit of a selfish agenda.

How do the best networkers behave?

It is important to understand the difference between 'doing networking' and 'being a professional networker'.

Someone who goes out 'hungry', to as many events as possible and with little thought for anyone else, is 'doing networking'. These people usually make contact because they want something.

Someone who wants to develop a long-term relationship for mutual benefit and who is prepared to work at that relationship can be called a professional networker. These people often become "friends".

To have a successful portfolio career you must become a professional networker.

Case Study A - 'doing networking'

A business owner attends a business seminar with a key speaker. The business owner's objective is to meet as many people as possible so he can to give out his business cards. Time is short so he rushes from one group to another. He pushes into groups, often interrupting conversations. He quickly says who he is and what he does, hands out his cards and moves on. It's easy to tell that he is not listening to other people because his face is nodding but his eyes are vacant. If he does identify a potential buyer he brightens up and focuses, ignoring everybody else.

Don't you just hate meeting this type of person? Imagine what he is doing to his business and personal reputation!

Case Study B - the professional networker

A business owner attends a business seminar where there is a key speaker. This business owner's objectives are to learn as much as she can from the speaker's presentation, meet a few key people and make a couple of useful contacts. She will be satisfied if she only meets 4 or 5 people during the whole event. She joins groups and makes sure she engages and participates in any conversations that are in progress, adding useful comments or questions. She demonstrates a natural interest in the members of the group and focuses on building rapport. She is not worried if she doesn't connect directly with people this time because she understands that their paths are likely to cross again. She only offers her business card if she feels she has established an element of trust and respect. She knows her business reputation is at risk if she makes a nuisance of herself.

Isn't this the person you would rather meet at an event?

In networking, it is important that your actions clearly demonstrate that you:

- like people
- are willing to spend time with the people
- are really interested in their issues
- are willing to share what you want
- are very willing to share useful information
- are the same person with everyone
- believe in friendship, trust and good, old-fashioned respect for others

Here is the good news! If all you need to do is hone your relationship skills, your success is in the bag. Think about it - there is one thing in this world over which we have complete control and that it is how we behave.

What is the case for networking?

Here are the top ten reasons for networking as defined by a group of MBA students:

1. It opens career doors.
2. It is a way of gaining industry knowledge.
3. It is a way of monitoring competitor activity.
4. It is a way to influence key people.
5. It is a means of creating a strong virtual team.
6. Listening to people is a way of creating new ideas.
7. It provides a forum where one can test out ideas and skills.
8. It is a way of creating a higher personal profile.
9. It is a means of developing your business.
10. It is a way to benchmark and exchange best practice.

There's one thing that networking is definitely not: **Networking is not selling.**

Networking does however create opportunities where a sale could take place. Networking is enigmatic yet it is a tried, trusted and proven form of business development. Networking can give you whatever your heart desires.

That is not to say that networking does not have its pitfalls, it does. The biggest two are finding the time to network and feeling confident it will create commercial results. These disadvantages can easily be turned round by reviewing the 6 steps to effective networking below.

My Six Steps to effective networking

I've studied thousands of people networking over the last decade, from those who are not very good at it, right the way through to brilliant networkers. From my studies and observations I can share with you the 6 things that every effective networker does to various degrees.

Step 1: You need a networking strategy

If networking is important to you then you need a simply strategy to keep you focused. Write down your answers to these questions:

- What are the job titles of your typical buyers e.g. CEO, CFO etc.?
- What geographical area do you want to focus on e.g. Manchester, Paris, Dubai, etc.?
- What industries and/or sectors do you want to focus on e.g. Technology, Media, etc.?

Networking takes time and energy and if you end up with a big list of people you want to meet, then sadly you will get frustrated pretty quickly. Keep your list very tight and focused, that way you will succeed quicker.

Based on you answers to these questions, the next 5 steps will form your strategy.

Step 2: Attend the right networks

Before you attend any networking event ask yourself:

1. Do you know enough of the 'right' people?
2. Do you need to meet more of the 'right' people?

If you know enough of the 'right' people personally I would spend more time with them on a one to one basis rather than putting in too much effort attending events. However, if a useful place to meet a number of your contacts is at their key events, then make sure you show up. This will increase your profile, keep you up to date with issues and keep you front of mind by demonstrating you understand their 'world'. If you don't know enough of the 'right' people then attending specific events will be extremely useful for you. All you need do is to find the best networks to meet the right contacts. So, how do you do that?

A word of warning. When you first enter the portfolio world of working you will meet people who have been in the market for some time getting all enthusiastic about the 'networks' they attend. This is where you can waste a lot of time and money.

Before you go anywhere go back to your answers in Step 1 – your strategy and who you need to meet. Before you attend any networking event make sure that the attendees meet your criteria. That sounds simple enough but I can guarantee many people slip into wasting a huge amount of time and money by not doing this.

A good search engine will help you discover the right networks for meeting exactly the right people for you. Things to search on should include:

- The job title of those you want to meet
- The industry/sector followed by key words such as:
    - Associations both Trade and Professional
    - Federations
    - Institutes
    - Networks

This combination will pull up some very interesting networking opportunities for you.

When you have a list of interesting 'networks' always check out the following:

- Do they have any special interest groups?
- How frequently do they meet?
- What is the membership criteria?
- How much does it cost?

If you want to find out exactly how to find the right business network to meet your buyers have a look at this link: https://www.udemy.com/find-business-networking-groups-anywhere-in-the-uk/#/

Step 3: What's your personal brand?

This is one of the most essential features of networking. It is also the most complex because it is about you projecting a clear message and those you wish to influence.

People still buy from people they like and trust first and foremost. They also buy from and refer those they 'get'. One of the most common mistakes made by portfolio workers is they try to be all things to all people.

You simply cannot afford to do that. Each of your 'communities' will want to see you in a specific way until over time they understand your wider skills.

Let's say your portfolio consists of being:

- A consultant
- A non-executive director (NED)
- A trustee
- A coach

We could easily bundle perhaps consultant and coach together for some of your contacts, but these same contacts are unlikely to make the connection about you being a NED or even a Trustee. Why? Because this is not necessarily part of their 'world'.

The best way forward with this is to create a clear brand/message for each of your 'buying communities'. Now this might sound like extra work, but to succeed as a portfolio worker, it is time well spent.

Jeff Bezos, CEO of Amazon said, "A brand is what people say about when you are not in the room."

This is exactly how you need to think about yourself when 'networking' with people. What would you like them to say about you when you are not there? The mistake people often make here is to focus too much on your skill set. Instead your brand should focus much more on your expertise and experiences. This is what people need to know about more than anything else.

People can't recommend you just because they think you're nice and a good team player – anymore than you could. People recommend others because of the problem they fix e.g. I need a 'networking' expert or a 'mobile data' expert (expertise/experience always comes first) who is a great team player and can motivate others (soft skills always comes second).

If you want to find out more on how to create your personal brand: https://www.udemy.com/practical-personal-brand-brands-that-create-opportunities/?dtcode=c7GxC4Y2Ga7R.

Step 4: How to work a room

This is the activity which causes the most angst! Why? Because it raises the specter of rejection. It is where we show our greatest weaknesses. We have to make conversation and interact with people. That may sound easy but we are under pressure - and that can show.

Remember that you are striving to:

- Build trust & rapport.
- Establish common ground with everyone you meet.
- Create the lasting impression of a warm, open & approachable person.
- Develop a reputation for being a conversationalist & communicator.

On first arriving:

- Acquire a guest list, if there is one.
- Decide who you might want to meet.
- Stand quietly on your own for a few minutes and watch the room.
- Pin your badge top right (easy for people to read – because they have just forgotten your name too).

How to make yourself more interesting:

- As soon as you meet someone give them your full attention.
- Shake hands - make sure it is a good handshake because it does matter.
- Only give your first name to start with - the rest can follow later.
- Stay focused on the conversation - however difficult that is.

- Mirror the body language of the other person for a while.
- If they make good eye contact you must too - if they don't, you don't.
- If you are going to talk about what you do, focus on your expertise.
- Only produce your business card if you have established rapport.
- Only go for their business card if you have something to add later on.
- Stay with someone until the conversation draws to a natural end.

Five key things to do:

1. Wear something distinctive (a good aid for later recall).
2. Make a point of saying hello to the organisers, sponsors and host.
3. Always build rapport, trust and interest; NEVER sell.
4. Always practice your communication skills.
5. Always spend a little time reconnecting with people you have met before as they are your virtual sales force.

Two great conversation openers for speaker lead events are:

1. If you meet someone prior to hearing the speaker: *What are you hoping the speaker will cover in their presentation?*
2. If you meet someone after hearing the speaker: *What did you find most useful about that presentation?*

Remember to always have your own answers ready!
   A simple technique for breaking into a group is: look for a gap in the group, make eye contact and move in.

Here are the key rules for breaking away from someone professionally (after all you don't want someone to feel dumped do you?):

- No matter how bored, you must always be respectful and give the other person your full attention (being ruthless here, you simply don't know who they might know).
- Let the other person finish their sentence/story and then move into a moving away conversation, for example:
  - *Are there other people you need to catch up with? I was wondering if we have common contacts here.*
  - *I've been hogging you all night and am sure you need to meet other people. Great to meet you.*
  - *It's been a really interesting conversation but sadly there are a couple of people I need to catch up with. Would you excuse me?*

If you want to learn more about how to work the room, go to www. howtoworkaroom.co.uk.

Step 5: Stay in touch

Now we move into a critical stage - the follow-up. What was the point in meeting me if you don't stay in touch to build the relationship, trust etc? People put a huge amount of effort into attending events and yet place little emphasis on the follow-up. The follow-up is where the networking pays dividends. This is how we build our personal brand and stay front of mind.

What is your experience of following-up a contact or being followed-up yourself – was it positive or negative?

Here are 10 different reasons why you might stay in touch with someone:

1. To exchange ideas or tap into someone else's experience.
2. They might make a good role model for you or for someone you know.
3. To learn about a different industry/sector.
4. To learn about different cultures or business models.
5. You like this person.
6. They might network you into their groups.
7. You might be able to network them into your groups.

8. They might make a good speaker or could contribute a good article.
9. They might help you find a new post.
10. You are new in town and want to build your network.

The principle to follow here is 'Givers Gain'; don't wait until you need something before you pick up the phone or send an email. If you build up a network of contacts that you can help at some point you may be able to call upon their help in the future.

Of course what we all want to know is whether there is a system that really works when it comes to following up. There is but it is something that you won't have heard before...

The follow-up
Firstly we need to understand the rules of engagement. Remember there are two sides to the same coin. Understand why you are doing this. Are you staying in touch because you want something (a job, a contract or to sell your products or services) or are you offering something that might be of interest them (an exchange of best practice, a good speaker)?

• There is only one reason why people take a call after they have met you and that is because they like you, trust you, respect you or simply feel positive about you at some level.
• To achieve this you need to find common ground when you first meet.
• To find common ground you need to ask questions that helps you understand their needs and if there is any way you could help them.
• If you have something to offer, you have a robust reason for contacting them again.
• If you would like to follow up the meeting, ask their permission to so and watch their response carefully.

Busy people often need a process
Great networkers excel at staying in touch and building relationships. So exactly how do they do this? Be warned there is nothing new here, only discipline!

- Every day they do something to add value to someone in their network.
- They think about their contacts and look to add value.
- They slowly educate their contacts about their expertise and any experiences that might be relevant.
- They don't sell, they educate.

What does this look like? What format do they use?

In every conversation they seek to ask and listen and then they pass forward:

- White papers of interest
- Articles of interest
- Contacts that might be useful
- Case studies that are relevant
- Initiations to events on a key issues

And so on. There is nothing new here, it just needs discipline and a desire to be useful.

Step 6 – Using social media

Networking has become very much easier as Social Media has grown. But so have the complexities and benefits. There is a whole new chapter covering this subject in detail so it is suffice to say here that social media is important and should be aligned to all previous 5 steps:

1. Create a strategy and align this to your business objectives.
2. Find the right social media platforms where your buyers are just as you do when attending networking events.
3. Build your personal brand online (make sure it all matches up).
4. The 'how to work a room' principles apply online; Be respectful and professional.
5. Social media is a great way to stay in touch.

A few key learning points

- Most people feel nervous when they first start networking.
- The biggest personal barrier is the fear of rejection.
- Allocate time to network.
- Don't waste time by networking in the wrong places.
- Most people are not natural networkers - they have to work at it.
- Most professional networkers have a low-key approach.
- It takes persistence and it is important to be consistent.
- Everyone can do it if they have the desire and willingness.

Successful and skilled networkers have their own follow-up styles but their follow-up letter, email or telephone call will be virtually instant, will often contain humour, will refer to their previous conversation and could contain something of potential interest. If they feel that there is a case for a professional relationship, they say so. They also keep their promises, send information and discuss opportunities.

From one networker to another, may I wish you every success and hope that you have lots of fun discovering 'the magic of networking'.

Heather White is an international Speaker, Coach, Trainer, Online Course, Author and Founder of Smarter Networking (www.smarter-networking.com). Heather has worked with FTSE 500 companies, Business Owners, Graduates, CEOs, Women's Groups, Senior Executives & Business Schools. Heather's approach is practical, teaching thousands of people how to network and thereby achieve great results for their careers, confidence and business.

Heather's clients include: Accenture, Cambridge University, KPMG, EY, London Business School, Rolls Royce and many other high calibre organisations. Heather was recently delighted to speak at a TEDx event in Oxford.

MARKETING YOU AND YOUR PORTFOLIO

BY BARNABY WYNTER

So there you have it. You're sitting in your tidy home office, pencils sharpened, note pad clean, your phone is gleaming. All is quiet. This is the new way ... Wait a minute – all is quiet! Very quiet. Unlike the corporate world, the noises of commerce do not happen automatically. You are those noises now. Nothing will happen unless you make it happen. It is time to market yourself – and that means you have to do it yourself.

The great news is that in making the decision to become a Portfolio Professional you already have a lot in place. What you need to do now is to package your 'youness' in such a way that you become a brand.

Defining brand for the Portfolio Professional

The word brand is in common usage, but to define what it means rarely leads to a clear common definition. Research confirms this with responses from, 'it's the name'; 'it's the logo'; 'the image'; 'the expectation'; 'the colour', etc.

For the Portfolio Professional, there are two key components. Firstly, there is the product which comes in the form of a promise of service from you. However, that promise will remain in your office until such time as when a prospect, the second key component, decides to buy 'you'.

Prospects don't just simply gravitate towards products, they go through a set of stepped decisions that bring them closer to the product until the time comes when they finally decide to buy. As they go through each step, the affinity towards the product strengthens until a purchase is made.

Your challenge is to build a relationship through a set of experiences that yields a 'BRAND YOU'. It is the strength of these experiences that govern customers' inclination to purchase so,

'BRAND YOU' is every experience that affects the relationship between you and your customer.

All of us hold in our heads a list of products which meet any given, need or circumstance. This ladder in the mind is governed by all the brand experiences and defines who is top.

Usually potential purchasers default to a choice they have made before – the easy option, the 'regular' choice made many times before. As a Portfolio Professional, you must break through some of these 'remembered' patterns in the mind of your prospects and establish new ones, so that your service becomes the preferred one.

Creating a BRAND YOU

No matter what the eventual choice, everyone goes through the same 6-step decision making process.

You will be shortly introduced to this 6-step model. It can be used to drive your sales and marketing efforts, to judge how well these are working and assist you in identifying communication strategies.

The challenge facing the Portfolio Professional today is greater than ever. Clients expect more from their business relationships – they have more choice, less time and more information sources. And with less money available, they all want to believe they are getting value.

There are now more product offerings than ever, making choice much harder. Getting information has become easier, but the sheer volume adds complexity to decision-making. The last fifteen years have seen more technological advances than in the history of mankind. More frighteningly, in the next fifty years, predictions say that 90% of what people will know has yet to be discovered. If you're planning ten years of portfolio working, you represent at least 20% of this new thinking! It doesn't bear thinking about.

The Brand Bucket® Model

The Brand Bucket® was developed in 1985 for people selling and marketing their products or services as a filtration process to help overcome information overload. It maps the journey all prospects go through when they make purchases and become loyal customers. When applied it ensures that buying decisions are directed towards the product or service you want to sell.

Figure 20. The Brand Bucket®

Why is the model shaped like a bucket?

Whatever the product, more people have heard of it than actually use it. As a result, the first step of the bucket contains the largest number of people, diminishing in numbers, until the 6th step when there are least of all. As people experience your brand, they move through the various decision steps and may decide not to proceed.

As a result, the top is wider than the bottom, a bucket shape.

The success of any business is how wide the bottom of the bucket is, not the size of the top!

The six steps of the Brand Bucket® are as follows:

Step 1: Awareness

Getting your name out there is not hard. All your friends and colleagues have spurred you on. Of course they'd give you work once you strike out on your own. You'd be exactly what they needed once released from the shackles of the corporate world. Hell, at times you've felt like a legend in your own lunchtime...

But there's a catch. Their willingness to spend their employer's money on you will be dampened by a process of justification, relevance, timing and budget availability. Sure you might already have customers but what happens when their contracts stop ... and they will! You need to create awareness amongst people who have no idea about anything about you. So the first job of a Portfolio Professional is to tell those who you think can use your services that you are there – to build the awareness of BRAND YOU amongst your prospects.

In isolation, this is not enough to change people's behaviour. It is fundamental to the process of buying because it establishes the relationship.

Whether you set up with a corporate identity, have multiple identities, or just use your own name, what any brand name says about you impacts on a prospect's understanding of you. However, just raising awareness is not enough; you need to provide more information to generate a relationship to get those people to engage with you further. Name awareness must be linked to Step 2

Step 2: Image match

Having created the awareness, now consider what you want your prospects to 'feel' about you. You need to create a sustainable image that allows your clients to integrate you into their own lifestyle needs.

Now what do we mean by 'image'? The strongest image anyone has of anything is that of themselves. Your own image is extensively nurtured and cared for. From the moment we awaken until we go to sleep, we constantly feed our image through our chosen lifestyles.

Lifestyle includes both home and work. The prospects you'll talk to are in jobs solely to meet their own lifestyle needs. So you need to present to, and engage them in ways that enable them to say, 'I see where you fit into my life'

Without this, people are able to reject the relationship or become attracted to stronger relationships that support their own personal image.

Brand image works best when it carries a promise of a benefit that meets the needs of the person to whom you are selling. Your prospects are invariably in work mode. It is important that you put yourself in the shoes of your prospects. How do they feel? Stressed, lost, unable to complete a task, over worked, out of their depth?

These factors are emotional issues that affect their ability to deal with life.

As a result, you need to match up with their issues:

Them	You
Out of their depth	You understand, you've been there before
Unable to complete task	You're here to help
Overworked	You're an additional resource
Stressed	Relaxed
Lack of Knowledge	You can provide the know-how

If you can convey an emotional benefit to an issue they are struggling with, then you will find they need you and probably straight away!

However, unless they are continually reminded of the feeling, reliance on solely creating an emotional response inevitably results in that same person 'forgetting' your brand.

Spend a disproportionate amount of time simply telling everyone you are there in a way that makes others feel good. Leave them with a real sense of what you do. Write yourself a short tagline which you say when you meet them, such as 'I make businesses grow' or 'I get people home earlier' or 'I specialise in long lunch hours'.

The author's corporate tag is 'I make your marketing work'.

Have fun with this. It will get you to the next step. Try it in a conversation about what you do! Do it at association meetings, clubs, when networking chats over lunch and dinner - but make sure you follow it up with step 3.

Step 3: Facts match

No business relationship can be formalised unless everyone involved knows what you offer, what you can do. It is also helpful if this is presented in a way that demonstrates how this might differ from other offerings.

Getting over what facts make your product or service good shouldn't be too difficult. The challenge is to know which ones influence the purchase decision. The stronger the links to the emotional promises in steps 1 and 2, the more likely the customer will continue their decision-making process. It is no good promising 'easy' and giving the customer a complicated result. It is no good offering cheap pricing when there are financial caveats that in the end put them off.

People already have a list of rational features against which they will mentally audit you. Knowing what these are, it is crucial that you turn all your features into benefits. Just ask yourself 'so what' about each of your features and use the answer to engage your prospect.

By this stage, with the right messaging, your potential customer should be saying, 'Now I know who you are and how you will benefit me.'

We must now ensure that the knowledge and understanding they have about your product or service is turned into a memorable experience provided by you.

Step 4: Response

Get your prospect to become involved with the product or part of your product offer.

Each 'sales campaign' should include a mechanism that allows prospects to experience your product, sometimes through an associated incentive. Tune it to the motivations of your target audience. The mechanism must enhance the brand promise and not simply be 'off the shelf'.

Such a 'test drive' creates the brand experience in its entirety. More importantly, it creates a new pattern of behaviour, exclusively belonging to you. Direct engagement with your prospect attains a far stronger relationship than those who sell similar solutions but have had no interaction.

You must get people to respond. Don't undertake work for someone that is free just to get them working with you. If you do this, then your so-called involvement will really act only as an awareness campaign. You must create a customer experience that leaves a new pattern in the customer's mind that might one day yield a sale. Whatever your promotion or experiential campaign, it MUST demonstrate your product or service and what makes it special or unique.

This step can be one of the most exciting. It can be the first point of real interaction between a prospect and Brand YOU. Develop something that leaves a residual 'experience' of your product or service. Audits, analyses with action plans, developing methodologies to tackle issues, are all good approaches. All of these offer your prospect real value but still leave a desire for them to continue working with you to make your recommendations happen.

In making such recommendations, you will set a pattern in people's minds, you will raise their expectations, you will appear to match up to your promise but now real effort must be placed on the next step.

Step 5: Usage

Too often, businesses establish a reputation that cannot be delivered at product or service level.

This is the real test. Does what you have said live up to its promise? If it doesn't, you'll have wasted all your previous investment getting the prospect to this point and potentially created a threat to your business.

However, fulfilling expectation is critical to the ongoing relationship between you and your customer. Customers need far less persuading to buy Brand YOU next time. The more they come to trust you, the less likely they are to be attracted to the competition.

Both presentation and delivery influences how people feel about their purchase and whether they'll buy your product again. Every communication opportunity should be used to enhance the product experience, especially the written word. Now is the time to get to grips with that new laptop, tablet and mobile as well as working in the 'cloud'. The more professional you appear the better. It removes potential criticism that you lack a corporate infrastructure around you.

When embarking on a brand relationship, Step 5 is one of the best places to start. Identifying what makes you different and using it to feed the relationship between steps 1 – 4 increases your chances of linking all the steps together.

Only in Step 5 do you get the sale. At last! Job Done!

True if you are selling a one-off, but if you are looking for a long-term relationship or simply a repeat purchase, then cutting loose at this point means you will have to effectively start again at the top of the bucket.

Now is the time to really look after your new customer.

Step 6 : Loyalty

If your customers have made it this deep into your Brand Bucket, they've become your most valuable asset in two important ways.

- The strength of the relationship with you means they are more likely to spend more money with you.
- As loyal users of Brand YOU, they have the potential to become advocates, one of your most valuable marketing tools – working on your behalf to direct new prospects into the bucket.

Think of your own experiences. How often have you gone through a similar process, only to find yourself totally ignored or treated to an 'off the shelf' aftercare package? The chances are that you became disenchanted very quickly, and certainly haven't recommended to others.

An existing customer is the most valuable person a brand can have. They will happily act as your spokesperson, telling others how good you are. You need to consult and look after them accordingly. They might then become a Brand You advocate.

Additionally you can incentivise them to tell others about you. Find something that you offer that they might like but wouldn't normally pay for. Explain to them that if they recommend you to someone else,, you could offer them a discount off future work. Alternatively you could offer an added value benefit, perhaps something in the original proposal they would have liked to do but didn't have the budget originally. Do that in exchange for a converted lead.

Practical ways to use the bucket

There are four key components to successfully applying the bucket model to your brand communication.

1. Define who will make your best customers.

The very essence of Portfolio Professionals is they do not have just one type of customer. As a result as prospects they come with differing hopes, fears, desires and needs. It is these that dictate the kind of relationships they want. Often a Portfolio Professional can service quite different target groups at the same time. It is important to listen to your prospects' requirements to ensure that you can meet their emotional needs first; then rationally match what you do to their needs. By doing this you can define who will make the best customers (and the most profitable!).

2. Analyse how Brand YOU is seen by the target at each level of Brand Bucket®.

Executing your own research can be very helpful here. Listening is fundamental to creating Brand YOU. Don't be afraid to ask your prospects for their expectations. Use Questionnaires, SWOTS, workshops, lunches, chats in the pub or over coffee. Not unsurprisingly, in seeking their advice you will find that they are not slow in coming forward.

3. Once you have this data, map it out against a Brand Bucket®.

Doing this will give you a clear steer on which hot buttons you can press to deliver a comprehensive service to your customer. After this analysis, you will have a visual shape of where the relationship with your customer is strong and where there is room for improvement.

Following use of the Brand Bucket® to audit over 450 brands, three shapes have emerged:

The funnel shape

This is where a brand has a strong awareness and image match amongst its target market BUT no-one knows what the product does. The net result -no sales. The chances are that amongst your friends and old colleagues, Brand YOU is like a funnel. Make sure they know what you can do by demonstrating some of the work you have done for others. Never assume they know, they won't.

The hourglass shape

This shape occurs when a brand has some loyal customers but there are others who have heard of the brand and do not use it. The result is often diminishing users.

It may well be that you are working with a department of an organisation. People from other departments may have heard of you or met you but for some reason they don't use you, despite the fact that you clearly already have a deep understanding of their business. This is an hourglass relationship.

To fix this, you need to demonstrate to other areas of the business exactly what you are doing for their organisation and engage them in a way that gives them a clear understanding of what you are doing for others. Find something that is of general interest to the whole organisation and offer to present it to other managers, a test drive, as described in Step 4 earlier.

The terrarium shape

This shape is fat at the bottom and has no opening at the top (the name is inspired by the glass bottles you grow plants in). This shape occurs when there is good understanding by existing customers of a brand because they are happily using it but no-one outside this group has any awareness of this brand.

It is most likely that in the early part of your portfolio working life you will very quickly create a terrarium. A few projects that keep you busy and distract you from the need to look for more work because you don't need any at the time.

This is the most dangerous shape to have because, if ignored, you might suddenly find the projects that are keeping you busy (in the bottom of your bucket) leak away and because there is nothing coming through the top you end up with no business. Always be mindful of the need to keep building emotional attachment with new prospects.

Once you have mapped Brand YOU against the bucket, it will become apparent which areas you are strong in and which areas need attention and effort. Make sure you are honest with yourself when you undertake this exercise. It is often helpful to ask a partner to help with this exercise as you will get an outsider's perspective and they often come up with things you have taken for granted.

4. Define what is important at each level of the decision-making process.

Having established the strengths and weaknesses of Brand YOU, now is the time to define what your key messages are at every level. You know what makes Brand YOU tick. Define your value proposition for each of the 6 steps, checking each time that they form an obvious link together through the experience you are going to provide.

It is important that each key message is as unique to you as possible. The more of these you can get, the more differentiated your offer becomes. If you cannot find anything different, then look again. Remember it is the collective value of all the differences that will dictate the strength of the relationship with you.

Marketing Brand YOU

Once you have a completed Brand Bucket analysis, now is the time to sit down and decide how you are going to tell your target market all this great news.

Firstly decide how many customers you need. Then allocate a budget. This will help you think creatively about how to spend the money and optimise getting your story across.

Write a PowerPoint presentation that you can print out and leave behind with people. Get a leaflet/brochure printed. It doesn't have to be expensive but can make you look much more professional. The chances are that you don't need that many customers so you don't have to produce thousands.

At each level of the Brand Bucket decide how best to get the message you have decided upon across to your prospects.

This is the creative bit, so be different. Just stick to your message and try to link each piece of activity together so that they all add up to a bigger story. Find a colour, a shape, a set of words, a look and feel or a piece of design that appears on everything you do. So each time you communicate with anyone on your contact list they get to know it's from Brand YOU.

And finally

Congratulations on getting this far. You deserve a chance at success. The Brand Bucket® is active today in the real world. It can really work for you. What have you got to lose by trying it? The customers will come. Good luck with your endeavours.

Barnaby Wynter is Managing Partner of The Brand Bucket® Company, a strategic and creative marketing communications agency. He has a BSc Hons in Psychology and Diplomas in Marketing and in Advertising and is a regional president of The Professional Speaking Association and a Founding Freeman of the Guild of Entrepreneurs. Barnaby recently became Dean for WorldAcademy.tv with his own video based ELearning Brand Bucket® Marketing Academy. The Brand Bucket® is a registered Trademark of The Brand Bucket® Company and is used here with permission.

SELLING

BY COLIN MCCRUDDEN

You may be clear on which roles you want in your portfolio and which you don't, but there is one role which you can't avoid – that of salesperson. Most new Portfolio Professionals have not sold before and they fall into one of three categories.

- They think they can't sell and never will.
- They think they can sell but probably can't ('we all sell, don't we?').
- They really can sell.

Selling is a skill, not a talent. You can learn and develop it just like any other skill. But, like any other skill, it needs practice. This means learning from your mistakes. In the case of selling, that can be a painful and confidence-knocking process if we fail to pick up business and income.

What is selling?

Every book on sales – and there are thousands – offers a different definition. In the end it comes down to money; that's why you're reluctantly out selling, to increase your income. But the majority of Portfolio Professionals will, by definition, be selling professional services and aiming for the longer term. That's why the essence of selling is the building of business relationships. At the right price, at the right time, anybody can make a one-off sale. Building relationships is more difficult for many, but should come more easily to those joining the Portfolio Life after years of experience of working in organisations where they related to those around them.

Selling is not networking and, in her contribution in Part 4, networking guru Heather White warns you that networking is not selling. Networking is essential to a successful portfolio, and contributes to the start of the sales process – it helps build your prospects. The same story applies to Marketing and Use of Social Networks, all set out in chapters within this book. Again they contribute. They help to build prospects but, in the end, like it or not, if you're to have a successful portfolio, you'll have to go out and sell.

Fears

You've set off on your portfolio life. You've decided on a brand, designed a logo, commissioned a website, had a brochure printed. Then … you come to the point where all this is merely window-dressing and you have to get out there and talk to real customers. Fear strikes you – fear of rejection, fear of failure.

All the sales techniques in the world are useless unless you can overcome those fears. Fear of failure is part of us, as is fear of rejection. At an early age we cried when we heard the word 'No', and it still hurts us in our lives today.

There's no easy answer to overcoming your fears, except to gird your loins, psych yourself up, call up all your reserves of confidence and get out there … and succeed. After all, without the fears how would we experience the fantastic thrill of sales success?

People Buy People First (PBPF)

It's a truism perhaps, but, but PBPF is key to your success in selling. What it doesn't mean is that you can carry on without techniques, with just your lovely self – and that they'll give you the business. That word 'First' is an important one. A customer liking you is the first hurdle to overcome, but it doesn't mean you get the business, just that they're happy for you to remain in the running.

However, PBPF reminds you that it's people skills, which work best. You're a warm, personable human being, so make sure that's how you're seen. You need to come over as empathetic, enthusiastic, on your customer's side, confident without being pushy. (No doubt you, the reader, have already mentally ticked off all these traits as being present in yourself.)

The customer's shoes

Good salespeople remember that they are customers too. How do you like to be sold to? What techniques make you squirm, and which do you respond to?

Spend time thinking about your customers.

Think yourself onto their side of the desk, understand their problems, issues and needs. What's in it for them? They have bosses and reviews, need pay rises and promotion, want to be mentioned in despatches. So they aren't necessarily driven solely by their organisation's goals. Unlike you who have escaped to the Unlimited life, they have to face company politics and personality clashes.

If you can get to the position where you are both 'singing off the same hymn sheet' then you're closer to making the sale.

Getting warmer all the time

Selling starts with a cold call, cold handshake or lead via Social Media or networking. It's about spotting an opportunity. From there it's your job to ensure that it gets warmer all the time. Every contact you have with your prospect or customer should have the objective of getting you closer and the relationship warmer.

Relationships are complex, but one basic is to have an interest in the other person, as well as demonstrating that you know and recall their interests, what they prefer and enjoy. At the early stages, their support for Blackpool FC may be sufficient. Later, you should know their favourite wine and their family. To gain real empathy and build a strong relationship, it's important to understand their job and their working life. Your own area of interest may only be part of a larger role for them. You should be aware of that and able to take a meaningful interest in their wider areas of responsibility.

This is customer care or, if you want to give it its modern description, Customer Relationship Management. The problem with that term is that it sounds data-driven and rather cold. To the Portfolio Professional, CRM is all about keeping notes from every sales contact of any kind and transferring them into a working database to build your knowledge of your customer.

Warm customers are more likely to say 'yes'; warm customers recommend you; warm customers come back again.

Prospecting

Every relationship has to start somewhere. There was a point at which you sold yourself to your husband, wife or partner. It was probably a cold call, walking up, introducing yourself, asking them out.

It's the first day of your portfolio; all the background materials are complete. Your networking has gained you a number of business cards – people you've at least met briefly and have some kind of access to. With these as a start you should build a Prospect List. Quality is preferred to quantity, but a healthy business needs a healthy Prospect List. If you're rejected by your one and only prospect, that's a disaster; if there are 100 more prospects to contact, then there's still hope of success. There's a selling term, 'well-qualified prospects', and you 'qualify' your prospects by researching them to establish how good the fit is between them and your service or product. Yellow Pages is not the way to a well-qualified Prospect List.

Of course, in a portfolio you'll need a separate Prospect List for each of the areas of your business.

Getting appointments

Your need is to get face-to-face with the prospect. Letters rarely succeed, so you will have to tackle the non-salesperson's nightmare: the cold telephone call.

A few rules:

- **Don't sell the service/product – sell the appointment.** There isn't time to sell, and you open yourself to rejection on the telephone. Give sufficient details to hook the customer and get the appointment.

- **Get the customer's name, and use it.** People like the sound of their own name. When somebody uses their name, they feel a step closer.

- **Use a script if it makes you feel more comfortable, but never let it sound like one.** Think of those annoying calls you get from large call centres, think what you don't like about them. They only go in the direction they choose; they have difficulty responding to your change of direction; they're too familiar; they tell porkies about 'research' or how long the call will take. PBPF.

- **Don't put your phone down without a date in your diary.** That's your objective, even if the date's further off than you wanted. Ensure you've made a step along the way.

- **Use time to your advantage.** Objections to appointments are usually based on 'busyness' rather than business. As a customer, it's more difficult to refuse an appointment where you're promised it will last 'a guaranteed maximum of 20 minutes'. On your side, even if that's not sufficient, it opens the door to further appointments and offers good learning time.

- **Keep notes.** On responses, on callback times, the names of those you spoke to, including receptionists, secretaries, assistants. If you have to call back, it's better to be able to name a person, rather than say 'I spoke to somebody in your office'.

- **Project enthusiasm and confidence without being over-bearing.** It's more difficult to project over the telephone. Recommended techniques include ensuring that you smile as you talk – use a mirror by your desk; and many people find that standing up increases their self-assurance and projection on cold calls.

- **Make calls in batches.** Once you've got yourself psyched up and set up, it's a waste not to make the most of it. Have a list of calls to make, and you'll find that they get easier, and achieve better results, as you work through them. If you're using a script and amend it as you go, it will be more effective by the end of the session.

It gets easier with practice. Most things do, but cold calling more than most. As the fear recedes and confidence grows, your performance will improve; you'll project yourself better, and have more success.

The sales appointment

You're a Portfolio Professional, so we know you'll present yourself well, be on time, and all those other small but important details. Every sales appointment is different and you'll have your own approach. But there are some important guidelines to bear in mind.

- **Professional, enthusiastic, confident.** You need to bring along the same qualities you used in your telephone prospect call. Timidity never won a sales pitch, but neither did over-the-top arrogance. PBPF.

- **Have a plan, but don't stick rigidly to it.** Build flexibility into your call plan. Listening and changing direction in response will open up new avenues to explore.

- **Use appropriate sales materials to illustrate your product or service.** Testimonials or a mini portfolio of your past work are better than glossy brochures. PBPF. For more detailed presentations, don't ignore the power of a personalised Powerpoint presentation to illustrate not only your service but also your knowledge of your customer's business. Alternatively, a short video presentation may be helpful, but ensure it's professional and left as a reminder rather than as an opening introduction.

- **Emphasise benefits not features.** Features are what your product or service has to offer – your degree, experience, your proficiency on the violin. But none of these are worth talking about unless they offer potential benefits to your customer.

- **Use open questioning:** How, What, When, Why – and listen to the answers. Too many salespeople use the time while their customer is speaking to prepare the next point they want to make. Even worse, they miss the buying signals.

- **Two-way discussion, not one-way sale.** Promote discussion during the sales call. When you start a meaningful discussion, you're not only having a dialogue, you're starting a relationship

- **Talk about their business, not yours.** The fact that you are portfolio-ing could be of interest, because many customers may be considering it for their own future. But if you want the sale, it's your customer's business you should be focusing on.

- **Silence is golden.** If you're silent, you might just hear something. If you hear something, you might learn something. That's why timeshare salespeople never learn.

- **Summarise the customer's needs** to show that you understand them, and to invite correction. It puts you on their side of the desk and reduces later objections.

The close

The most dangerous stage. If you've been taught a 'powerful closing technique' and you play it wrongly, then your empathetic PBPF approach can suddenly turn into a hard sell and alienate your prospect. Closing means asking for the business, rather than fading meekly out of the appointment after a pleasant chat. It's a matter of judgement when you close, but close you must if you want to succeed. The amazing thing is that customers expect to be asked to buy, and closing is simply that.

Here are three guidelines.

- If you get buying signals at whatever stage of the appointment, use them, don't wait. 'I'd really like one of these, please.' 'No, I'm sorry, I've got another 50 benefits to tell you about before I can take your order.'
- Ask for the business and stop talking. Silence is a difficult but powerful ally in sales. Put your proposition to the customer and force him or her to react.
- On average, it takes three closes to get the order. Don't give up after the first rejection.

If you and your customer have not reached a stage where you can ask for the business – more information required, more research – then don't leave without agreeing time and agenda points for a follow-up appointment.

Objections

Before you can close, you usually have to overcome objections. Whether they are going to buy or not, customers, especially professional buyers, must show themselves not to be easy touches.

A simple rule of thumb for handling objections is:

- Welcome the objections as an opportunity to prove your service/ product further.
- Ask questions to clarify and explore each objection. Briefly summarise them all.
- Respond with benefits. Cover each objection in turn.
- Confirm with the customer that you have covered each of his or her objections.
- Return to your sales proposition.

Having answered each of the objections, you should be in a position to go forward to the close.

Buying signals

They're important; they lead to sales, you must listen and watch for them. They can be verbal and non-verbal. Is the prospect with you or not? Have they switched off? Through their manner, body language and comments you can judge how warm they are. If you're facing a cold prospect, use open questions to get them talking more about themselves and their business. If you're in a warm situation, summarise the benefits and ask a more pointed open question. If they're hot – sitting forward eagerly, agreeing with what you say, adding positive comments – move quickly to the close.

Listening

The forgotten technique. So many salespeople are so busy selling that they never hear. They go in with a well-prepared list of benefits that they simply have to get across in the time allotted, and they deliver them – 1, 2, 3. The customer adds the occasional comment which is ignored as the benefits (all good, no doubt) are trotted out. The often small signals are simply not heeded. The salesperson doesn't change track or emphasis – and they fail.

Listening is at the heart of selling. Customers have problems. Unearth the problem and you're much closer to a sale. If you don't listen, you won't find out what's really bugging them and where you could help. It's not just a case of appearing to listen in order to impress and letting their words flow over your head. Real listening is needed, because real listening should change your response. This is why too formal an agenda is not ideal in sales calls.

The finish

Two things to remember once hands are shaken at the close:

- There may be a walk to the lift or to the exit, so have some small talk ready to avoid being off-guard.

- The meeting's not finished until you're off site; a great close can be destroyed by being glimpsed afterwards loosening the tie, lighting a cigarette, making mobile calls, scratching the anatomy.

After the sale

Whatever the outcome, you have some action points to follow up on.

- Keep to any commitments you made – they must be on time and as promised.
- If it's positive, confirm the outcome by email or letter within 24 hours.
- If you didn't get the business, write to thank the prospect for their time. Confirm any further planned meeting. It's all part of building the relationship.
- Update your records with all the useful material you gathered.
- Assess your selling performance and note action for improvement.

Selling always has an edge to it, vital for keeping the adrenaline flowing. But, with practice, patience and persistence it can become a natural and even enjoyable part of your life as a Portfolio Professional.

Colin McCrudden chose a Portfolio Professional role after a successful business career, latterly as Chief Executive. His Portfolio Life comprised a 'stimulating diversity of roles' as non-executive, consultant, catalyst and communicator. He sadly died in April 2010 after a short illness contracted whilst doing what he loved, travelling to see his family and experiencing the wine regions of the world.

THE POWER OF SOCIAL MEDIA AND HOW TO HARNESS IT

BY PAUL MCCRUDDEN

You've already read about the importance of *relationships* in a previous chapter. Never have they been more important. Social media gives a power to individuals to connect with each other and organisations around the world, resulting in new ways for how consumers interact. Now any individual can have an instant – *real-time* – connection with a company. They expect a real-time response. It's not enough as a consumer to wait for days to receive a reply. A reply is expected within hours, and ideally quicker. Managing relationships with your customers and prospects has become sharply focused on the quality of your social communications with them. Do it right, you'll reap the rewards. Do it wrong, and the world will be told about it.

And doing it right is about employing much of the advice in this book, but doing it in an online context. You can use social media to build relationships in an honest and personable way, to network effectively, to read consumers' intent and to sell at the right time. And most importantly, to step change your life. To cross that bridge.

You would have already seen lots of different words used to describe people. Consumers, customers, prospects, fans, followers. Just as in the physical world, you should develop a strategy for how to use social media – and all of its available tools – to take people through the funnel for your business' success.

The central tenet of social media – publicly sharing our everyday lives – is often alien to many people as they transition from the corporate world to a portfolio lifestyle. But this has become normal. Become, not becoming. For people and companies across the world, this sharing nature is opening new doors and opportunities. For many, it's the default way of connecting and maintaining relationships.

Initial reluctance to immersing yourself in the world of social media, and its marketing benefits, may be fuelled by the endless jargon that accompanies it. Always-on, all-year-round, tweet, re-tweet, post, comment, vine, pin, hashtag, real-time, trend, promoted trend, opportunity-to-view, pay-per-click, cost-per-engagement: the list is never-ending. It's a new form of communicating, and a new dictionary that goes with it.

But it's crucial to remember that it's not just a younger generation (however that's defined) that is using social media. People of all ages – including those moving from a 20 year career in the corporate world onto their next adventure – are taking advantage of the revolutionary benefits that social media provide. Recent research shows an increase in usage of social media across three years of 40% in 35-45 year olds and 80% in 55+. *(International Business Times : Facebook Gets Older')*

The benefits of social media

What are the benefits? How can they really change the way you think about communications, about relationships, about business? The best way to think about the benefits that social media provides you, is to consider it as the closest way to discovering more about the things you love. Whatever your hobbies, interests, passions, social media enables you to quickly, and easily, discover more than you currently know, whilst forming friendships with other people sharing a similar passion. Every time we click, Like, Tweet, View, Share we are connecting globally with each other via our interests. This is known as your Interest Graph, and it's worthwhile taking that into consideration when planning the best way to express your portfolio self in social media. What do you want to share with others? What will you be interested in discovering more about from people local and far away? What are the interests around which you want to connect with the world?

For business, social media is a growing phenomenon. It's become an industry adage that if you think your business isn't active on social media, you're wrong. Even though you aren't talking about your business, somebody else very likely is. Which means if you don't have an official presence, you're missing out on being a part of a conversation about YOU.

Imagine that on a personal level. Imagine there was a conversation online – accessible to anyone in the world – about you and you weren't part of it. As soon as you heard about it, you'd go and have a look to find out what was being said. And after that you'd join the conversation and make sure the stories that were being told were accurate and truthful. It should be no different for a business. If there's a conversation going on online about your business or industry – and there's a fair chance there is – you should be part of it. Participate. Be active. Steer the conversation in a direction you want it to go.

The benefits for Portfolio Professionals

As you know, the life of a Portfolio Professional encompasses many areas. That's the joy and challenge of it. You'll likely have multiple roles with multiple responsibilities. You'll have irregular working patterns and juggle a range of deliverables and customers, while also networking, auditing and selling at the same time. And you've now got to add social media to the mix?

Well, you'll be pleased to know that social media is an ideal bedfellow for being a portfolio professional. Here are just a few ways in which Twitter, Facebook, YouTube, Vine and whatever other platform you may use allow you to build your portfolio career. You can:

- Manage multiple profiles (for your multiple interests and businesses) in an easy way.
- Control when and to what degree you participate in conversations, at a time that suits you and your specific requirements.
- Network with whoever you want, it's easy to find and connect with people with similar interests.
- Create communities to help manage your prospects and customers in a productive way.
- Communicate 1-to-many and 1-to-1 at any time depending on your business need.

Social media enables you as a Portfolio Professional to be flexible when dealing with customers. The deeper you immerse yourself in social media, the greater the range of ways you find to engage consumers. One example of this is the tenet that you should be active on platforms used by your target audience , not just wait for them to be active on the default platform you're on. In other words, there's no point having a Facebook page if most of your target customers are on Twitter. In social media, one size does not fit all. Appreciating this allows you to develop a flexible approach to connecting with consumers that will match the flexibility your portfolio career requires.

Your shift to being a highly active social media contributor is well timed. The rise of mobile technology means that you adopt a practical approach to all the things mentioned, and do them any time, any day wherever you are. Right now. You could set up your individual or business profile on any social media account within seconds. The power to succeed is in your fingertips. And what's more, smartphones and cloud technology mean that you don't need to be in an office to run your portfolio career. On your mobile device, social media can be the glue that sticks the different elements of your portfolio life together. This lightweight approach can re-energise the way in which you act and do business, and provide a freshness to your social communications.

And the most important thing about mobile is that's how people now interact. Consumers are now primarily mobile, using social media throughout the day, every day of the year. Various research studies prove this, and that people unlock their mobile phones on average anywhere between 100 and 300 times every day. When you think social media, think mobile.

And if you're still not sure about why social media is so appropriate to the life of a portfolio professional, then remember this. Social media is a highly personal form of expression, from how you act online, your tone of voice, who you interact with to how your business manages marketing, sales and customer service. The wide spectrum of opportunities that social media provides means that you can find your comfort zone without the need to be on anyone else's terms. It keeps you in control of you.

How Portfolio Professionals use social media

The power of earned media has changed the landscape for businesses large and small. Nowadays it's not just the print, radio and billboard ads that market your business. It's people.

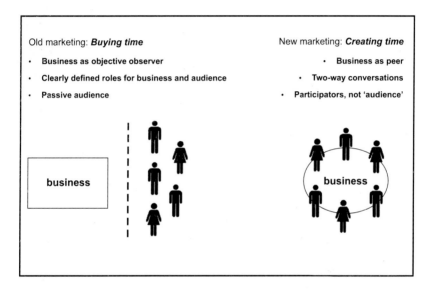

Figure 21

Social media is commonly split into three distinct areas. Your business should have a strategy for each. They are:

1. **Owned media**: your official, active presence on any platform (eg. Twitter, YouTube, etc). Also referred to as 'organic'.
2. **Earned media**: people talking about you, which in turn connects their social network to your business. Think of this as 'word-of-mouth'.
3. **Paid media**: the promotion of your owned media so that you can reach a larger audience than would organically see your content

More new words, eh! Which means it's important to be confident in each of their meanings so that you can properly create a strategy and measure effectiveness in everything you do in social media. The more you participate, the more you'll get out of it. It's as true for a business as it is for an individual.

So how should you use social media? What are the ways in which it can enhance your life as a portfolio professional?

From a high level view, there are three key elements:

1. **Strategy**: plan the most appropriate route to achieving your business goals
2. **Execution**: participate in a pro-active and reactive way
3. **Measurement**: analyse the performance of your social interactions against your strategic objectives

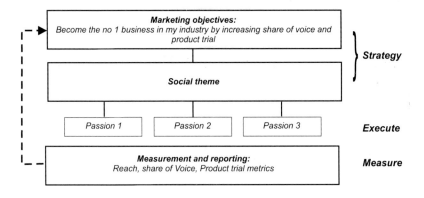

Figure 22

Starting at the top, describe your business vision and objectives. Then state how this should be interpreted to appeal to your followers in social media. This helps to add the human element to your content and will make sure that your profile is an appropriate fit for the personable nature of social media. Next, plot out a series of content pillars – say three – that will show the topics and themes you will share content and participate in conversations about. On another page, you can then write down a more detailed description of these topics to help guide you further. Give each of these content pillars a distinctive name – something that only your business would use. It'll help give your content ideas a tighter focus. Finally, add how you intend to measure the effectiveness of your social media content. We'll explore this further shortly.

You'll see that this plan fits neatly into your plan for Strategy, Execute, Measure all on one page.

Let's look at the three elements in turn:

1. Strategy/Planning

A good starting point is to decide why you and your portfolio needs social media – what role will it serve for you, and what benefit should it bring to your followers? There are typically three ways that it could provide a service: for Entertainment (ie. advertising your brand), for Information (ie. news), for Utility (ie. a useful service). Decide which of these is most appropriate for your business. Pick one or two – that way you'll start to narrow down the role that social media can play for you.

An important factor in this decision is to consider the various business functions that social media serves. On any given day you can use it for networking, marketing your product or service, selling and customer care. And sometimes all of those things could happen in one tweet – an effective response to a customer service enquiry could lead instantly to marketing a related item and cross-selling it, which can also serve as a form of networking if your customer then re-tweets it to all of his or her followers. Social media has the power to do this in a simple tweet.

Whatever the size and nature of your activities its worth creating a social media strategy that is aligned to your objectives. Above all else, this will help you to remain focused on what you're trying to achieve in social media and measure how effective it's working for you.

Consider your approach over a number of phases. What journey do you need to go in in social media in order to achieve your objectives? Plan out the phases that are aligned to your business goals. Here's an example:

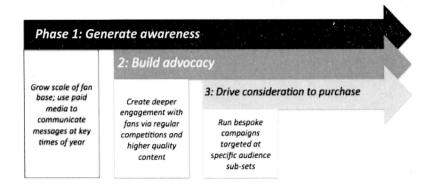

Figure 23

There are four basic steps you need to consider at this stage .

a) Which social media platforms to use

These may gradually increase as you move from one phase to the next. The platform rationale should be dictated by where your target audience is. The best way to understand this is to conduct **social listening** and analyse where people that talk about themes related to your business and your competitors are active. Fashion communities, for example, are highly active not only on Twitter but also on Instagram. If you're selling clothes you wouldn't want to miss out on all the conversations and content on that platform.

b) Planning the content

Once that's in place it's time to start planning the range of **content** that you'll share. What will you talk about to engage followers? How will this convert them into customers and advocates? Or, if you've decided that your business' social media role will be to provide a useful service for your customers, how does this affect what content you post on a daily basis?

c) What tone to adopt

Next, it's time to define your **tone of voice**. How is your business going to speak online? What makes it distinctive in how it communicates with people? A good way to do this is to list out all the words that do and don't show how you'd speak in social media. While remaining authentic, be as distinctive as possible so you stand out from the crowd, but above all adopt and avoid the following:

✓ Positive	✗ Superficial
✓ Approachable	✗ Fantastical
✓ Glass half full	✗ Pessimistic
✓ Confident but never arrogant	✗ Childish
✓ Opportunistic	✗ Happy to be normal

To support this, take some time to write out example posts that you would and wouldn't make. It'll help refine your business' tone of voice and be good practice for when you actually come to start publishing your content.

d) Planning the campaign

Then comes the fun bit! It's time to write your first campaign plan. This should be a calendar month – or week if you prefer – that includes all the specifics of the content you'll share with your followers. Because so many conversations in social media are about events that happen in people's lives, it is useful to include any key events that are coming up in the month which you think will be relevant to your business or followers. Then get writing! To ensure that your campaign plan is fully aligned to your social content model, you could colour code the posts you write so that you can see the role of each piece of content and how it ladders up to your over-arching business objectives (for example, allocating different colours to each column in the following table).

	Week 1	Week 2	Week 3
Role for marketing	*Introduce product*		*Raise awareness*
Content hub	Introductory post & link to LinkedIn post	Share information about product	New content every day: • video vignettes & extracts • guest blog post from influencer
LinkedIn	Form group; invite others to join Post about product, and purpose of group (be provocative)	New post: Share information about product	
Twitter	Follow influencers and relevant parties Join conversations with followers / following Introductory tweets Retweet / Favourite relevant conversations Start using hashtag, and use on-going for pro-active tweets	Ongoing participation in relevant conversations CTA to sign-up	New content every day: • video vignettes
Medium	Post about product and purpose of group (be provocative)	New post: • share information (different to LinkedIn post)	

	Week 4	Week 5	Week 6	Week 7	Week 8
Role for marketing	Promotion		Engage community		
Content hub	Regular content & links to content shared on other channels				
		Infographic	Guest blog post	Infographic	Guest blog post
LinkedIn	Promoted posts Posts with link Incentivise influencers to tweet about the product	Video vignettes; infographics			
Twitter	Promoted Tweets with CTA to buy Targeted at appropriate audience segment Incentivise influencers to tweet about the product	Video vignettes; infographics Ongoing participation in relevant conversations Reply to influencers and relevant parties, with link to buy Targeted Promoted Tweets, with buy CTA			
Medium			New post		New post

The campaign plan should include the copy of your post, any visual content such as an image, video or link, and which platform you intend to publish it on. Do this for the full month and judge whether you have the content in the right order, whether you're using the correct tone of voice, and whether the ratio of your content pillars is appropriate. If you think you've nailed it at the first attempt, you're probably wrong. As with any creative work, review and refine the drafts to make it as tight as possible.

An important point from that last paragraph to stress: include visual content such as images, videos. It helps build emotion and engagement in your business, bringing it to life in a way that words alone may not have the power to do.

When it comes to actually posting the content online, make sure you commit also to reply to any responses you get. And to join other conversations your followers are having with other people. Remember, they don't just care about what you've got to say. You need to build relationships over time for all this content planning to then be effective in the long-term.

2. Execution

Execution covers networking, connecting, selling and customer care.

Let's look at each of those functions and explore how to get the most out of them using social media.

a) Networking

Heather White's chapter in this book sets out the principles to adopt in raising and developing your networking skills and you should bear them in mind when using social media. Good networking starts with identifying who are the right people to connect with. This can be done by natural curiosity on social networks, or more formally through **social listening**. There are tools available – some free, some paid – that allow you to filter all the conversations happening on Twitter and other platforms to whatever topic you choose. Even without these tools, you can simply search on the platforms using whichever keywords you want. Either way, at the touch of a button you could have a list of potential customers who you can then contact immediately via their social media profile.

What's more, you can instantly discover more about these people by looking at their profile page and history, to read their personal description, see the content they've shared, and what their interests and passions are. And better yet, many platforms allow you to then see who they connect with – often, other people that you will be interested in networking with too. It's all seamless, available for you to access and will be a major boost to your networking abilities.

When analysing who to connect with, try to get a sense of who the influencers are in any given communities. This may simply be whose content is shared, or re-tweeted, the most. Or it may be someone who has the largest number of followers. Whatever way you judge influence, start dissecting your networking list into different groups so that you have a greater focus on exactly how to connect with them.

b) Connecting

Once you've conducted your social listening, the next step is to start connecting with people and building a relationship. There are simple ways to do this:

- **Join existing conversations**: on **Twitter** and other platforms this is done by using *hashtags* – topics around which conversations take place. You can reply to people who have used hashtag topics you're interested in with a relevant comment, or tweet using the hashtag too. Over time, aim to build a rapport with your network through sharing your views and interests.

- **Start a new conversation with someone**: Many platforms allow you to instantly connect with one or more people in a simple way. On Twitter this is done by including that person's @ name in the tweet (eg. for Richard Branson it is @RichardBranson). This results in that person being notified of your tweet. They can then choose whether to reply to you.

- **Direct messaging**: many platforms allow you to send a private, direct message to an individual.

In all cases, it is imperative that when you start or join a conversation you add value in some way. Make the conversation better, not worse. This could be done by sharing a link to an interesting related story and giving your point of view on it. Or by sharing image or video content for people to watch and swap opinions about. However you want to do it, make sure you bring something to the party.

It's important to stress here that every social media platform is different, and they each have their own quirks of usage. The methods above are relevant on **Twitter** and various other platforms. As a platform that distinguishes itself as public and conversational, many businesses are attracted to using it because of the ease in which people can connect with one another.

LinkedIn is another good tool for networking. It has a less public conversational quality but allows you to easily search and find a fellow professional with whom you want to form a connection and network. It has a messaging facility and it is important to adhere to the basic rules of networking when inviting people to connect with you - give them a reason join your network. It also has a facility to create communities of interest, which can be a powerful shop window for your activities.

Facebook is primarily a private network, meaning that it is harder to use as a networking tool unless you already have a strong relationship with someone in the first place.

As an individual user of social media you'll participate in conversations naturally, just as you would when you speak to people elsewhere in your life. As a business user, social media requires greater strategy. One key element remains constant though: be human. Don't suddenly put up a mask and use corporate language. It won't work. After all, you're using social media to connect with people on a personal basis whether that's to network, market, sell or provide customer service. Behind every social profile is a person like you!

c) Selling/generating business

As with all efforts to generate business, there are tips and tricks that can be used to make the sale. As relationships are so important in social media, it is highly likely you'll be able to judge when to push someone closer towards a sale in the same way that you would in the physical world. As your business gets bigger over time, generating sales becomes more of a 1-to-many approach in social media, in many cases becoming much more focused on sharing links to a sales page of your website for people to instantly buy online.

As you construct the copy of your tweets, think about the way in which your language guides the user to a certain feeling or intent. For example, if you ask a question it is likely that you will receive answers. Whereas if you make a statement it is more likely you'll receive a view, Like or Favourite (more social media jargon!) but not necessarily a reply. Both serve a valid purpose. From a selling point of view, now consider how to use phrases that are a call-to-action. These are often short and straight to the point, to entice the follower into doing what is being requested. "Download now...", "Click here...", "Buy this...". Add a link to navigate the follower to somewhere they can act on that intent. Used at the right time and supported by other effective, and less intrusive, content you should find that this will result in a larger number of interactions than a softer approach. To stress, only do this when (a) you're happy with the content you've already shared and relationships you're building, and (b) when there is something for the follower to act on.

Various studies have shown that the number one way in which people want to interact with a business on social media is to receive offers and discounts. The irony of this is that it's not exactly the number one thing most businesses want to be doing day in day out on social media. But it's important to remember that getting the sale, albeit at a discounted rate, can lead to positive word-of-mouth from your followers to their friends, which in turn can lead to increasing your number of followers and potential customer base. It's an example of where your sales can also provide some of your marketing. Earned media – and if you get the sale, you've definitely earned it.

Much of social media is a constant test-and-learn. What worked, what didn't. The good news is that for things that prove less effective you can tweak and evolve them the next time without too many people realising the changes you've made. A billion tweets are shared every two days, so there's plenty of opportunity for you to win that sale the next time.

d) Customer care

It's become second nature for people to take to social media to vent their frustrations at a company for failing to satisfy their customer needs. Social media has changed people's expectations about customer service. It's imperative your business accepts that as social media is a good way to win business, but it's a bad way to lose business. For the reasons just highlighted, earned media can result in people talking positively or negatively about you based on their most recent experience. The threat of people talking negatively about your business is a risk. Above all else, you should be rigorous and disciplined in using social media as a customer service channel.

Responding to issues in an open, authentic and honest way is an effective strategy. Even if you don't yet know how to solve the customer's actual problem, make sure you reply saying that you're investigating it and will be back in touch. The reason why this is so important? Because the conversation you're having is public. Treat this customer right, and it gives greater scope for everyone else who sees this conversation to judge you in a positive way.

Some platforms – including Facebook and Twitter – allow you to take the conversations private. This is highly recommended, so that you can sort out the detail of the customer issue in a way that doesn't instantly share all the dirty linen. As part of your first response, you could inform or ask the customer that you'll send them an email or direct message to resolve the issue.

3. Measurement

With so many functions to consider, how should you best measure the effectiveness of everything you do in social media? How to judge the success of those numerous interactions and conversations so that you can keep improving month-on-month?

There are a number of free tools that give you instant access to various results about your social profile. These range from the volume of mentions you receive through to the sentiment of the conversations. It's useful to track these results to see where you can improve as part of your never-ending test-and-learn approach.

Beyond this, you should measure the success of social media against your business objectives. Use this simple model to plot out your objectives (and phases), what components can be measured against them, and the dependencies at to what might affect the results.

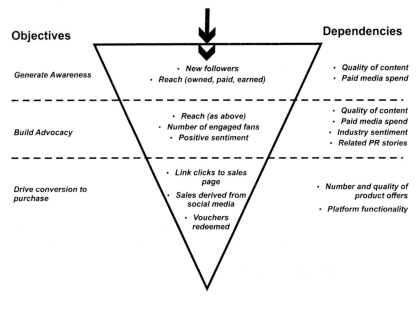

Objectives

Generate Awareness

Build Advocacy

Drive conversion to purchase

- New followers
- Reach (owned, paid, earned)

- Reach (as above)
- Number of engaged fans
- Positive sentiment

- Link clicks to sales page
- Sales derived from social media
- Vouchers redeemed

Dependencies

- Quality of content
- Paid media spend

- Quality of content
- Paid media spend
- Industry sentiment
- Related PR stories

- Number and quality of product offers
- Platform functionality

Figure 24

The more you immerse yourself in the social media world, the more you'll learn about the multitude of ways you can measure performance. To start you off, consider the following:

- Volume of mentions/conversations
- Impressions of your content
- Reach (unique people) of your content
- Volume of new followers
- Number of clicks/interactions on your content
- Positive/Negative sentiment analysis
- Cost per engagement or click

Not all free social measurement tools provide the same techniques, so you will need to choose which metrics you want to track and choose accordingly.

.....and finally

Woah. Some networking, marketing your product or service, a bit of selling, responding to customer issues... how are you going to have time for all this? The simple answer is pace yourself. Walk before you run. Master one thing at a time and build from there. Continue to evolve what you do in social media, and as your experience and knowledge grows so too will your performance.

And if it doesn't? Then hey, I'm sure you'll connect with some great people on the way who share your interests and passions. And that too is fundamental in your life as a Portfolio Professional.

Do's and Dont's

It's an oft-quoted line that being in social media is like being at a party. Don't be the person that stands at the side of the room shouting in trying to get people's attention. Instead be that person in the heart of the party having interesting conversations on different topics with lots of different people. In other words, don't just shout out about your business all the time. Social media is a two-way form of communication – you have to participate in other people's conversation topics just as much as your own in order to build effective relationships.

Here's a list of Do's and Dont's to help you at the world's biggest party:

Do:
- Be authentic, be yourself
- Be transparent – own up to mistakes if you make them
- Commit to participating every day – that's how you'll get most out of it
- Plan your content – keep it fresh and distinctive
- Reply to people who respond to you

- Participate in relevant conversations even in unusual circumstances such as during a TV show or live event
- Test and learn
- Evolve regularly. If you're doing what you did a year ago, you're probably missing a trick
- Connect your social media activity to your other online communications – eg. incorporate your social profile into your website and eCRM

Don't:
- Run before you can walk – there's no need to have a presence on every platform straightaway
- Master each platform you're active on. They each have their quirks, learn them and be comfortable with how to use them
- Hijack hashtags that aren't relevant to your business – ie. just because a lot of people are talking about a certain topic don't bulldozer your way in if it's not appropriate for you to join
- Be a corporate voice. Show you and your company's human side. After all, you are the best person to do it

Useful links

Keep up to date with the latest news and trends in social media at www.socialmediaweek.org.

Case studies

Discover a wealth of interesting case studies at the following sites:

- https://biz.twitter.com/success-stories
- https://www.facebook.com/business/success

Paul McCrudden is an award-winning social media enthusiast. Previously Head of Social Media for a leading advertising agency, he is now in a senior position at a leading social network.

SMART MOVES FOR EXERCISE AND HEALTH
BY MAGGIE HUMPHREYS AND LES SNOWDON

Exercise – does it matter?

To me the outdoors is what you must pass through in order to get to a taxicab.
Fran Lebowitz

A British Heart Foundation report found that lack of exercise can be as bad for us as smoking 20 cigarettes a day, or having high blood pressure or high levels of cholesterol. A Royal College of Physicians report found that levels of fitness are so low that many Britons are left panting after a brisk walk. One reason for people taking less exercise is that they have become increasingly sedentary.

Wherever people practise a western way of life, they become more inactive. 'The civilised man has built a coach and lost the use of his feet,' lamented the American poet, Ralph Waldo Emerson, writing in the 19th century. The horse, the coach, the railway, the omnibus and finally the motor car have robbed us of our natural birthright. For Homo Sapiens read Homo Sedens – and that's official. It's not the passing years but a passive lifestyle that's the problem.

This is where we came in

Before we became portfolio workers, we had fallen into the same sedentary trap. With busy jobs and lifestyles, we were overweight and unfit and we were tired of trying every exercise and diet routine under the sun – jogging, cycling, swimming, squash, skipping, exercise bikes and a dozen other exercise and diet routines available in print and video. We were part of the 90 per cent of people who continually fail with new exercise routines. We were tired, bored and we had made little progress in getting fit and losing weight. Until we discovered fitness walking.

We had always loved walking, but we had tended to walk at weekends when we had more time. Discovering fitness walking was like finding the Holy Grail of fitness. Instead of waiting for the weekend, we decided to get out and walk four or five times a week, starting at our own front door and doing a circuit around the block and back. And we set out to walk at a brisker pace, stepping up our speed to 4 mph. Within a month, we were regularly doing 30 minute walks and we had more energy to get through the day. We felt fitter and more alert and by revamping our eating habits, the pounds were beginning to drop off.

We were so thrilled with the benefits of regular fitness walking that we put our fitness walking experiences down on paper. They became a popular best seller, The Walking Diet, published in Britain and eight countries around the world.

Exercise and a healthy diet do matter. So here's our portfolio prescription for exercise and healthy eating.

Getting into an exercise mode

The human body is the perfect exercise machine. It is designed for movement and activity. When kept active, joints maintain mobility and muscles keep their elasticity. And the body's systems – circulatory, respiratory, digestive, etc. – all function at peak efficiency only when kept active with regular exercise. However, modern work patterns often require long times sitting at a desk and in front of a computer screen, putting undue stress and strain on the body. As we need a business strategy to run our business successfully, so we need an exercise strategy to maintain our body in peak condition.

The place to begin is our work environment. Three key influences require our attention:

- the working posture of the upper half of our body
- work station design
- our working habits.

Are you sitting comfortably?

People have always sat down, but in recent years there has been a dramatic increase in neck, shoulder and arm problems in sedentary workers, often grouped under the name RSI – repetitive strain injury. It is estimated that 90 per cent of headaches are caused by neck tension due to poor posture. Add to that back pain, and the modern office and home worker is plagued with complaints that reduce his or her effectiveness. For optimum concentration and efficiency, the body needs an upright sitting posture to maintain quality breathing, circulation and oxygenation of the brain. The place to begin is with your chair. A suitable chair should, swivel and be height-adjustable, have a seat large enough to suit your own body shape and have a back rest with firm low back support.

Your work station

Once you have a suitable chair, adjust the seat height to the work surface at 'elbow height'. Both feet should be flat on the floor or on a footrest. At the correct height you should be able to slip two fingers easily under your thigh. If not, use a couple of telephone books or a footrest to raise your knees level with your hips. Failure to do this can cause poor circulation and discomfort in the feet and lower legs.

Other factors in your work environment to consider are:

- an ergonomic keyboard to offer your hands and wrist a more natural working position, or a keyboard and mouse rest for your current keyboard

- a sloping workspace to reduce strain to the neck, shoulders and upper spine
- a copyholder to aid correct head and neck posture and reduce muscle tension
- ensuring the primary light source, such as a window, isn't shining onto your face or directly onto your screen and lights are suitable for the task and not too bright – a glare-free screen could help protect your eyes
- a well-ventilated workspace.

Working habits

To avoid stress building up during the day, and to head off fatigue and loss of concentration before it strikes, it's a good idea to adopt a 'best practice' approach to working habits. Whilst concentration spans vary, an optimum attention span of 45 minutes to one hour is a good rule of thumb. High concentration tasks requiring shorter periods may require greater attention, and enjoyable, interesting tasks may allow you to work longer. The ideal time to take a break is just prior to a reduction in concentration. The following will help you improve your working habits.

- Avoid focusing on a screen for extended periods of time – take regular breaks.
- Change posture regularly while sitting to improve blood circulation and breathe correctly – deep from the diaphragm, not restricted and shallow from the upper chest.
- Take frequent short breaks – stand often and move around the room.
- Perform a few desk stretches – shoulder circles, neck exercises and jaw relaxers.
- Take regular exercise breaks – go for an energy-boosting walk.
- Don't work too long at one task – vary tasks.
- Eat a healthy diet with regular meal breaks.

Home alone – maintaining motivation

The toughest part of working from home is working alone. Leaving the day job behind, we lack the ready support and camaraderie of co-workers. There's no one to listen to our jokes, discuss the score in the previous night's football match, or share work problems with. So we need to find other ways of maintaining our sanity when we are home alone! Here are just a few ideas you might want to try.

- Network with other home based portfolio professionals.
- Start a lunch-time club.
- Go for a walk and make it a regular habit, have a beer, meet in the park and kick a ball around.
- Start an online e-group.

Getting started

Walking is the perfect exercise for portfolio workers. It's simple and the only equipment you need is a pair of well-cushioned, supportive shoes, and you're in business. If you're reasonably fit and active and don't suffer from a medical problem that will affect your ability to exercise – if in doubt, do check with your doctor first – then do a circuit for 5 -10 minutes around the block along a familiar route at a normal, comfortable gentle speed. Then turn around and come home. It couldn't be easier, and you can take a break at any suitable time during the day to stretch your legs, get some fresh air and get some high quality oxygen pumping through your veins.

If you are comfortable with a 5-10 minute walk, then increase your time to 15 minutes and try walking at an easy, but faster than normal pace. You should be able to hold this pace without getting out of breath. The following 7-day walking plan will help to keep you motivated. It helps to have a goal to aim for.

Day	1	2	3	4	5	6	7
Pace	Gentle	Gentle	Easy	Easy	Rest	Brisk	Brisk
Time minutes	10-15	10-15	15	15-20		15-20	20

After 7 days, either repeat the programme, or continue adding another five minutes to your walk each week. A good goal to aim at is 3 miles in 45 minutes, 5 times a week – enough to keep your body trim, your muscles strong and your energy high. The more you walk, the more you can walk. Practice builds strength and stamina.

Make walking part of your life

To keep your interest and motivation going, it's a good idea to explore new ways to make walking part of your life – so here are seven creative ways to get the most out of your walks and keep them varied and above all – fun!

- Walk to get the paper and energise yourself for the day ahead.
- Get off the bus or train one or two stops early and walk.
- Leave your car a distance from your destination and walk.
- Walk instead of having a coffee break – walking gives a better 'lift' than coffee.
- Try lunch time walks – invite a friend or start a lunch time walking group.
- Walk in the evening to work off your dinner, relax and de-stress.
- Use weekend walks to visit the country, seaside or some special place.

Nutrition – boosting the benefits of exercise

Tell me what you eat and I will tell you what you are.
Brillat-Savarin

As a portfolio worker who has taken the initiative to become more active, you are now faced with the prospect of organising your own meals at home. Perhaps used to business lunches, a corporate dining room or simply having the choice of a wide range of cafés, restaurants and take away places close by, suddenly panic sets in! How will I manage? I'd like to eat healthier foods, but just what exactly are healthier foods? And what to shop for? So here are a few ideas to help you revamp your eating and shopping habits and boost the benefits of exercise.

The most important thing is to eat fresh foods and cut down on processed foods. Ready-made meals may seem an easy answer but a quick glance at the breakdown of most ready meals will show large amounts of salt, sugar and fat. Fresh foods are not only nutritious but can be very quick to prepare. Now that you are balancing your lifestyle you will have more time to both visit and be selective in the supermarket. If you plan ahead, you will have plenty of wholesome and appetising foods at hand to maintain a healthy balance in your diet.

A healthy balance

- Eat lots of fruit and vegetables – sometimes raw and if possible with the skin on.
- Have moderate amounts of fish and lean meat.
- Wholemeal bread, rice and pasta are excellent staple foods.
- Use moderate amounts of dairy foods – for cooking use olive oil rather than butter.
- Eat only small amounts of sweet foods – chocolate, biscuits and cakes.
- Drink plenty of water throughout the day – it is important to keep up your intake of fluid.

Eat healthily, but don't beat yourself up trying to get it right all the time. So you have an odd craving for a chocolate bar or a bag of chips! If you follow the 80/20 maxim, and try to eat healthily at least 80 per cent of the time, then you should not go far wrong. The key is to aim for a healthy balance in your diet.

Breakfast is very important to give a kick-start to the day. You will be less likely to feel hungry mid-morning if you have eaten a good breakfast. After a morning's work you need a break and something to eat. The best combination is a walk followed by a nourishing and attractively presented lunch. Space precludes the addition of detailed recipes and suggested breakfasts, lunches and snacks but we have a number of ideas to help you plan your meals and these can be found in either our books or website.

How to plan a low stress lifestyle

From the moment we wake, to the moment our head touches the pillow at night, most of us are tuned into the vibrations happening all around us – radio, television, etc. And noise – endless noise. It is more and more difficult to get away from it all – even on holiday. You can take your office with you and be in continual contact anywhere in the world. Connected by an invisible umbilical cord to the information superhighway, you are always on call. Somebody is always waiting to talk to you. Something is always urgent.

But, I hear you say, I'm a portfolio worker now. I've left the corporate whirl behind – I can manage my own life and working day. Surely life is going to get a little easier now?

As a portfolio professional, begin by focusing on your lifestyle and try to identify the key areas of possible stress. Rank them in order of the most severe stressors and imagine how a more positive approach to exercise, diet and relaxation techniques could help you take control of your life. The following winning ways will help you organise your week and plan a low-stress lifestyle.

The Working Day

- **Wake up and stretch.** Your heart rate is slow, body temperature is low, muscles are stiff and your mind is not fully alert. Rather than a cup of coffee, five minutes doing a few wake-up stretches will energise you and put you in a positive frame of mind.

- **Eat lots of carbs.** Carbohydrates release energy gradually stimulating the brain to produce serotonin, a feel-good chemical which promotes feelings of calm. Begin the day with cereal or porridge.

- **Focusing in on your time**. How you spend your time is how you spend your life. Tackle poor time management. It can be a major stressor. Success depends on being prepared, organised and focused on the important tasks that make a difference.

At the end of the day make a To Do list for the next day and prioritise in order of decreasing pay-off.

Evening and Weekend

- **Focus on the inner you.** 'Tension is who you think you should be. Relaxation is who you are,' says a Chinese Proverb. The evening is a time to relax. Find time to slow the pace and get in touch with your 'calm centre'. As a Portfolio Professional, you will work at odd hours. Just five minutes deep breathing or a massage will connect you with your inner rhythms and re-vitalise you. Massage can reduce stress and tension, improve circulation, calm and relax your nervous system, and activate your body's own self-healing mechanisms. And it can take years off you.

- **Walktalk.** Freud called his therapeutic technique 'the talking cure'. No need for a therapist, ask your partner or your best friend. Go for a walk together. The healing power of rhythm unlocks harmful emotions and creates harmony out of discord.

- **Family fitness**. Many people feel that the greatest threat to their families is the lack of time they spend together. Taking to the outdoors with the family can be a way to strengthen family bonds and family bodies. It's said that the family that walks together talks together. Alternatively, go cycling or swimming together, or take up a participative sport.

- **Connect with nature.** 'Time for you' is a key part of the portfolio life balance. Spend it connecting to the whole of nature. There's that feeling of 'coming home' and 'belonging' when you're in the presence of hills, mountains, rivers, oceans and wildlife. It reawakens the senses. The great outdoors makes us more mindful, more aware of our surroundings.

How to plan a low stress diet

What does stress have to do with diet? Plenty. Stress depletes the body's resources and our bodies use up nutrients faster and less efficiently than they normally do. It's during these times that we tend to binge on unhealthy comfort foods which sabotage our bodies. To strengthen our body's defences against stress and eliminate harmful toxins, we need to eat more foods which are high in stress-busting nutrients, and fewer foods which contribute little or nothing to a healthy, nutritious diet.

A stressbusting diet should include vitamins, carbohydrates, proteins and plenty of water. Equally a stress busting diet should avoid or limit too many fatty food, sugar and salt. Too much caffeine and alcohol will promote anxiety and act as a depressant.

We have a number of ideas to help you plan a range of stressbusting meals. These and ways to get and keep active can be found in our website www.walking.org.

Maggie Humphreys' first book with Les Snowdon was **The Walking Diet** *which was published in more than 10 countries. Maggie has been a teacher for over 25 years and she is co-creator with Les of the DTI award-winning educational website* www.edontheweb. com *as well as their walking website.*

Les Snowdon was the UK manager for an American geophysical company for nearly 20 years and a keen walker. Les and Maggie have co-written several books on fitness and healthy eating and have done more than 200 features and interviews in magazines and the press and on TV and radio.

ACKNOWLEDGEMENTS

We'd like to thank the many people without whom this book would not have reached publication.

We are especially grateful to all those who have shared their Portfolio Journeys, and to our specialist contributors. We appreciate the wisdom and the time they have donated, and thank them on behalf of all the readers who have benefited and will continue to benefit. They have contributed generously from the early stages of planning the book and through to this latest edition.

As new authors we had the excellent support of our first editor, James Alexander – a source of encouragement and font of fine stories – and for the latest editions, the experience and guidance of our publisher, Nick Dale-Harris. Their faith in the book, and their appreciation of how it can really change lives for our readers, has been important to us.

Our thanks too to those who have read parts or all of these pages (often at fairly unreadable early draft stages) and given their views, comments and expletives deleted. Special thanks go to the Bourne, Lyons, and McCrudden families.

We are also indebted to everyone at The Success Group for their time, good advice and use of material.

The models used in Chapters 4-8 are proprietary to The Success Group, and are part of The Portfolio Package coaching programme. Some of the models have been adapted from the work of others, including Dan Sullivan, Jinny Ditzler, Graham Alexander and Ben Cannon, and Robert L DuPont, Elizabeth DuPont Spencer, Caroline M DuPont.

There are many others too numerous to name who have inspired and accompanied us on our own journey of experiencing the portfolio life, writing the book, and bringing it to this new edition. Perhaps the others will forgive a special mention to Charles and Elizabeth Handy, who we had the privilege to share thoughts with and who have been generous in their praise of our book.

Finally, we must say a particular thanks to those who have given us feedback on how our earlier book inspired and assisted them in their own career change. This has been, and will continue to be, the real reward for us as authors.

Adrian and Christopher

344

CONTACTS

Downloading the models & charts

For your copies of the models and charts used in the book visit our website: www.PortfolioProfessionals.org.

Keeping in touch

We'd like to keep spreading the network of Portfolio Professionals. By registering on our website, you will be joining a fast-growing community.

We also welcome your input. Use the Contact page on our website, www.PortfolioProfessionals.org to give us your comments and contributions, or email us.

- Adrian Bourne: adriantb@portfolioprofessionals.org
- Chris Lyons: chrislyons@portfolioprofessionals.org

The authors are available to give advice and support to assist your move to the Portfolio Life.

The contributors from Part 4 are available for advice on their specialist subjects.

- Chris Collingbourne: chrisc@portfolioprofessionals.org
- Maggie Humphreys: maggie@walking.org
- Richard Jones: Richard@rgjsolutions.com
- Chris Meggs: chris.f.meggs@gmail.com
- Cliff Russell: cliff@cliffrussell.com
- Les Snowdon: les@edontheweb.com
- Heather White: heather@magicofnetworking.co.uk
- Barnaby Wynter: barnaby@comms-unit.com

BOOKS AND REFERENCES

Part 1 : Introducing the Portfolio Life

Barr, Jeff, *1001 Golf Holes You Must Play Before You Die*, Ronnie Sellers

Carr, Allen, *Allen Carr's Easy Way to Stop Smoking*, Penguin Books

Coelho, Paulo, *The Alchemist*, Harper Collins

Handy, Charles, *Taking Stock: Being Fifty in the Eighties*, BBC

Handy, Charles, *The Age of Unreason*, Arrow Books

Handy, Charles, *The Elephant & The Flea*, Hutchinson

Williams, Nick, *The Work We Were Born To Do*, Element Books

Part 2 Charting your Portfolio

Hopson, Barrie & Scally, Mike, *Build Your Own Rainbow*, 4th ed, Management Books 2000

Nelson-Bolles, Richard, *What Color is Your Parachute*, Ten Speed Press

Part 3 Implementing your portfolio life

Cameron, Julia, *The Artist's Way*, Pan Books

Collins, Jim, *Good To Great*, Random House

Comfort, Max, *Portfolio People*, Century

Peters, Tom, *The Brand You 50*, Random House

Schultz, Patricia, *1000 Places to See Before You Die*, Workman Publishing

Part 4 Running your Portfolio Life

Garratt, Sally, *Going It Alone*, Gower Publishing

Jones, Tony, *Taxation Simplified*, Management Books 2000

Toogood, Granville, *The Articulate Executive*, McGraw Hill

Warner, Janine, *Creating Family Web Sites For Dummies*, John Wiley

Useful further reading

Baker, Diane, *Running a Home Based Business*, Kogan Page

Dixie, Alan, *Working From Home in 90 Minutes*, Management Books 2000

Johnson, Spencer & Wilson, Larry, *The One Minute Salesperson*, Harper Collins

Lambert, Tom, *High Income Consulting*, Nicholas Brealey

Lazear, Jonathon, *Meditations for Men Who Do Too Much*, Aquarian Press

Leach, Robert, *Running Your Own Business*, 6th ed. Management Books 2000

Santella, Chris, *Fifty Places to Fly Fish Before You Die*, Stewart, Tabori & Chang

Schaef, Anne Wilson, *Meditations for Women Who Do Too Much*, Harper & Row

Sheehy, Gail, *New Passages*, Harper Collins

Please visit www.PortfolioProfessionals.org to see other useful books and websites

INDEX